I0800220

BLACK AMERICA SERIES

ELBERT COUNTY
GEORGIA

BLACK AMERICA SERIES

ELBERT COUNTY
GEORGIA

Aurolyn Melba Hamm

ARCADIA
PUBLISHING

ISBN 978-0-7385-1757-5

Published by Arcadia Publishing
Charleston, South Carolina

Printed in the United States of America

Library of Congress Catalog Card Number: 2004113561

For all general information contact Arcadia Publishing at:
Telephone 843-853-2070
Fax 843-853-0044
E-mail sales@arcadiapublishing.com
For customer service and orders:
Toll-Free 1-888-313-2665

Visit us on the Internet at www.arcadiapublishing.com

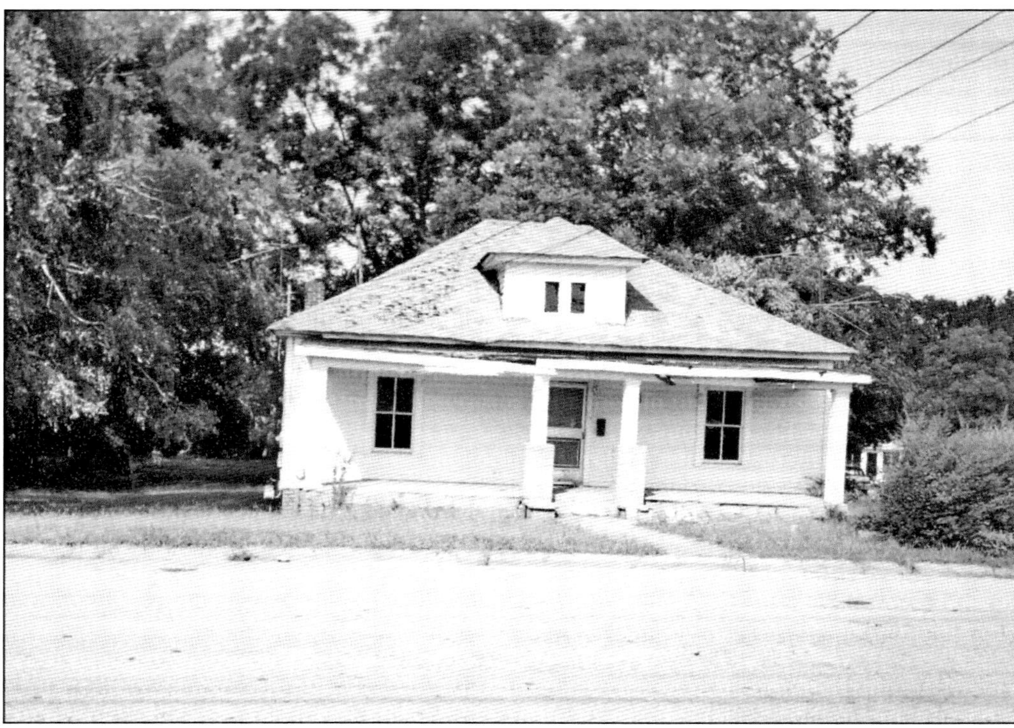

First Hospital. In the early 1900s, African Americans used this house as a hospital.

Contents

ACKNOWLEDGMENTS

If not for my sister, Janice Hamm Gallimore, introducing me to the *Black America Series: Greene County, Georgia* by Mamie Lee Hillman, this work would not exist today. I might have never realized the opportunity to write such a book on Elbert County. I also would like to thank my other brothers and sisters—Terry Joseph Hamm Sr., Patricia Hamm Allen, Barbara Lois Hamm, Sandra Hamm Gibbs, and "Jelani" William Michael Hamm—who have encouraged me always. I would like to recognize my son, Alan Hamm, has been very supportive. My daughter, April Michaela Hamm, gave insightful comments, editing and critiquing much of my material.

Many other people assisted me in this endeavor by sharing local history, pictures, newspaper clippings, and precious time with me. I am grateful to everyone who entrusted me with the care of his or her documents, including, but not limited to, Minnie Winston Abner, Bettina Odister Allen, Genora Hamm Biggs, John and Mary Morrison Clark, Azalee Biggs Dye, George 'Mike' Fortson, Joe and Diana Demoss Glaze, Joe Allen Harper, Emma Bradford Heard, Mozelle Mattox, Deborah Lucinda Rucker, Nell Barnes Rucker, Brenda Hughes Trimble, Georgia White, Wilbert and Henrietta Taggart Williams, and Sara J. Willingham.

Jimmy O. White, president and founder of the Jim-Ree African-American Museum, Inc., shared his personal photographs as well as pictures from the museum's archives. I am most appreciative of all of the time that he set aside from his busy schedule to assist me in going through pictures from his collections. Rev. John Wayne Strong, pastor of Lofton Grove, and Carolyn Bolton, historian of Lofton Grove, shared photographs from the church's archives that I am more than proud to use. John and Rudine Phelps's oral history of the Civil Rights movement in Elbert County gave me insight into a time period that I would otherwise not have had. Mary Frances Harper Allen's, Genora Hamm Biggs's, Azalee Biggs Dye's, Joe Allen Harper's, and Nell Barnes Rucker's oral recollections of the history of Elbert County schools were important. Nelcena Thornton Tharps's recollection of Fifth Sunday Choir was valuable.

I would like to thank Susan Gilbert from Alumni Relations at Harvard University, who provided me with information on William Miles Brewer. John S. Page, associate dean of the Learning Resources Division at the University of the District of Columbia in Washington, D.C., provided a picture of William Miles Brewer and other invaluable information on the native Elbertonian. The Moorland-Springarn Research Center at Howard University in Washington, D.C., provided me with William Miles Brewer's obituary. I would like to thank the processing archivist, Stacy Swazy Jones, at Robert W. Woodruff Library, Atlanta University Center, for the *gratis* biographical material on Bishop William A. Fountain Sr. I would also like to thank Alexis Scott, of the *Atlanta Daily World*, for giving me permission to use the family picture of Bishop William A. Fountain Sr.

The copyrighted electronic publication *From Slavery to the Bishopric in the A.M.E. Church* by William Henry Heard, provided by the Academic Affairs Library at the University of North Carolina at Chapel Hill, was priceless; it provided me with insight into the education of African Americans immediately after slavery in Elbert County, Georgia. The electronic publication *In Those Days: African American Life Near the Savannah River* by Sharyn Kane and Richard Keeton, provided by the Corps of Engineers, also provided invaluable historical data. The website www.ancestry.com was useful in finding birth and death dates and draft card information from World War I; it also led me to the book *Who's Who of the Colored Race: Volume One: 1915* by Frank Lincoln Mather, which I located at Emory University Library. This book provided me with background information on Alfred P. Allen, William A. Bell, Paul J. Blackwell, William A. Fountain, and William H. Heard.

Introduction

Just as a tree without roots is dead, a people without history or culture also becomes a dead people.
—Malcolm X

Looking back, while working on my family tree and searching for historical data that may have affected my ancestors, I was reminded of the West African proverb, "When an elder dies, it is as if a whole library has burned." My mother died in 1997 at the age of 76, and my father died in 2000 at the age of 86. Though my mother was originally from New Orleans, she had lived in Elberton for over 40 years and was just as knowledgeable as my father about the history of African Americans in Elbert County. My paternal grandmother, my only grandparent to live long enough for me to know, died when I was 16 years old. The people they spoke of, the stories they told about people who did great deeds, and the testimonies they made about their own lives are incoherent fragments that I cannot quite fit together. I find myself wanting to ask my parents and grandmother questions, but I waited too late to take advantage of their knowledge of the local history. Oh, how I wish that I had listened more intently, that I had asked more questions while they were living!

One thing that I do remember is a superstition of my father's mother, Mary Wall Hamm (1889–1972). In order to keep uninvited spirits from taking up residence in her home, my grandmother would turn all unoccupied chairs to the wall and tilt them against the wall. The rocking chairs on the porch and even the chairs to the kitchen table were treated in this manner. A similar custom existed in West Africa, where a stool, instead of a chair, was tilted against a wall. This coincidence led me to wonder how far removed my grandmother was from Africa. My paternal grandfather's grandfather was born in Africa, but I do not know the origins of my grandmother's parents and grandparents. During slavery, parents, children, and even names were taken from African-American slaves when it financially suited their owners. When slaves were sold, their names changed, sometimes their first names as well as their last names. It was customary for slaves to take the surnames of their owners, making it impossible for many of the slaves to know and keep up with their genealogy.

In these modern times, with so much information only a keystroke away, I was ultimately disappointed by the lack of readily available information online. At the county's public library, I found only slightly more information than I found on the Internet, using my own personal computer. Imagine my disappointment when I searched the local newspaper archives housed at the library and found that it had been sanitized of information relating to African Americans until well after the forced integration of schools in Elbert County. Stories about crimes committed by African Americans remained in the archives, but positive articles and general current events contained in "Colored News" and later "Black News" and finally "Society News" were expunged from the local archives. In addition to these sections, certain years, such as 1915, were also missing from the archives; this was the year that a local African -American hero, Dr. James Paul Thompson, was killed by a white doctor and merchant, Dr. Alfred S. Oliver, who was exonerated of this crime by the local judicial system. Reportedly, the story was covered in the local newspaper, but it does not remain in the archives housed at the library today. The library also houses quite a few books on Elbert County, but only a few of these contain information about the African Americans who helped to mold their county and their country.

This distressful state of affairs can only be attributed to laws that permitted the enslavement of people who were spoils of wars in Africa and to laws that created communities based on skin color. When the 13th Amendment freed African Americans from their physical chains in 1865, they were ultimately ensnared by a judicial system that deemed African Americans inferior to white citizens. The Civil Rights Act of 1875 gave African Americans the same basic rights as whites, but the Supreme Court ruled it unconstitutional in 1883, declaring that congress had jurisdiction over the states but not individual citizens. Subsequently, the birth in the Southern states of "Separate but Equal" laws, or "Jim Crow" laws, legally banned African Americans from many public facilities. African Americans were required to use separate and often inferior accommodations. Politically, African Americans had no voice, and they were openly mocked in public. They were completely discounted as human beings. Poorly educated, many African Americans continued to depend on the oral documentation of history rather than the written documentation. "Jim Crow" laws gave many white-owned publishers justification for not including anything positive about African Americans in their publications. These circumstances help to explain why African-American news was not maintained in local archives.

In addition to this political degradation, educational standards were lower for African Americans than for whites. In fact, immediately after slavery, educational opportunities for blacks in Elbert County were almost nonexistent. There were no schools in the county matriculating African Americans, and the only education available to African Americans was a short summer session held at the courthouse. Although the courthouse was centrally located in Elberton, it was 10 or more miles from the homes of many of the African Americans living in Elbert County.

In spite of these political and educational obstacles, many of the Americans born in slavery persevered and made real contributions to Elbert County and to the United States. Two such men were Alfred James Allen and William Henry Heard. Alfred James Allen was born on September 11, 1859, on Singleton Allen's plantation in Elbert County. His parents were David and Frances Allen, both slaves. He was educated in the public schools of Elbert County. He graduated from Atlanta Baptist College with degrees from the normal department in 1885 and from the theological department in 1887. He was an ordained Baptist minister and educator. He taught in several Georgia public schools, and he was the principal of Benevolence Institute, in Shellman, Georgia, from 1910 to 1914.

Bishop William Henry Heard was born on June 25, 1850, on Thomas Jones's plantation. His parents were George W. and Parthenia (Jones) Heard. After emancipation, William Henry Heard learned to read and write by hiring himself out and accepting reading and writing lessons for pay. He ran for the Georgia House of Representatives from Elbert County in 1872 and lost, he claimed, because of stolen ballots. In 1875, he ran for the South Carolina House of Representatives and won, only to have his victory overturned after serving one year of his term. He attended South Carolina University, now known as the University of South Carolina (1876–1877), Clark University in Atlanta (1878), Atlanta University (1879), and Reformed Episcopal Divinity School in Philadelphia (1889), and received an Honorary Doctorate of Divinity (D.D.) from Allen University, in Columbia, South Carolina, and from Wilberforce University in Ohio. He received an Honorary Doctor of Laws (LL.D.) from Campbell College in Jackson, Mississippi. Heard believed that he had earned the honorary degrees because of his position as a bishop of the A.M.E. Church rather than for knowledge. He served as a consultant to Liberia for four years from 1895 to 1899. Heard also authored two books: *The Bright Side of African Life* (1901) and *From Slavery to the Bishopric in the A. M. E. Church* (1929).

Even when schools serving African-American students opened in Elbert County, the quality of education was much lower for black students than for white students. African-American teachers received less pay than white teachers, and African-American schools received used supplies and out-of-date textbooks. There were no transportation services, and because there was only one high school for African Americans in the entire county, many African Americans did not receive an education beyond the seventh grade. They simply lived too far away to walk to Elberton Colored High School, and they could not afford to board with someone living in the city of Elberton or to pay the yearly fee charged to county residents attending the city of Elberton's colored high school. It was not until 1956 that the city and county schools merged to become Elbert County Schools.

The "Jim Crow" laws may have prevented African Americans from receiving an education comparable to that of whites, but these laws did not prevent them from learning altogether. The segregated black school produced leaders such as Dr. James Paul Thompson, the first African-American physician in Elberton; William Miles Brewer, the third editor of *The Journal of Negro History*; Bishop William Alfred Fountain Sr., fifth president of Morris Brown College in Atlanta, Georgia; William Augustus Bell, president of Miles Memorial College in Birmingham, Alabama (1912–1913); and Rossie Thompson Hollis, one of the first African-American women from Elbert County to graduate from Paine College in Augusta, Georgia, in 1910, and who later became a professor at Paine College.

After the defeat of the Civil Rights Act of 1875, another 81 years would pass before African-American rights as full citizens of the United States would be reinstated with the Civil Rights Act of 1964. The first step towards equal education in Elbert County occurred in 1965, 11 years after the Supreme Court ruled the "Separate but Equal" laws unconstitutional in Topeka, Kansas. In 1965, the Freedom of Choice Act allowed three brave African-American high-school seniors to leave Blackwell Memorial High School to attend Elbert County High School, then an all-white school. Within a few days, two of them returned to Blackwell Memorial High School, and Deborah Lucinda Rucker became the first African-American student to graduate from Elbert County High School in 1966.

In spite of the evils of racism, the African Americans of Elbert County did not give up and formed their niche in the community. Without God, hope, and faith that tomorrow would bring a better day, blacks would not have survived their tumultuous experiences. At the end of slavery, many churches split, not for religious differences but for racial differences. One local church that was unique and did not follow this trend was Saint Mary's Catholic Church. When Marie Parker Hamm moved with her husband and her then four children from New Orleans, Louisiana to Elberton, her husband's hometown, she searched for a Catholic church and found one. In 1951, the Marie and her family entered the then all-white congregation and were immediately accepted. There were no back doors to enter the church through. There were no special pews to sit on. There were no separate catechisms. There were no separate communions. Moreover, when Marie Parker Hamm's children made their first communions, they participated in the same program that the little white children participated in, and at the end of the ceremony, all of the African-American and white children stood together and posed for a picture to be posted in the local newspaper. When the newspaper owner mailed the picture back, refusing to publish a picture with African Americans in it, the white families of Saint Mary's Catholic Church shrugged their shoulders and did not mention it to Marie Parker Hamm or her children until many years later. Churches were not only havens for religious worship, but they were also places where African Americans could interact with others as equals.

The 20th century brought many changes for African Americans in the United States. Our ancestors cleared many pathways for us to travel on, making it easier for us to obtain the places in society that we now have. This work is my effort to chronicle the history of African Americans in Elbert County. It is by no means a complete record but a glimpse. It is my hope that we continue to pay homage to our predecessors by documenting and archiving their achievements.

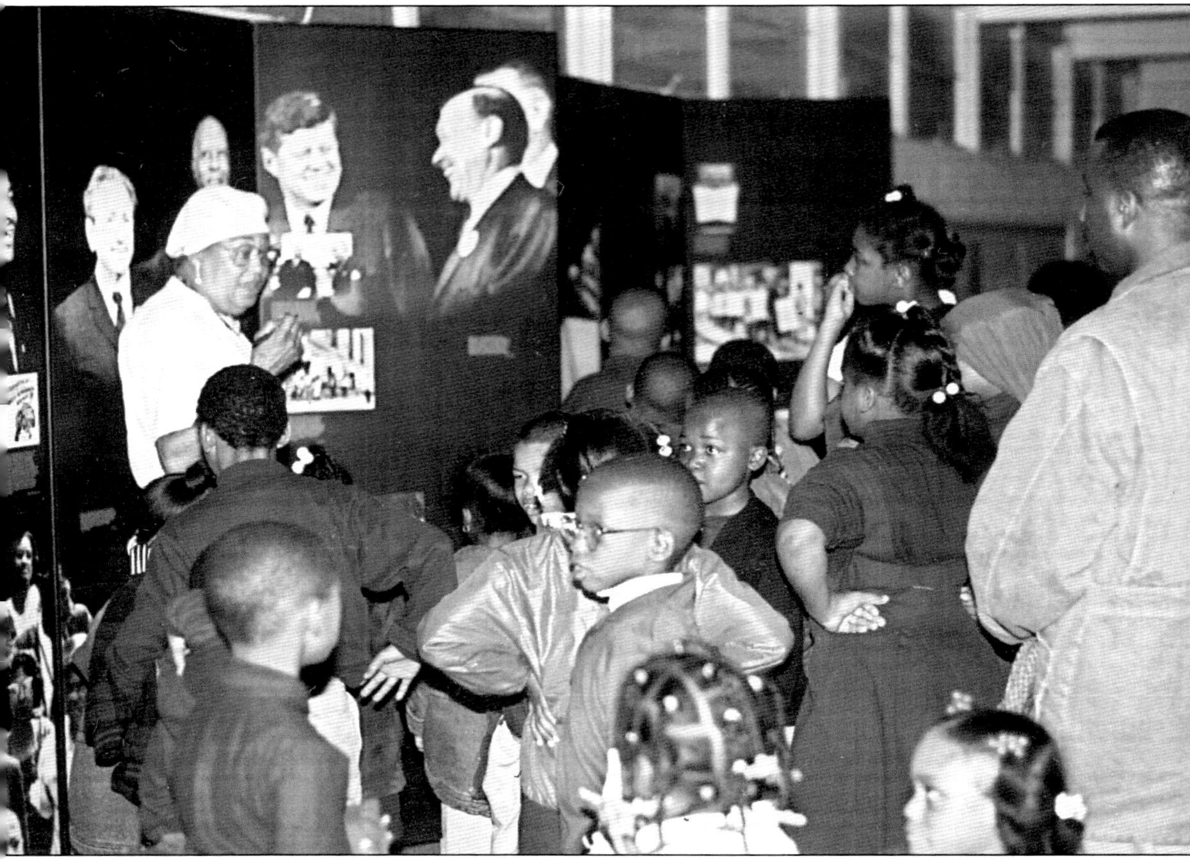

I dedicate this book to the youth of Elbert County. Here, Imogene Willis Holland presents to visitors an A. Phillip Randolph Institute visiting exhibition at Blackwell Memorial Cultural Center.

One

LEADERS DREAM TOMORROW'S REALITIES

I have a dream that my four little children will one day live in a nation where they will not be judged by the color of their skin but by the content of their character.
—Martin Luther King Jr.

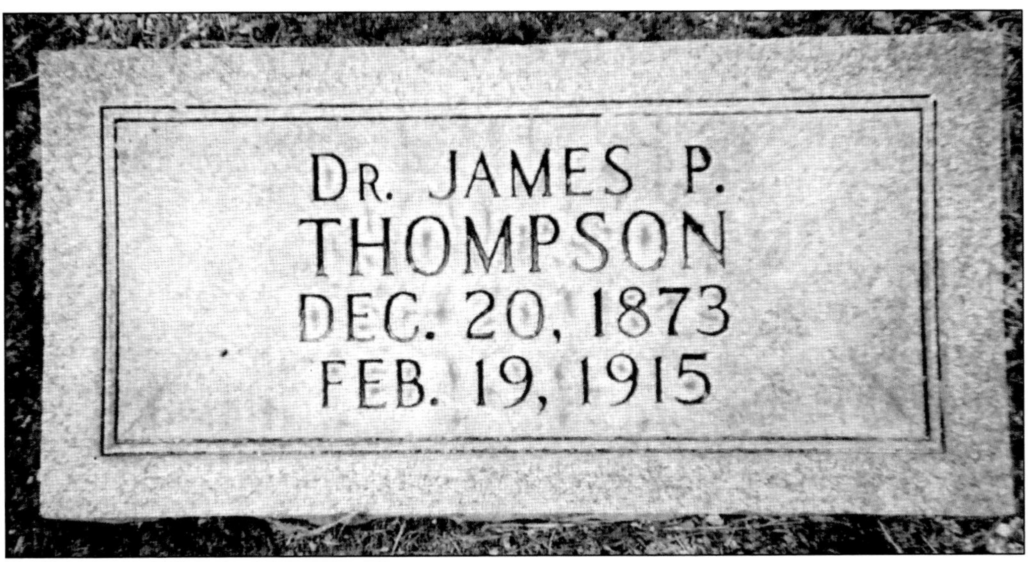

DR. JAMES PAUL THOMPSON, M.D. Thompson, a native of Elbert County, was the son of Lloyd and Betsy Thompson. Throughout his life, Thompson stood up for African Americans' rights. He was the founder of Emancipation Day celebrations in Elbert County. Some African Americans of the time believed that when Thompson correctly diagnosed a young white female as having scarlet fever, rather than the common cold Dr. Alfred S. Oliver had diagnosed, Thompson had signed his own death certificate. The trial that followed was speedy, and Dr. Alfred S. Oliver's version of accidentally shooting Thompson in the chest at close quarters was accepted. (Courtesy Charles and Marie Hamm Collection.)

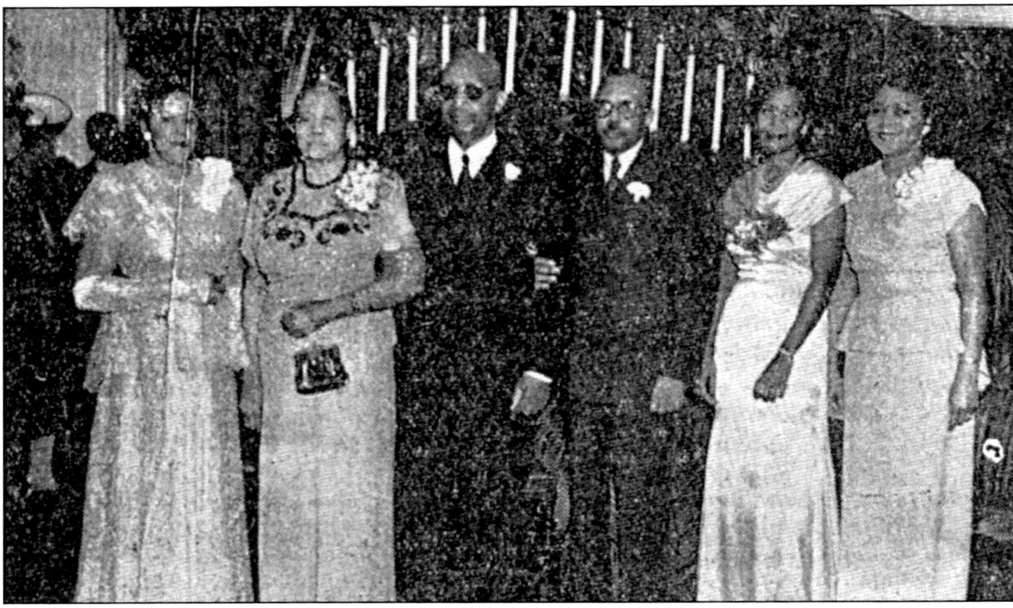

Bishop William Alfred Fountain Sr., (A.M., S.T.B., LL.D., D.D.) 1870–1955. Fountain was born in Elberton to Richard and Virginia Harris Fountain. Richard Fountain was a shoemaker, and Virginia was a housewife. Fountain was ordained a minister in an A.M.E. church in Elberton in 1892. Pictured are, from left to right, Louise Fountain Perrin, Julia A. Fountain, Bishop William A. Fountain Sr., Dr. William A. Fountain Jr., Julia Bell Jackson, and Suejette Fountain Crank. (Courtesy *Atlanta Daily World*.)

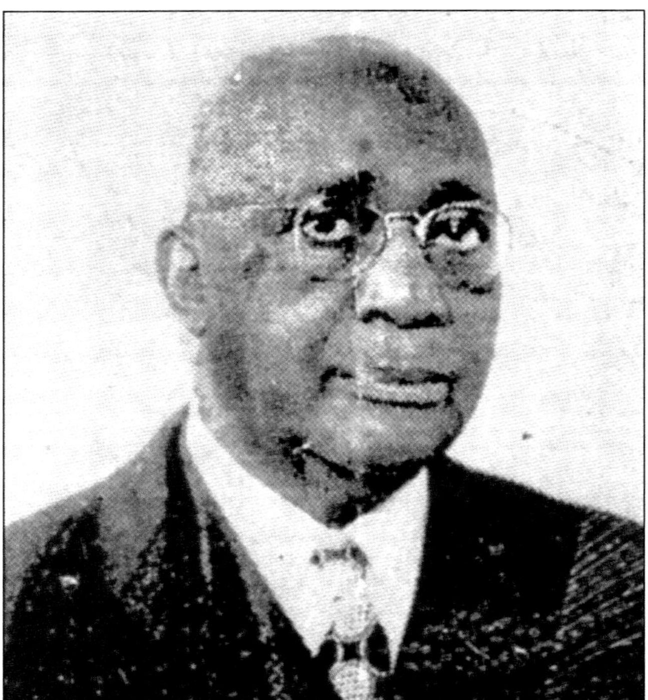

Fifth President of Morris Brown College. Bishop Fountain distinguished himself as president of Morris Brown College from 1911 to 1920. In 1920, he was elected the 32nd bishop of the A.M.E. Church. He was chairman of the board of trustees of Morris Brown College from 1928 to 1948. As the chairman, he and his son, Dr. William Alfred Fountain Jr., seventh president of Morris Brown College, accomplished many goals. (Courtesy Robert W. Woodruff Library Archives at Atlanta University Center.)

The Social Studies Department

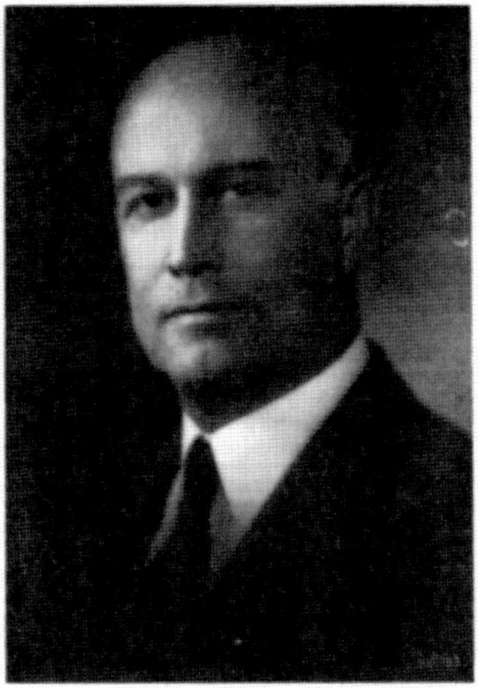

Mr. William M. Brewer

From The Lamp, 1950, yearbook of Miner Teachers College, Washington DC.

WILLIAM MILES BREWER, AUGUST 13, 1889–OCTOBER 7, 1970. "Willie" William Miles Brewer, born in Eliam, Elbert County, was the seventh child of Rev. Robert and Martha Dye Brewer. He received his early education in Elbert County, and he earned his bachelor's degree in 1919 and master's degree in 1929, both from Harvard University. Brewer's teaching career began at Johnson C. Smith University in 1919. He also taught in the public school systems of St. Louis, Nashville, Baltimore, and Washington, D.C. Distinguishing himself as the third editor of *The Journal of Negro History* from 1951 to 1970, he was awarded the Bancroft Prize in 1938 and in 1944. He received honorary doctorates from Johnson C. Smith in 1951 and Virginia Union University in 1963, and he worked as a secretary of the Colored Work Department of the YMCA at Camp Sevier, South Carolina, during World War I. (Courtesy University of the District of Columbia.)

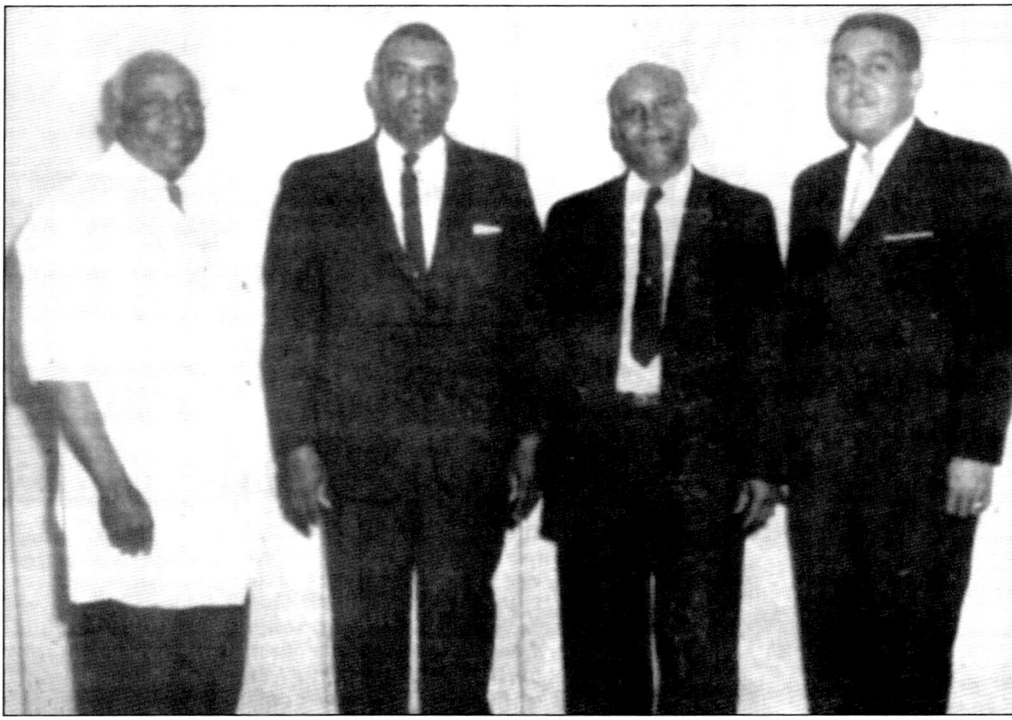

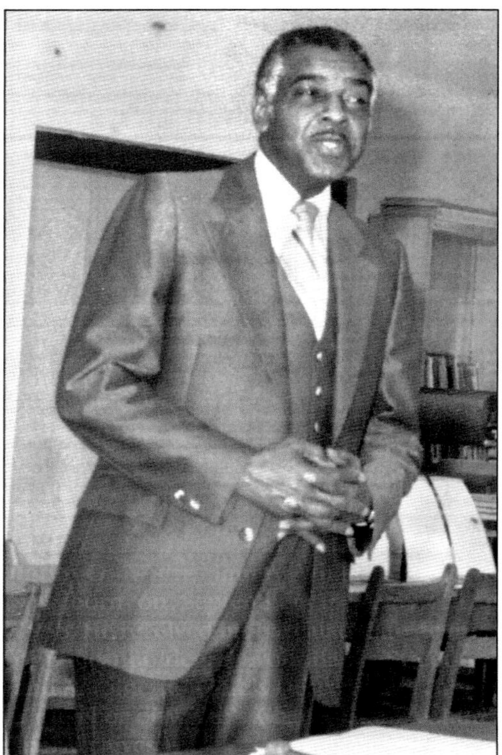

Dr. Rembert C. Jones, February 18, 1900–November 25, 1965. Dr. Jones was the third African-American physician to practice in Elbert County. From Wilkes County, he moved to Elberton after graduating from Howard University Medical School in 1930. Though a general practitioner, he was known as a "good skin doctor" and a "good obstetrician." Dr. Jones also owned Jones Dry Cleaning on Elbert Street. Pictured from left to right are Dr. Jones, Charlie Tate, R.T. Allen and James Hawes Jr. (Courtesy Georgia White.)

Dr. Horace Tate. Dr. Horace Tate was born and received his early education in Elberton. He received his bachelor's degree from Fort Valley State College. In 1960, he became the first African American to earn and be awarded a Ph.D. from the University of Kentucky, where he was elected to the Education Hall of Fame. He was the first African American to run for mayor of Atlanta. He served on the Georgia General Assembly from 1975 to 1992. (Courtesy Jim-Ree African-American Museum, Inc. Archives.)

CHARLES AUGUSTUS HAMM SR., DECEMBER 23, 1913–AUGUST 26, 2000. The fifth child of Mary Wall and Luther D. Hamm, Dr. Charles Augustus Hamm graduated with honors from Elberton Colored High School in 1936. He received his bachelor's from Paine College in Augusta, Georgia, in 1942, and his bachelor's in pharmacy from Xavier University in 1951. A veteran of World War II, he was the first African American elected to public office in Elberton and Elbert County. (Courtesy Marie and Charles Hamm Collection.)

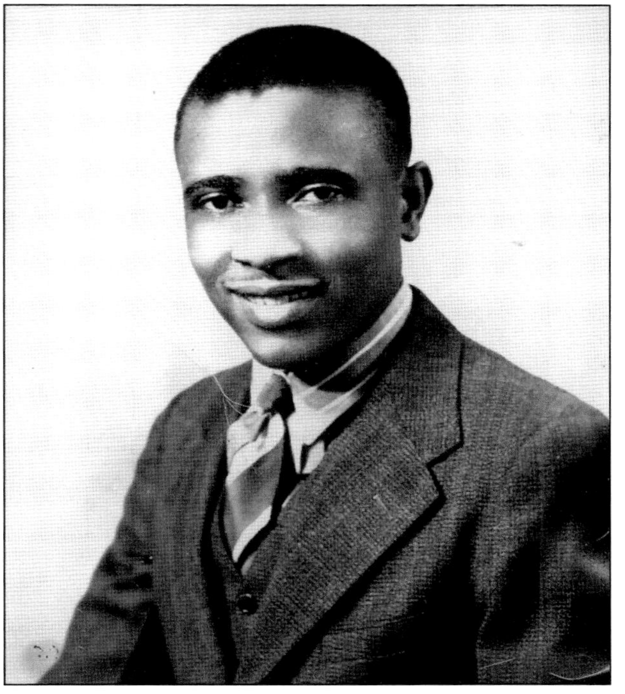

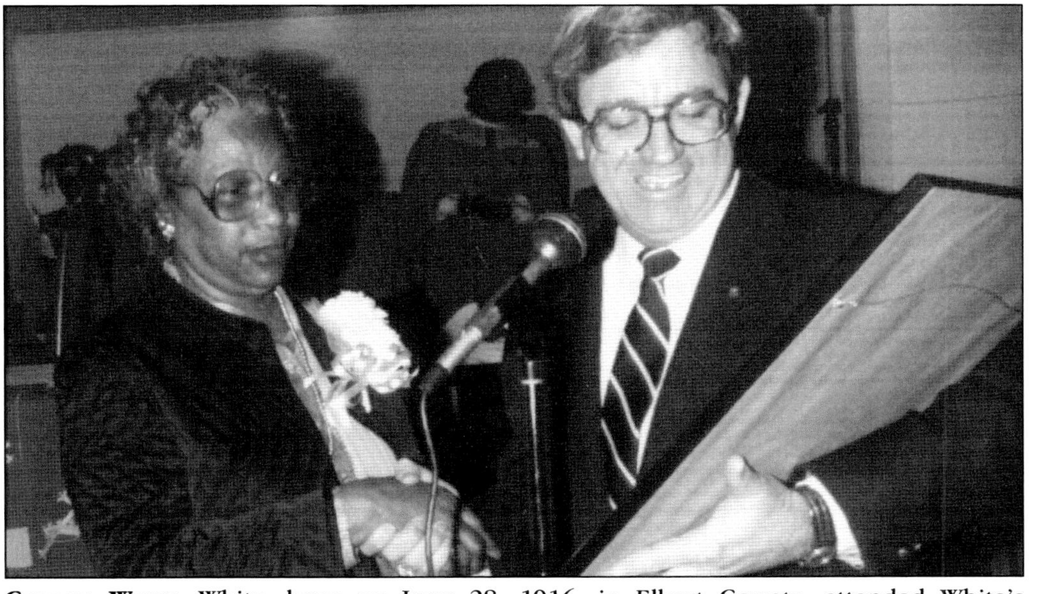

GEORGIA WHITE. White, born on June 28, 1916, in Elbert County, attended White's Chapel's Primary School and Elberton Colored High School, graduating in 1938. She was a nurse for Dr. Jones from 1942 to 1965, owned and operated the Casino Grill from 1965 to 1970, and worked as a nurse at Nancy Hart Nursing Home from 1971 to 1990. White was the first African American woman elected to public office in Elbert County. Here, she receives recognition from Major Joe Fendley for being an outstanding citizen. (Courtesy Georgia White.)

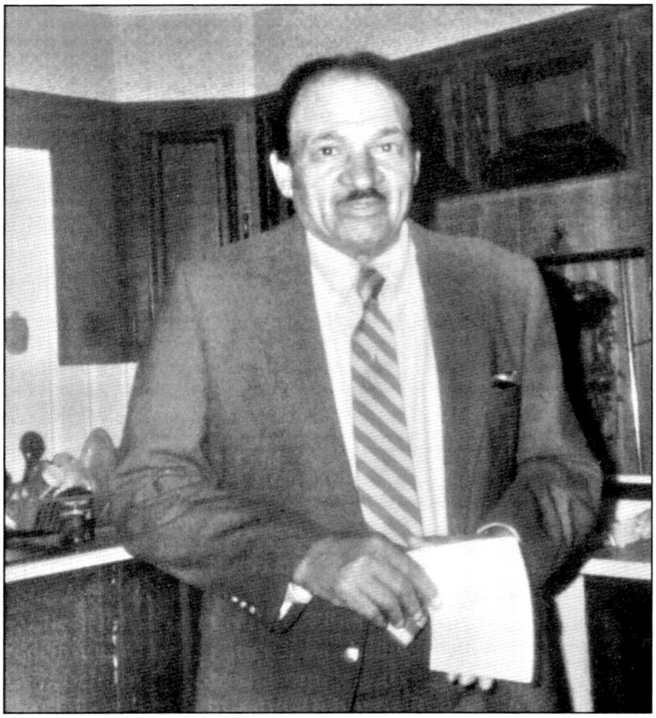

George "Mike" Fortson. Fortson was born in the "Sweet City" area of Elbert County on February 26, 1932. He attended Piney Grove Elementary, a one-teacher school under the guidance of Mrs. Fannie Biggs and Elberton Colored High School under principal Paul J. Blackwell. He served 21 years in the army and the army reserves. Using rubble, pieces of discarded granite, he created a business for himself. He is known for his charitable contributions throughout the community. (Courtesy Mike Fortson.)

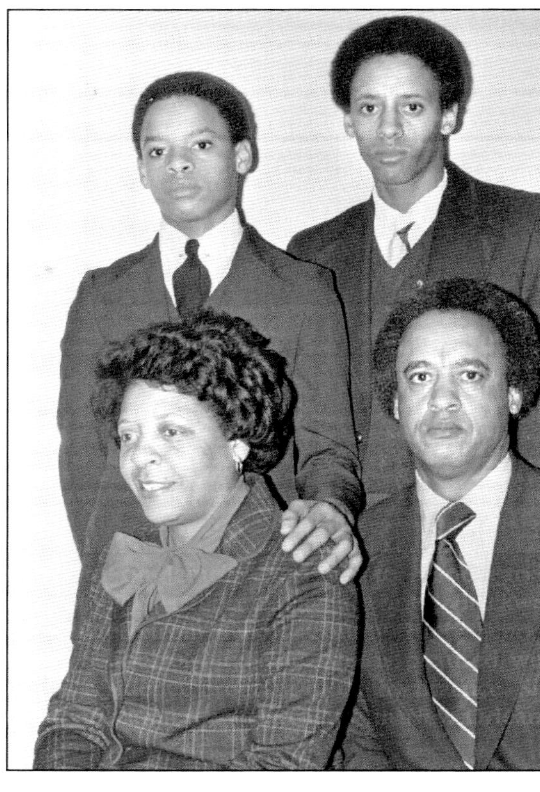

William Elliott Dye. William E. Dye, a 1950 graduate of Blackwell Memorial High School, received his baccalaureate degree from Southern Illinois University in Edwardville. He served as a state policeman in Illinois and later became the chief of police of East Saint Louis. He also served as chief of police of Champaign, Illinois, and Columbia, Missouri. Pictured are, from left to right, (front row) Azalee Biggs Dye and William Elliott Dye; (back row) Robert William Dye and Elliott Hoyt Dye. (Courtesy Genora Biggs.)

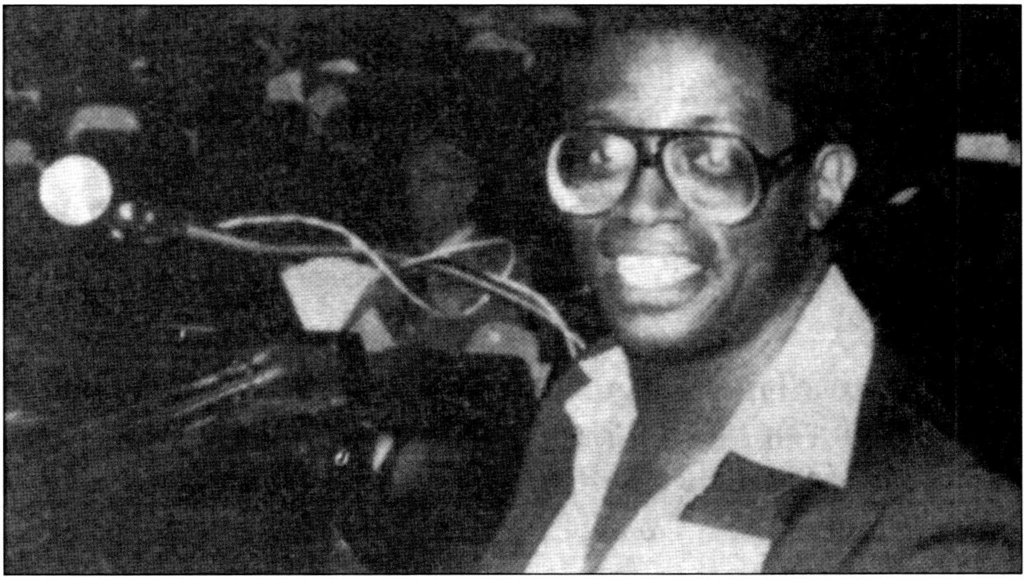

Dr. Judge Jefferson Cleveland, 1937–1986. Judge Jefferson Cleveland was educated in Elbert County, graduating in 1954. He was a music student of Willie Lorraine Grippon Smith. He received his bachelor's in music from Clark College, his Master of Music from the School of Music at Illinois Wesleyan University, and his Doctor of Musical Arts from Boston University's School of Arts. He was the executive editor and chief contributor to the hymnbook *Songs of Zion*. (Courtesy Marie and Charles Hamm Collection.)

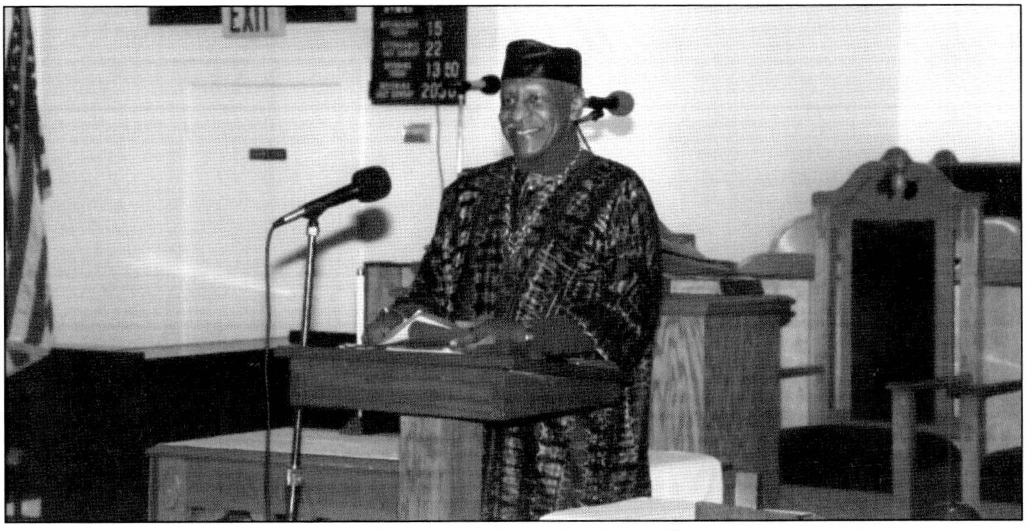

Jimmy O. White. Jimmy White, founder of the Jim-Ree African-American Museum, Inc., was born on September 15, 1939. He graduated from Blackwell Memorial School in 1958. He received his baccalaureate degree from Albany State College in 1964 and his Master of Education degree from Banks Street College of Education in 1972. He initiated the Sam and Antoinette White's Descendants Family Reunion, and like his fraternal forefathers, he is a member of White's Chapel C.M.E. Church. (Courtesy Jim-Ree African-American Museum, Inc. Archives.)

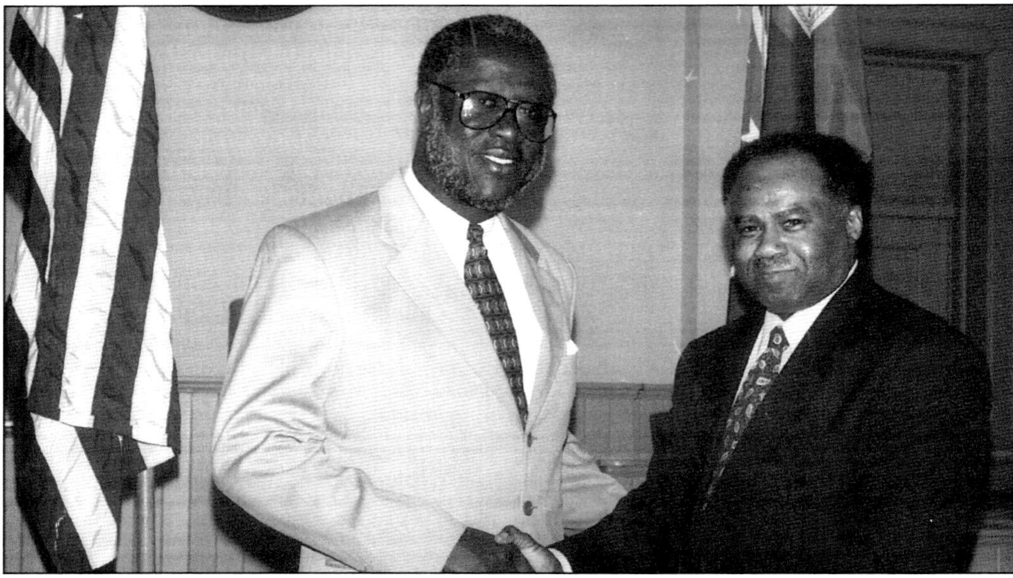

Justice Robert Benham. Attorney John Clark greeted Justice Robert Benham at the Elberton Bar Association. Benham, from Cartersville, was the second African American to graduate from the University of Georgia's School of Law, the first to establish a law practice in Bartow County, and the first to win a statewide election in Georgia since reconstruction, when voters chose him to serve on Georgia Court of Appeals. He is the first African American to serve on the Georgia Supreme Court. (Courtesy Mary and John Clark.)

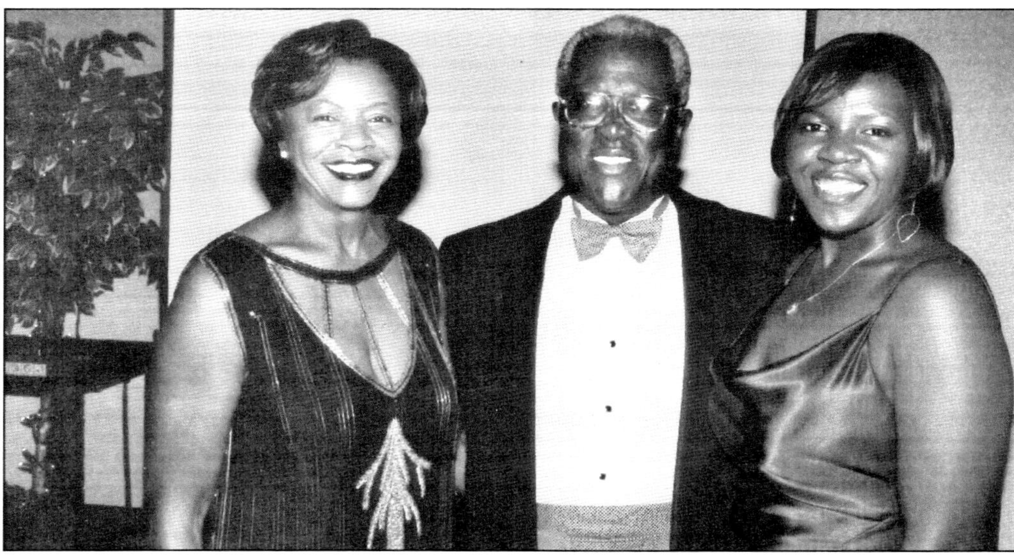

Attorney John Clark. Clark, the fifth child of Freddie J. and Otis Clark, attended public schools in Oglethorpe and Clarke Counties. He is a Vietnam veteran who graduated from Savannah State University with honors in 1975. He became the first graduate from Southern University School of Law in Louisiana to pass the Georgia Bar and the first African American to open a law practice in Elbert County. Clark is pictured with his wife, Mary Morrison Clark, and his daughter, Nefertara Clark. (Courtesy Mary and John Clark.)

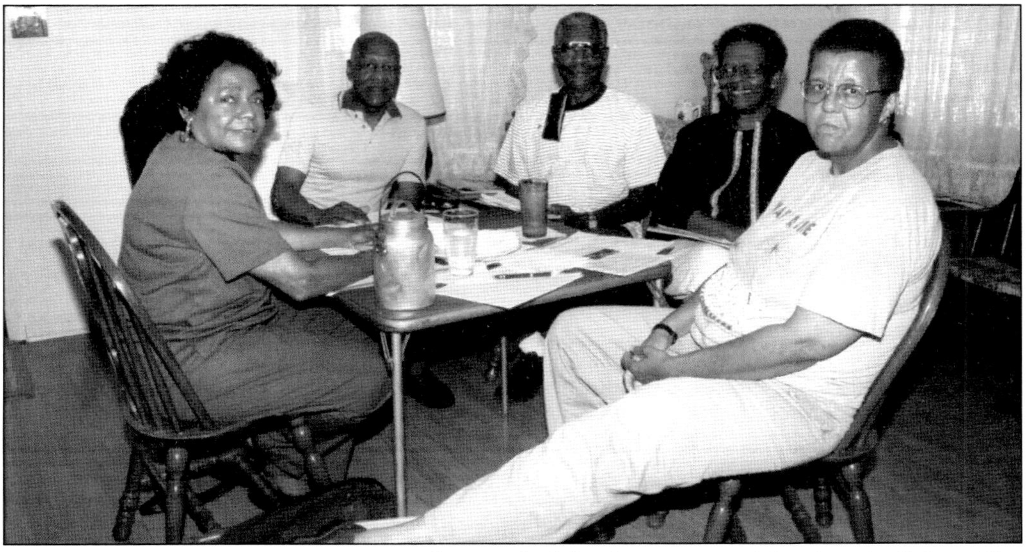

Deborah Lucinda Rucker. Attorney Rucker worked for Georgia Legal Services in Gainesville. She later worked for a program for families and children in crisis initiated by Governor Miller. Rucker retired to Elbert County when her health would no longer allow her to continue to work. Rucker worked with Jim-Ree African-American Museum, Inc. in designing a brochure. Pictured from left to right are Rudine Phelps, Jimmy White, Willie Heard, Sara J. Willingham, and Deborah Rucker. (Courtesy Jim-Ree African American Museum, Inc. Archives.)

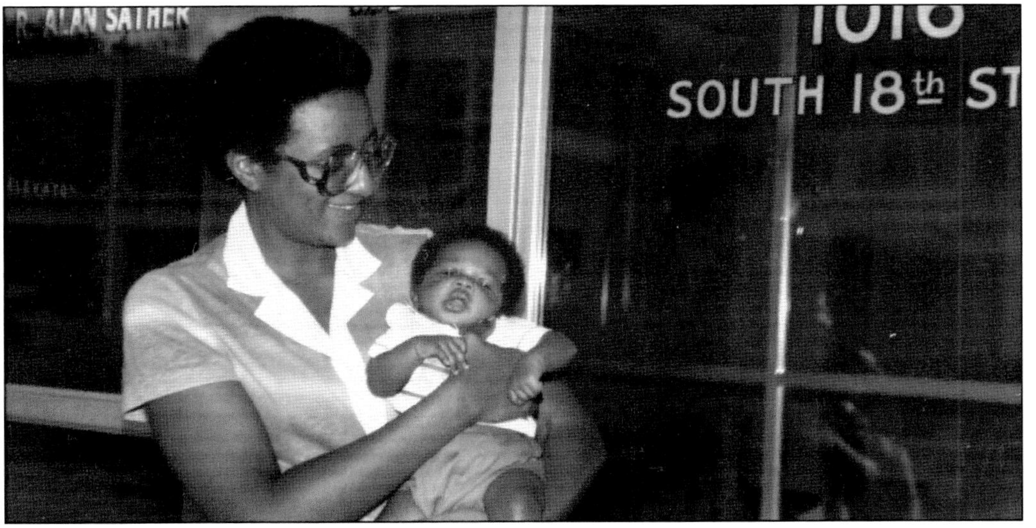

Dr. Barbara Lois Hamm, M.D. Hamm was born on January 3, 1954, to Marie Parker and Charles Augustus Hamm Sr. The fifth of eight children, she attended Blackwell School through the eighth grade and graduated from Elbert County High School, Mount Holyoke College, and Duke University School of Medicine. She is pictured with Chiemeka Azubuine, a child she delivered in a residency program in family practice. She later completed a residency program in child and adolescent psychiatry in New Orleans. (Courtesy Barbara Hamm.)

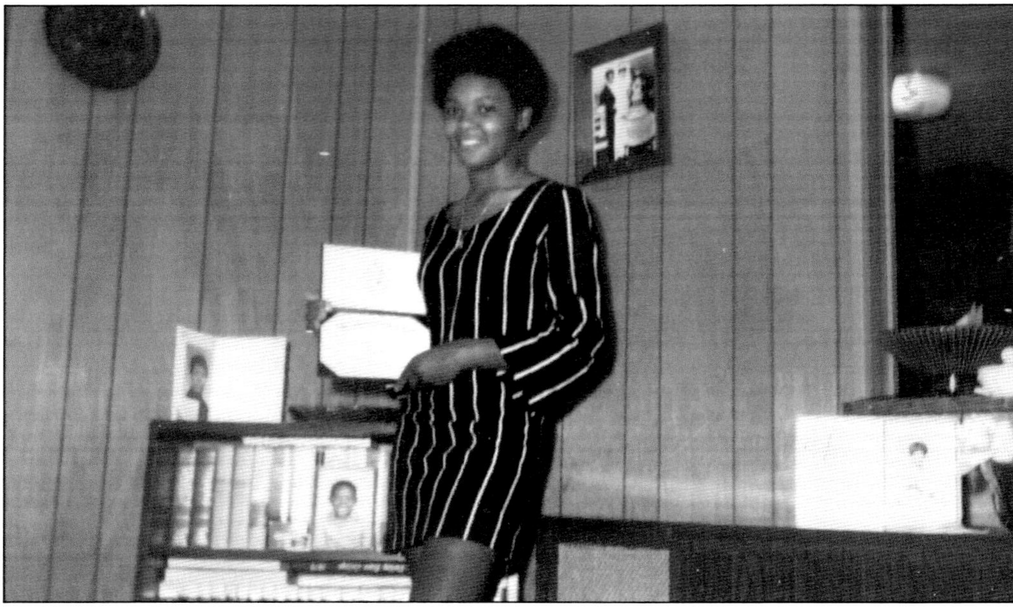

Peggy Glaze Burch. Peggy Glaze Burch was educated in the Elbert County School System. She entered Elbert County High School her senior year, when the local schools were integrated. She is a graduate of Savannah State College and is an owner-operator of an Allstate Insurance Agency in Cary, North Carolina. She is pictured holding her high-school diploma in 1971. (Courtesy Barbara Hamm.)

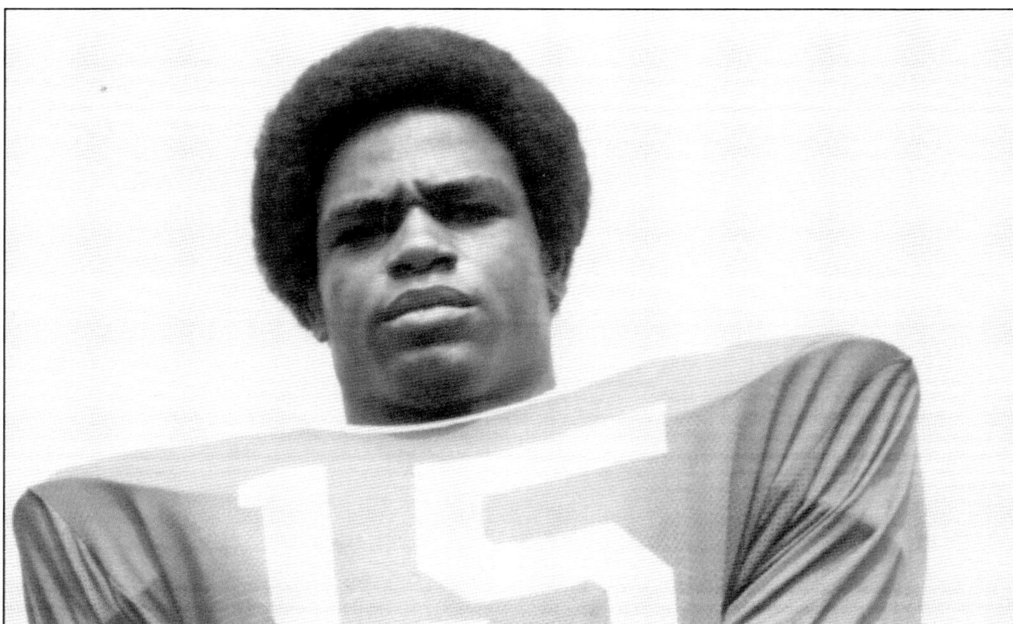

Clark Gaines. Gaines, educated in the Elbert County School System, went on to play professional football as a running back for the New York Jets and the Kansas City Chiefs. (Courtesy Jim-Ree African American Museum, Inc. Archives.)

JOHN CALHOUN. John Calhoun graduated from Blackwell Memorial High School in 1955. The class president, he was voted the most intellectual and the best speaker. He became the director of media relations at the White House and distinguished himself as a special assistant to President Gerald Ford as an advocate for African Americans. Taking the position in 1975, he had two main concerns: the renewal of the Voting Rights Act and strengthening traditionally black colleges and universities. (Courtesy Jim-Ree African American, Inc. Archives.)

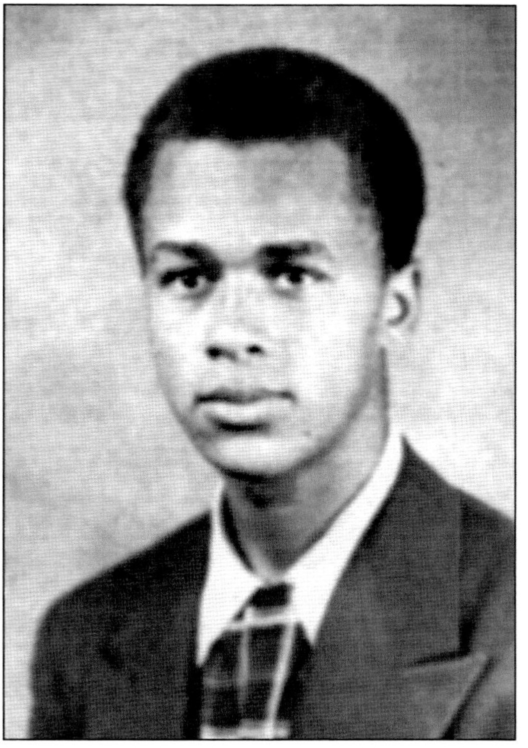

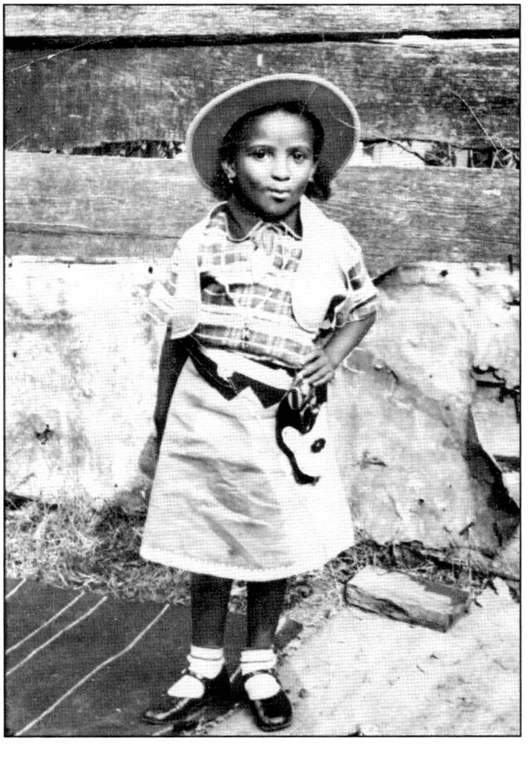

JANICE MARIE HAMM (GALLIMORE). Hamm dreamed of moving to Texas to tame wild horses. By her senior year at Blackwell Memorial High School, she had decided to become a diplomatic translator. With her bachelor's degree from Clarke College, she was accepted to the Peace Corps as a diplomatic translator, but ultimately she joined John Hancock in Atlanta, Georgia. She distinguished herself by becoming an executive director with Prudential Insurance Company and by becoming the chairman of the board of education in Greene County, Georgia. (Courtesy Marie and Charles Hamm Collection.)

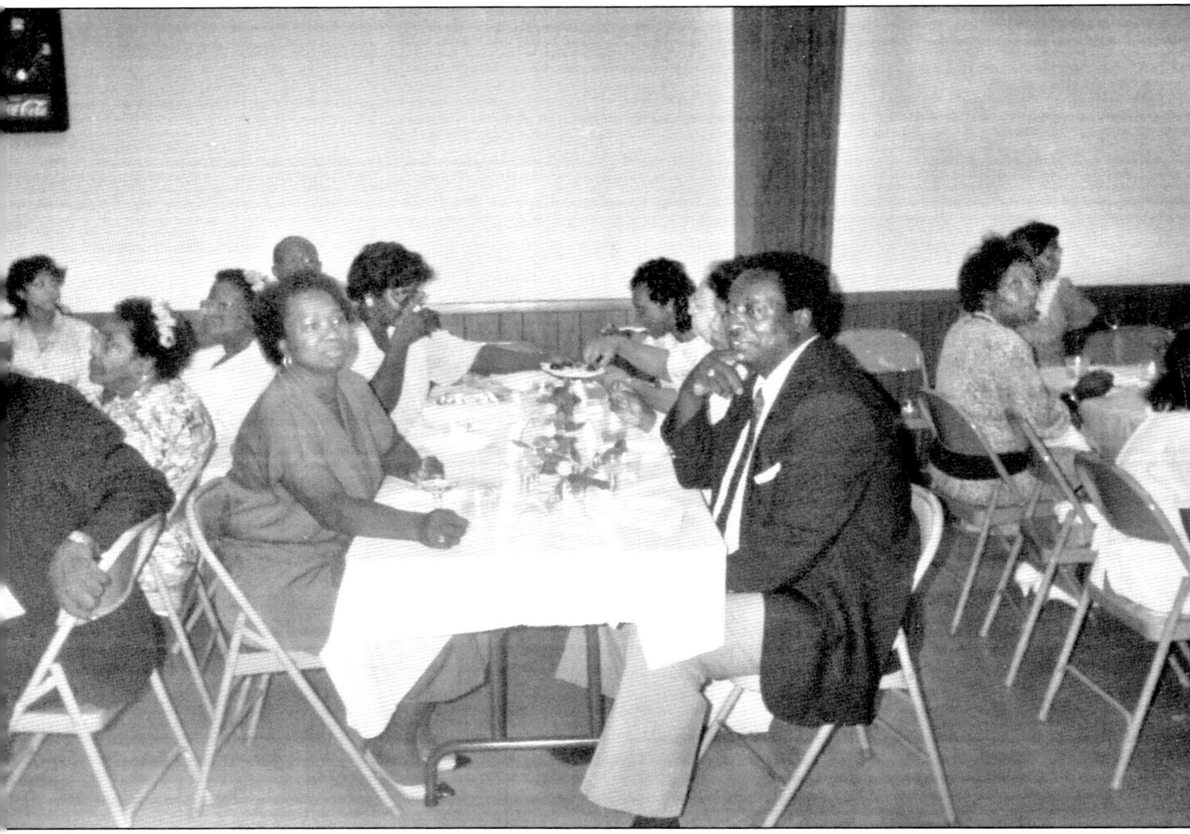

Spotlight. Barbara and Charlie McLendon distinguished themselves early in their professions as educators who cared about their students at Blackwell Memorial High School. Both graduates of Benedict College, Barbara was a science teacher and Charlie was the music and chorus director. With the integration of the public schools, their reputations as excellent educators remained intact. Barbara McLendon left the classroom to become an assistant administrator at Falling Creek Elementary. She is an activist, and though she has never been elected to public office, she qualified to run in several different elections at the local and state levels. Charlie McLendon, a native Elbertonian known for his love of music, left a legacy rich in music appreciation to his former music students and to his community. (Courtesy Mike Fortson.)

Two

The Church is the Heart of the Community

Everybody can be great because everybody can serve.
—Martin Luther King Jr.

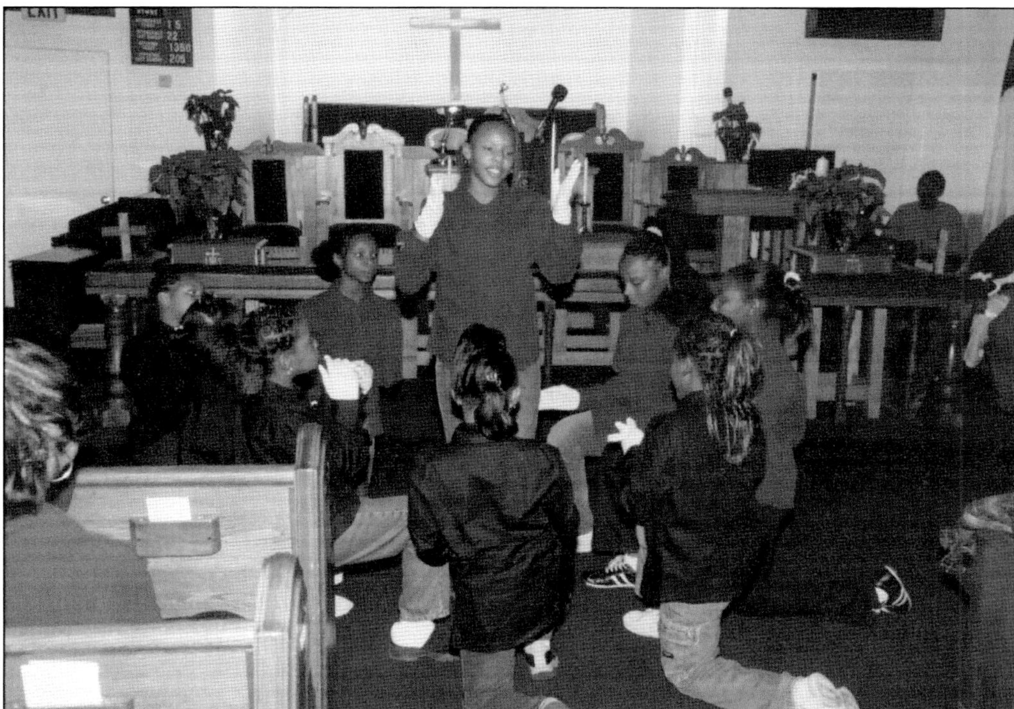

Dancing for Jesus. The youth step team at White's Chapel C.M.E. Church performs for the congregation. Churches provide leadership and service positions for all of their members. (Courtesy Jimmy O. White.)

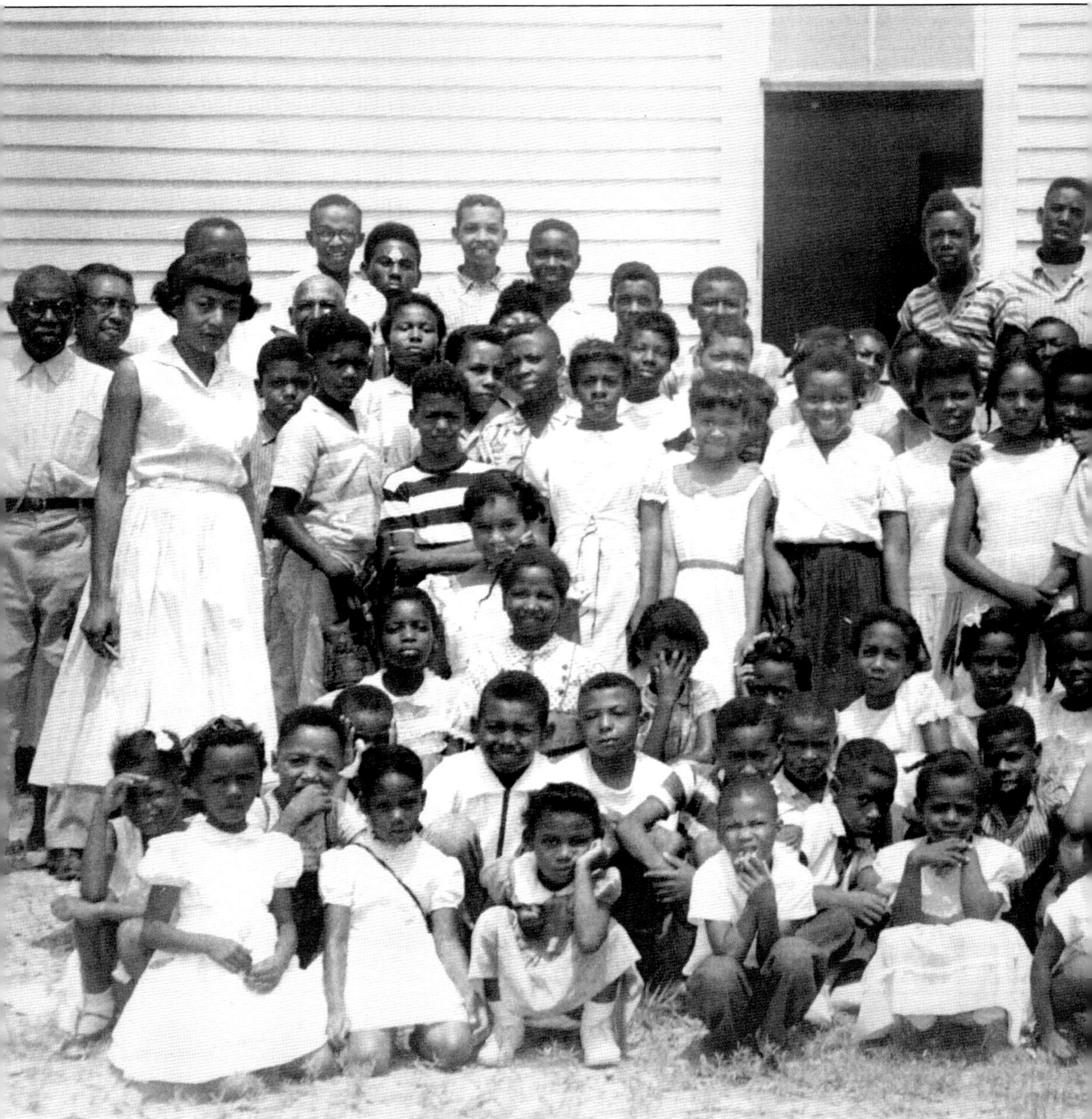

Vacation Bible School at White's Chapel C.M.E. Church. Children in the community attend vacation bible school the summer of 1958 at White's Chapel C.M.E. Church. The bible school

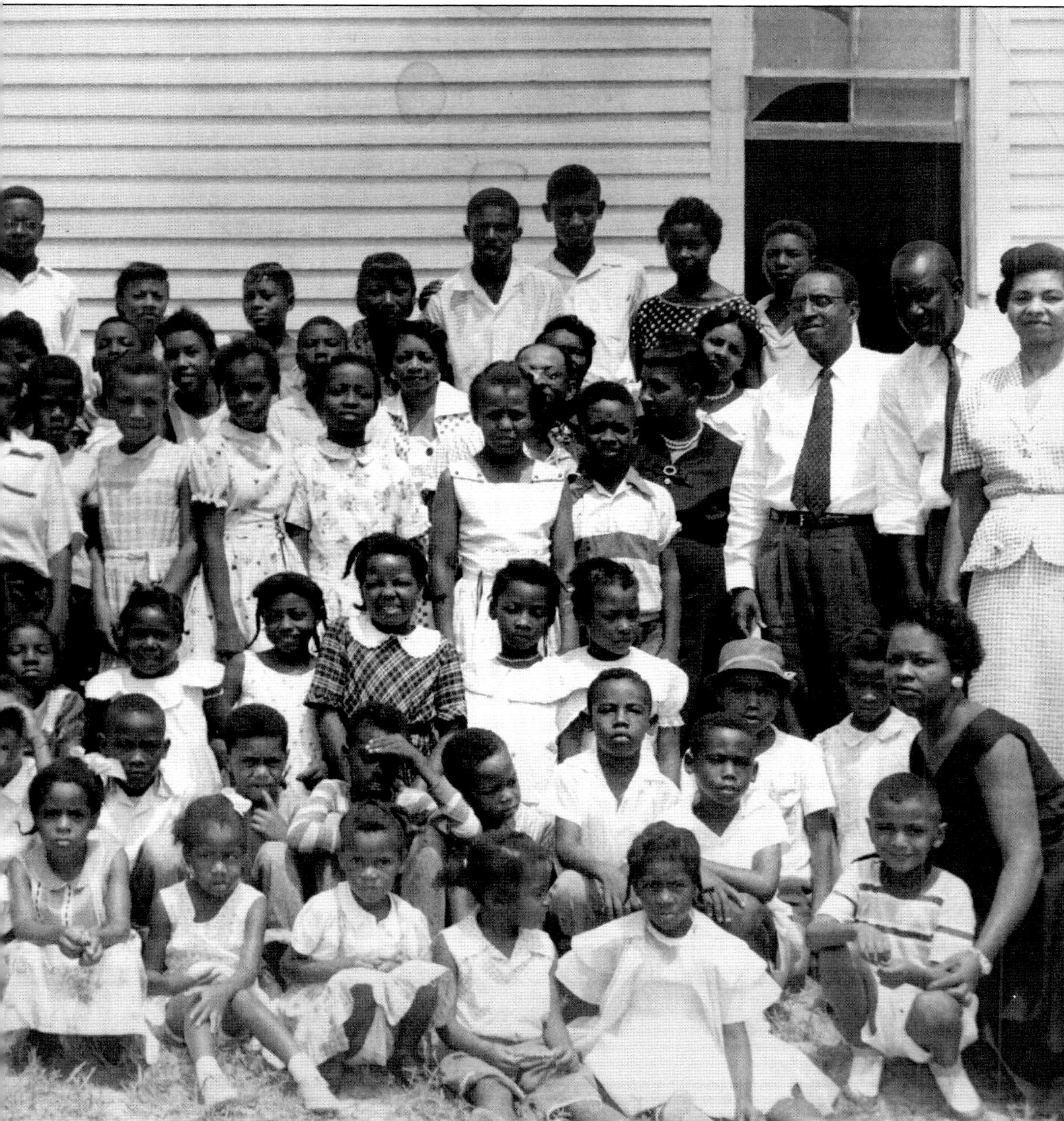

was a joint effort between White's Chapel C.M.E. Church and St. Mary's C.M.E. Church. Any child in the county could attend. (Courtesy Jimmy O. White.)

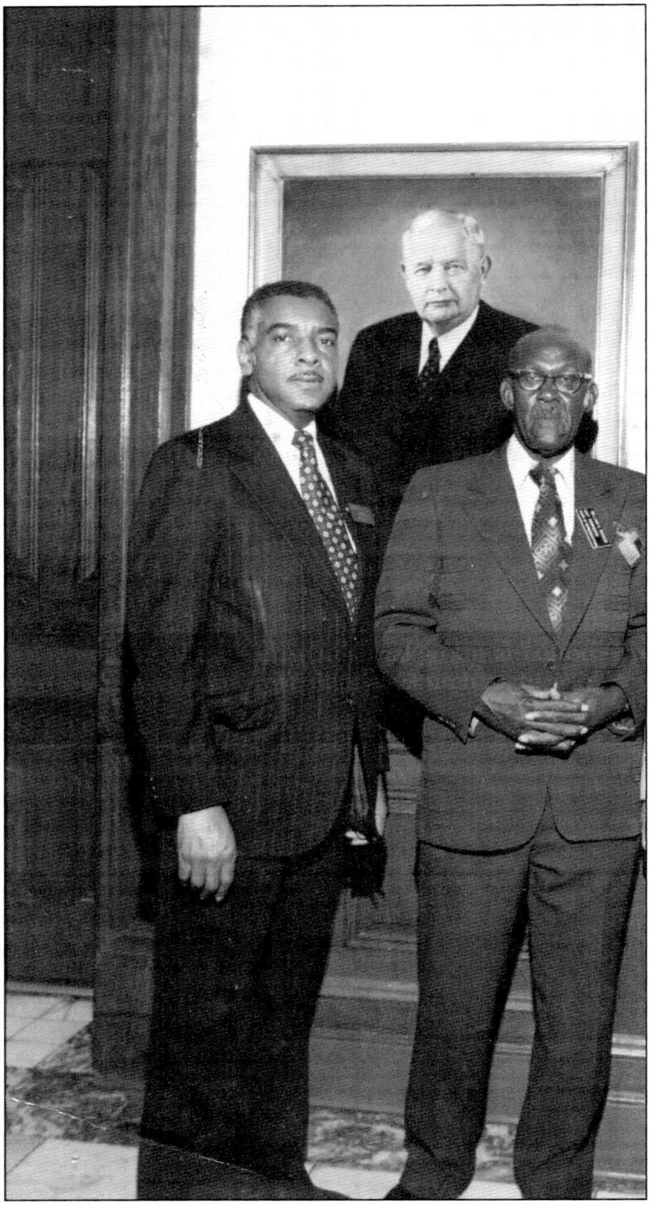

Rev. Billy Rucker, April 27, 1913–February 16, 2004. Rucker attended Hulme's Chapel C.M.E. Primary School and Elberton Colored High School, graduating in 1936 from the 11th grade. He attended Paine College, Johnson C. Smith, Theology A.M.E. School, and Syracuse University Simmons School of Embalming and Mortuary Science. After working as a mortician in Connecticut, Rucker returned to Elbert County, where he became a full-time farmer, raising cattle, pigs, cotton, and grains. He was a World War II veteran and a member of the NAACP; the Elbert County First Silvered Hair Levitates, a Georgia senior friendly organization; and active in other community organizations. In the 1970s, he was a doorkeeper at the Georgia State Capitol in Atlanta during legislature. Pictured are Horace Tate, left, and Billy Rucker, right. (Courtesy Nell Rucker.)

Rev. Estee Echols. Reverend Echols was elected pastor of Union Grove Baptist Church in 1963 and implemented many changes to the church building. He was a pastor at other churches, including, but not limited to, Fork Bethel Baptist Church, Arnold Grove Baptist Church, and Clark Grove Baptist Church. In 1986, he left Union Grove to become the pastor of Cades Chapel Missionary Baptist Church. He is pictured with his wife, Johnnie Lou Echols. (Courtesy Marie and Charles Hamm Collection.)

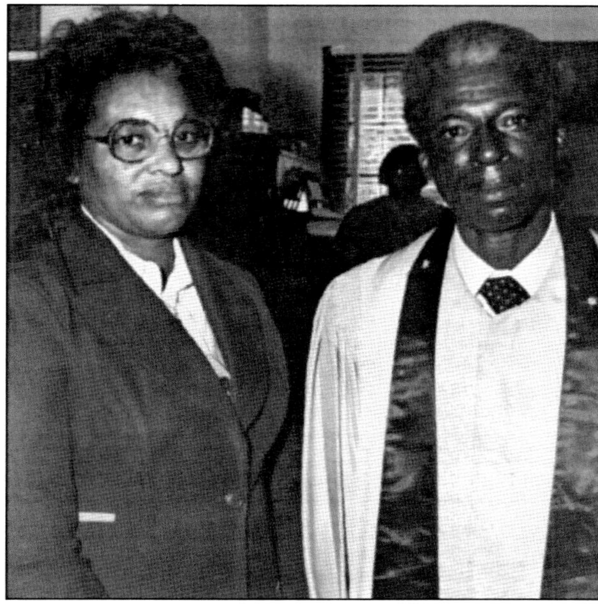

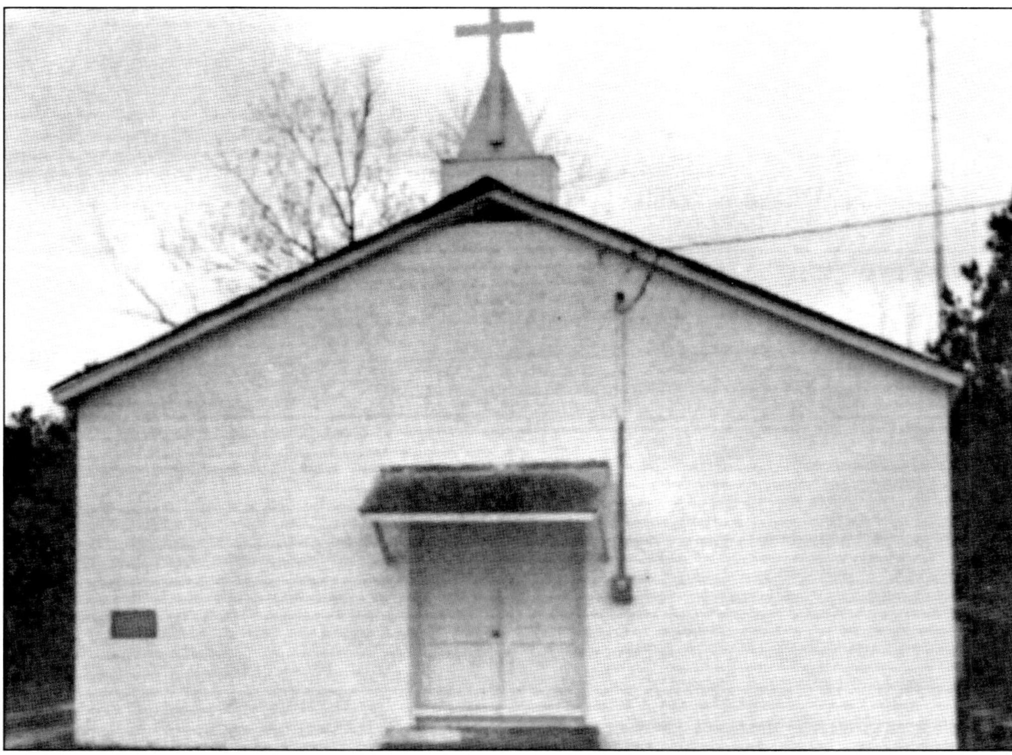

Union Grove Baptist Church. Wagonload by wagonload, Union Grove was moved in 1955 from the Highpoint community off of Lexington Highway to its present location on Pulliam Street. This move was implemented by Rev. D.C. Bell. The new site was a more central location for its members. (Courtesy Marie and Charles Hamm Collection.)

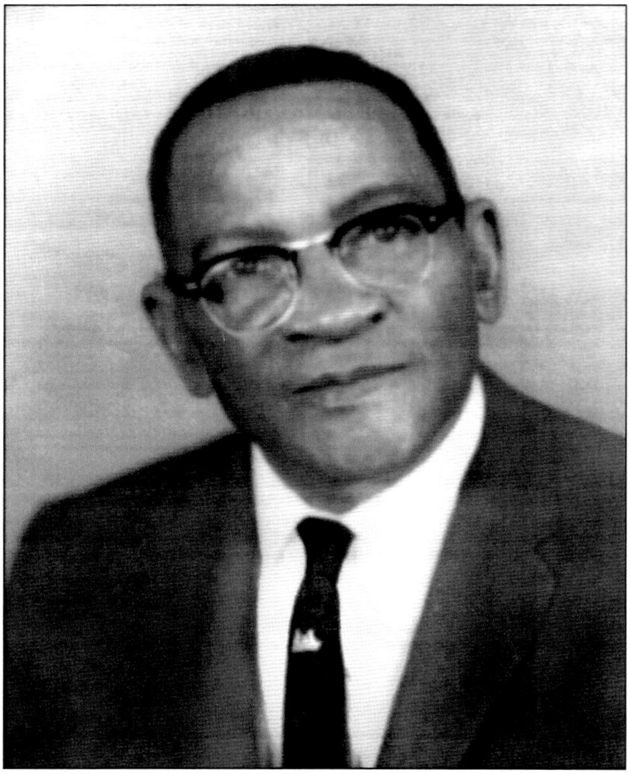

REV. JOHN R. MCKINNEY. Following his father's footsteps, McKinney became an embalmer and ultimately owned the McKinney-Rucker Mortuary. He also became the minister of the church that his father founded. John McKinney's love of God and music prompted him to start the tradition of Fifth Sunday Choir at Lofton Grove Baptist Church, which became popular with other Baptist churches in Elbert County. Baptist churches around the county would take turns hosting choir performances. (Courtesy Lofton Grove Baptist Church Archives.)

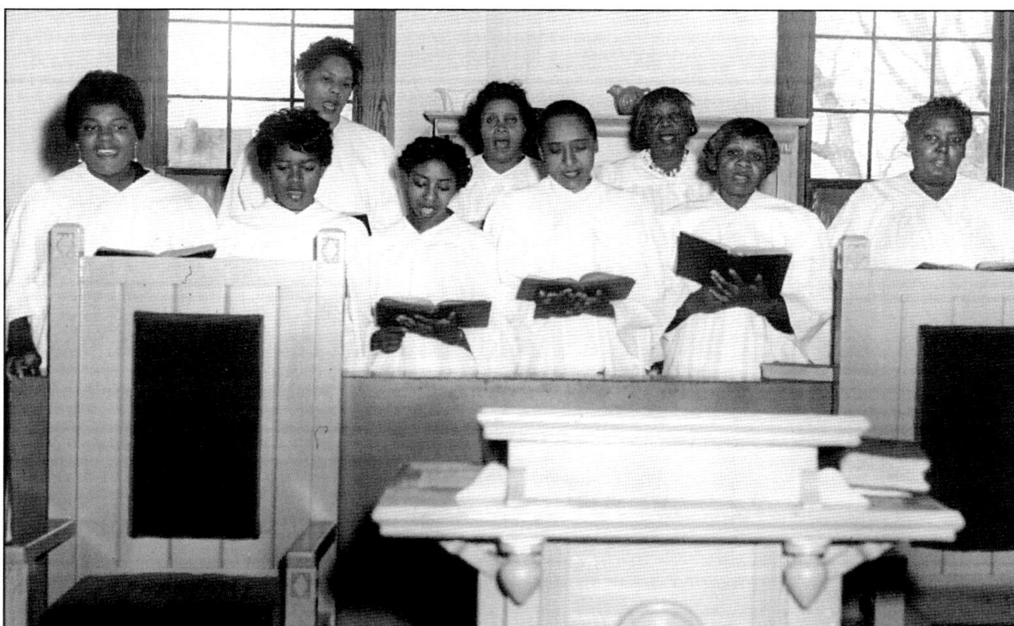

CHOIR AT LOFTON GROVE BAPTIST CHURCH. The choir sings praises for God. (Courtesy Lofton Grove Baptist Church Archives.)

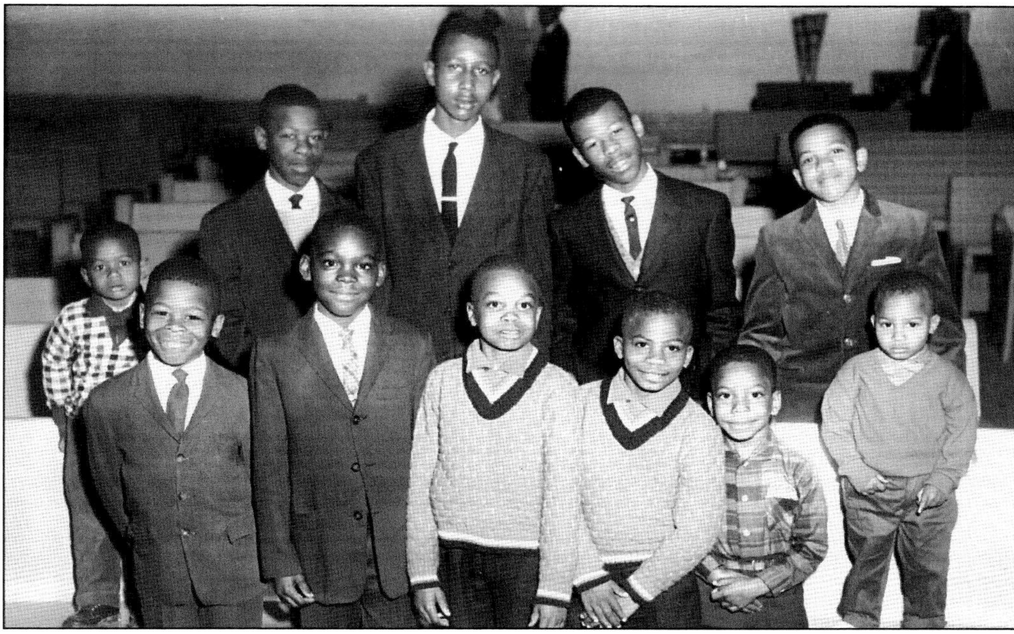

Boys' Youth Group. Members of the Christian social group at Lofton Grove Baptist Church pose for a picture. (Courtesy Lofton Grove Baptist Church Archives.)

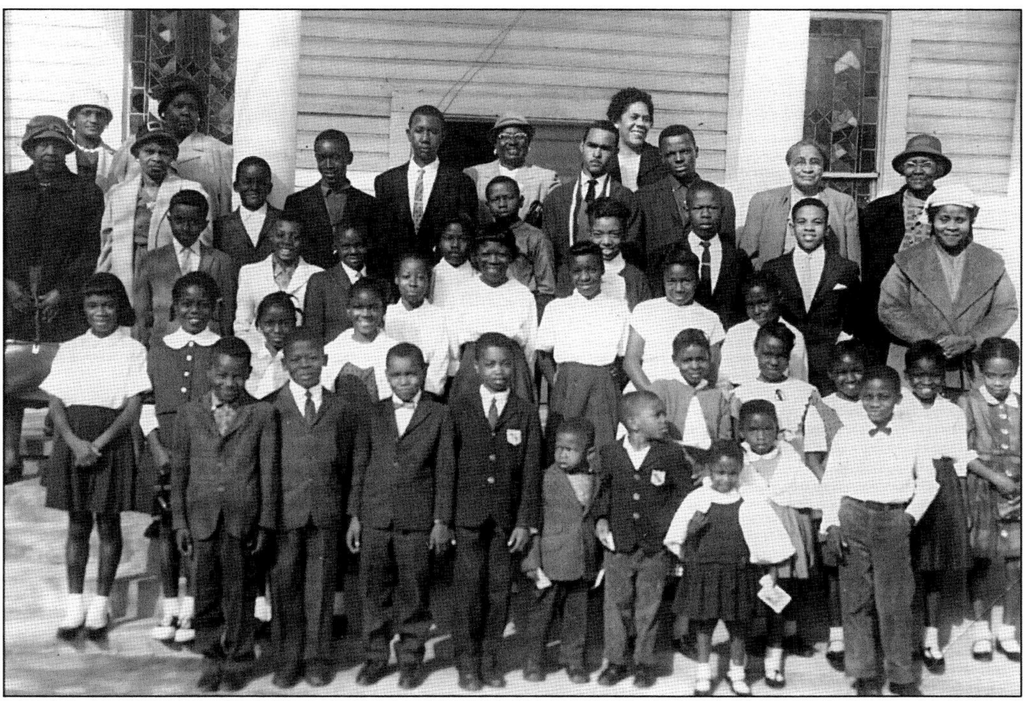

Sunday School. Some of the members of Lofton Grove Baptist Church attend bible study. After church, they pose for a picture. (Courtesy Lofton Grove Baptist Church Archives.)

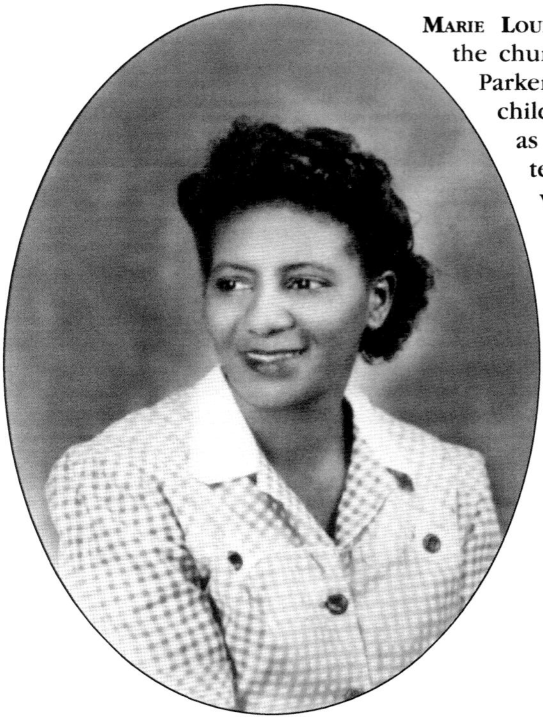

Marie Louise Anne Parker (Hamm). To marry with the church's blessings, Charles Hamm and Marie Parker had to sign an affidavit stating that any children that they should have would be raised as Catholics. Though race relations were terrible, this did not stop Marie Hamm from walking with her four young children about half a mile from her all-black neighborhood to an all-white neighborhood to attend mass. (Courtesy Marie and Charles Hamm Collection.)

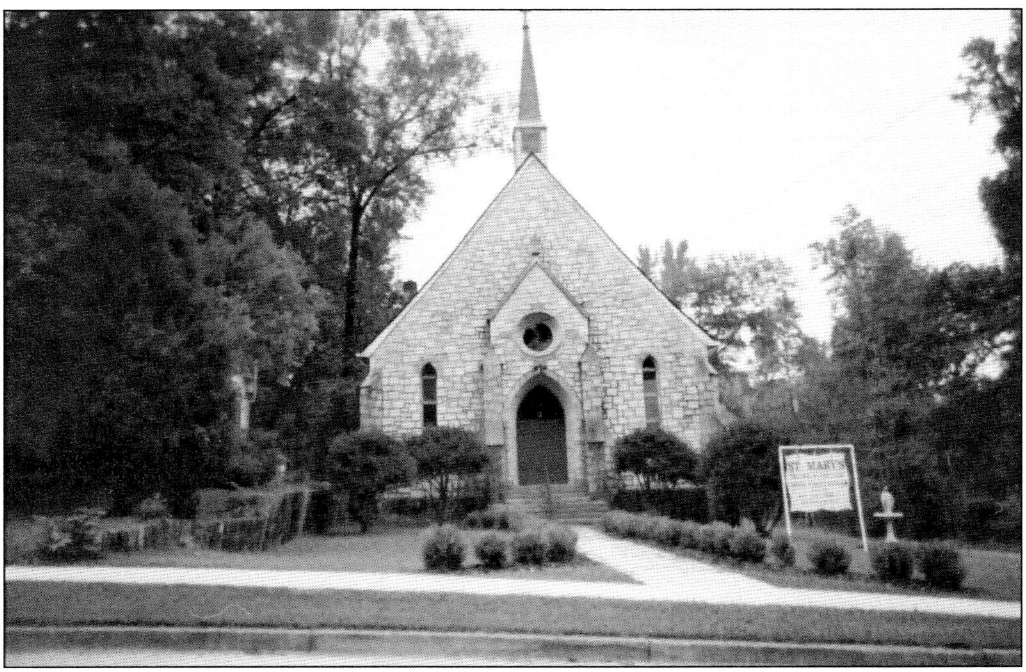

St. Mary's Catholic Church. The church—Father Walter, the nuns, and the congregation—welcomed its first African-American family in 1951. (Courtesy Marie and Charles Hamm Collection.)

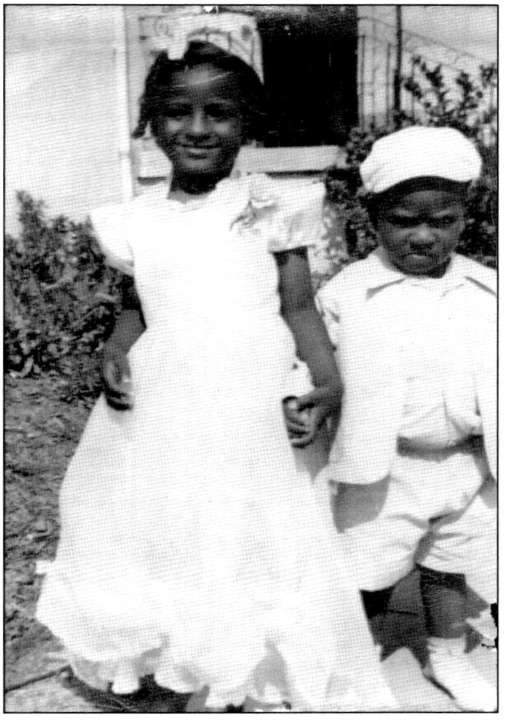

Click. Janice Marie Hamm and Charles Augustus Hamm Jr. pause for a picture after service at St. Mary's Catholic Church in 1952. (Courtesy Marie and Charles Hamm Collection.)

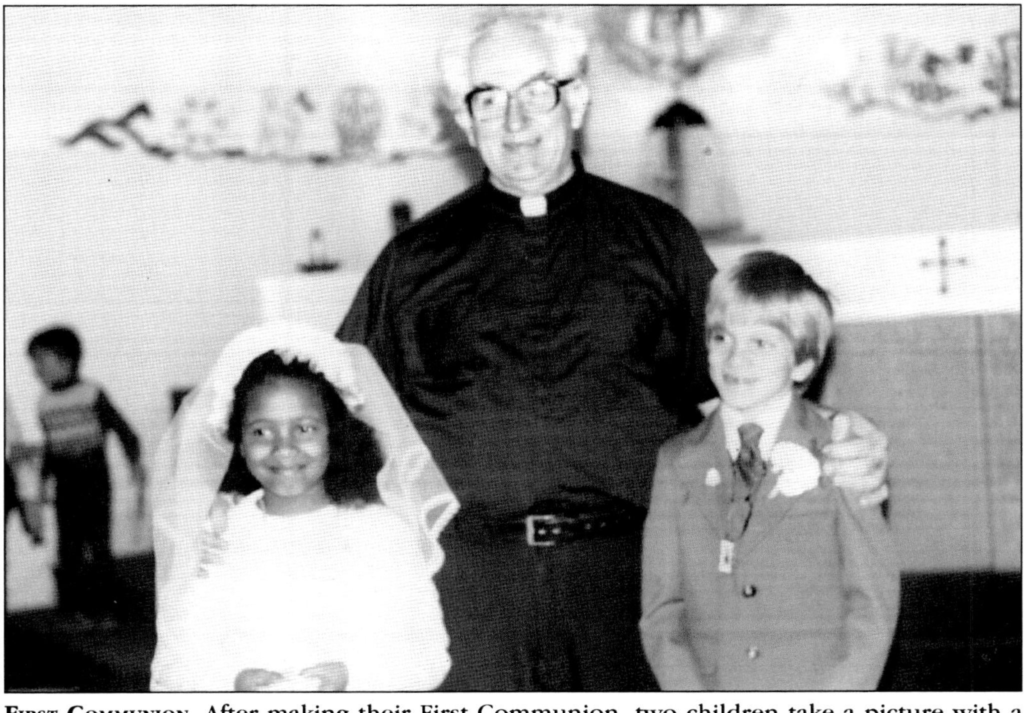

First Communion. After making their First Communion, two children take a picture with a priest at St. Mary's Catholic Church. (Courtesy Patricia Hamm Allen.)

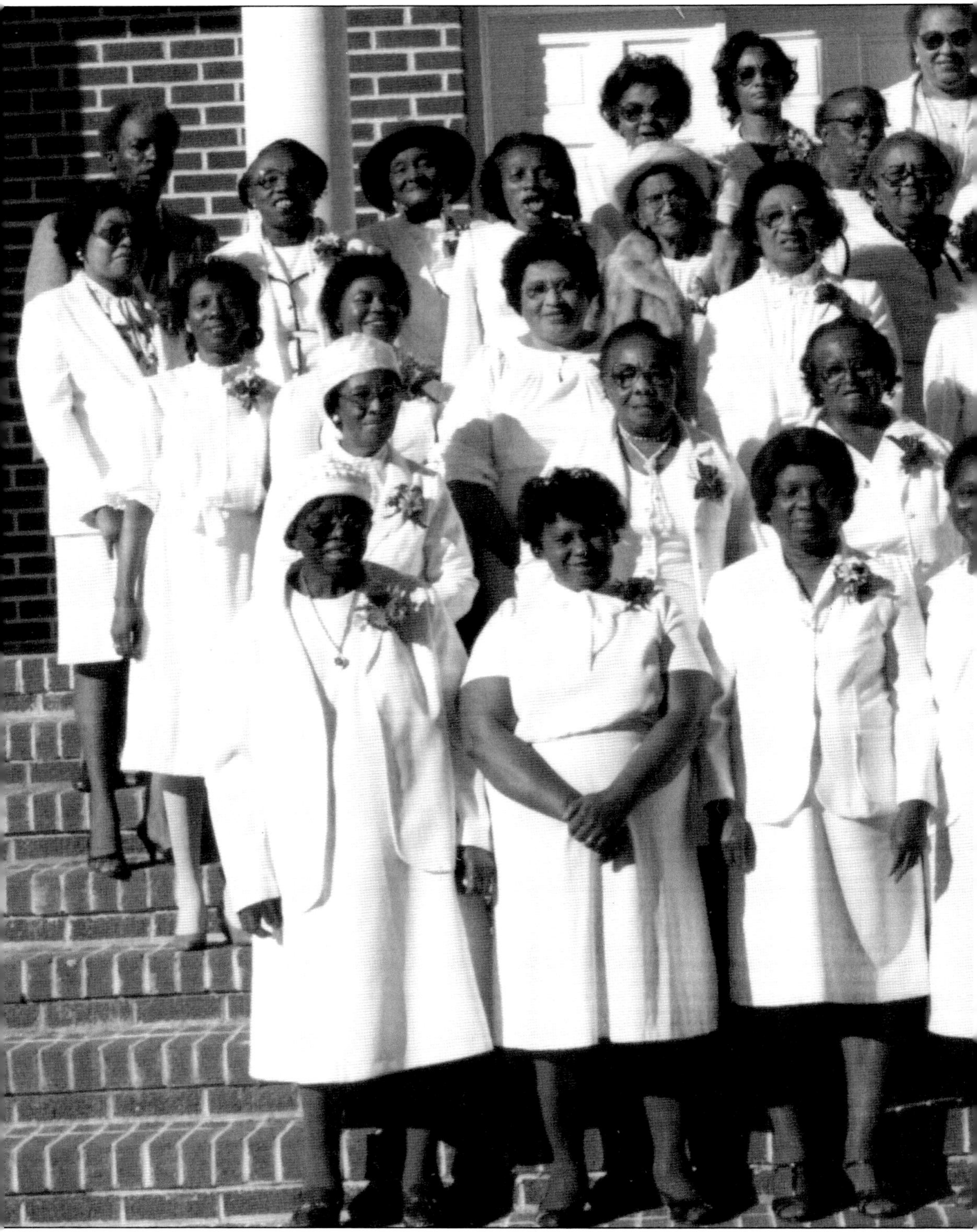

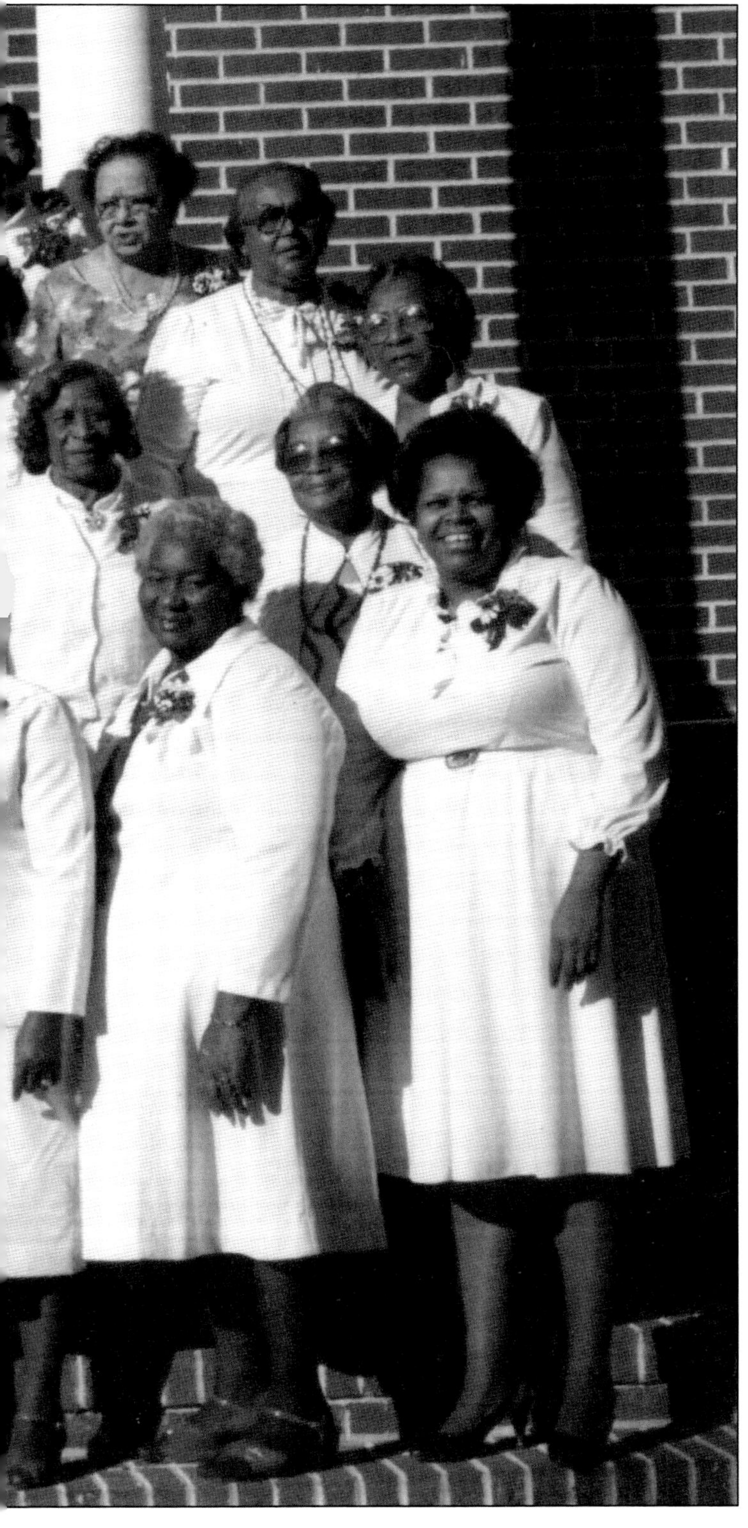

Women's Eighth District Missionary Society. Women from Vance Creek, New Era, Martin Grove, Mt. Calvary, Union Grove, Carlton Grove, Oak Grove, and Bethal Grove meet at Carlton Grove for an Eighth District conference in 1982. Pictured are, from left to right, (first row) Mozelle More, unidentified, Minnie White, Jasper Lu Allen, Mary Allen, and Vertis Mcintosh Martin; (second row) Ruby Banks Brawner, Drucilla Banks, Sallie Lee, Waterbelle Hughes, Lula Hughes, and Hester Mae Harper; (third row) Doris Hughes, unidentified, Janie Smith Bone, Genora Hamm Biggs, Janesta McKinney, and Willie Sue Syphore; (fourth row) Minnie Winston Abner, Molly Jones, Ida Henry Heard, Rosa Fortson, and Hattie Dye Johnson; (fifth row) Rev. S.T. Echols, Odessa Allen, and Lillie Pressley; (sixth row) Laura Lee Perrin, Shirley Dubose, and Imogene Holland. (Courtesy of Genora Hamm Biggs.)

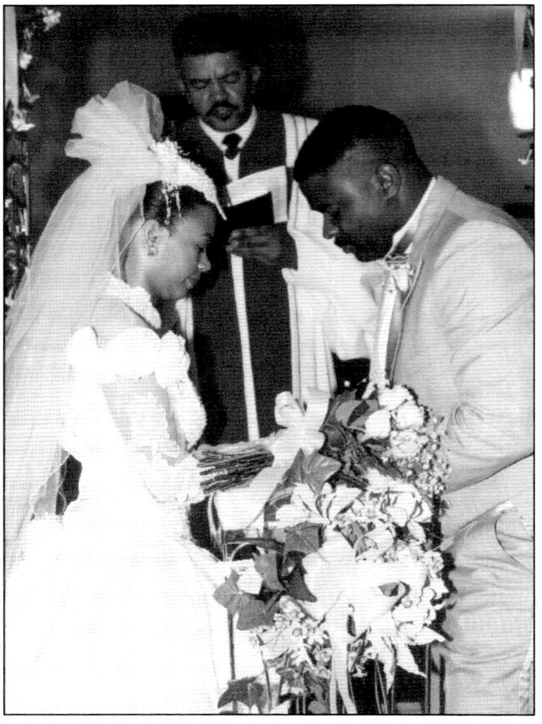

Nuptials. Rev. Thomas Jackson performs the marriage ceremony for Pamela Fortson and Charles Benefield at Saint Mary's C.ME. Church. (Courtesy Mike Fortson.)

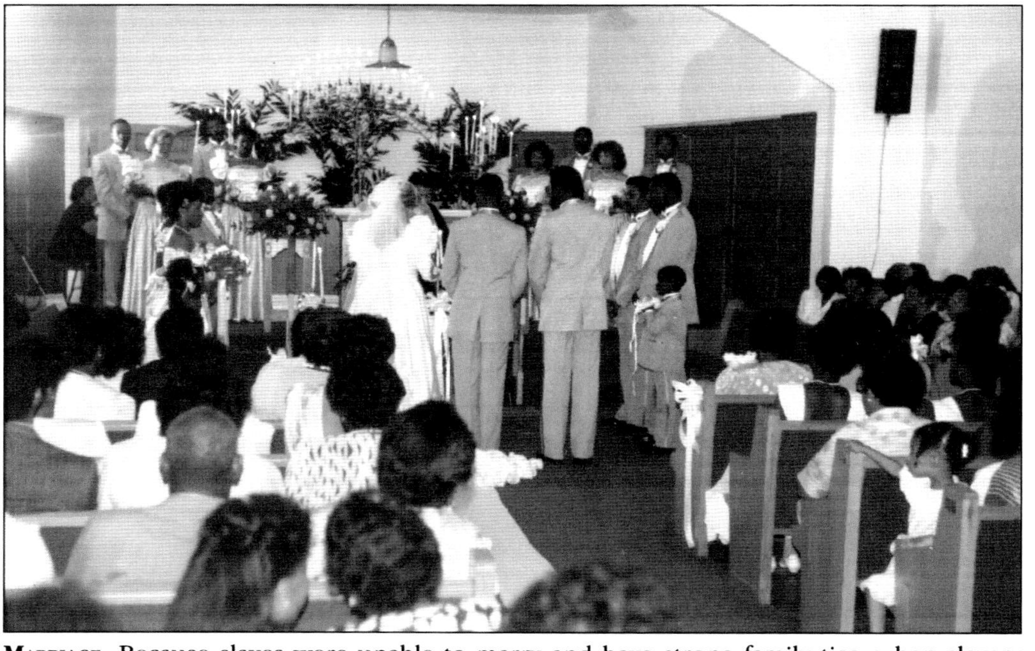

Marriage. Because slaves were unable to marry and have strong family ties, when slavery ended, marriage and family, for many former slaves, were synonymous with freedom. A couple exchanges vows at New Era Baptist Church. (Courtesy Marie and Charles Hamm Collection.)

TRUE BELIEVERS OUTREACH MINISTRY. True Believers Outreach Ministry is non-denominational. Rev. Herman Glaze, the pastor of the church, and first lady Jewell Glaze are pictured. (Courtesy Diana and Joe Glaze.)

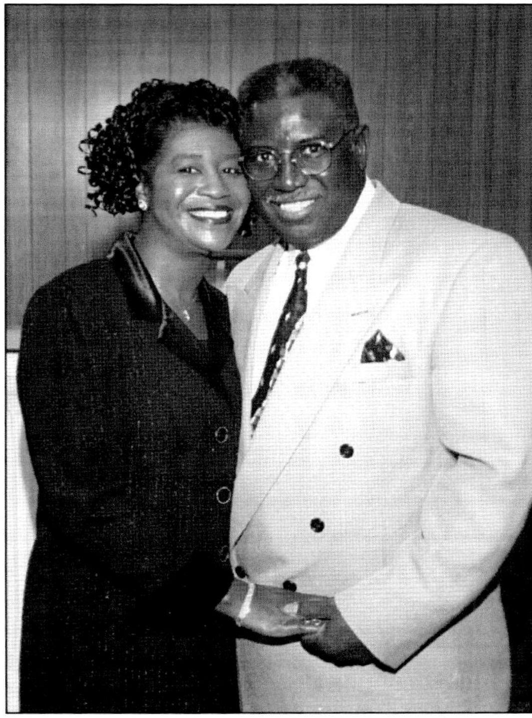

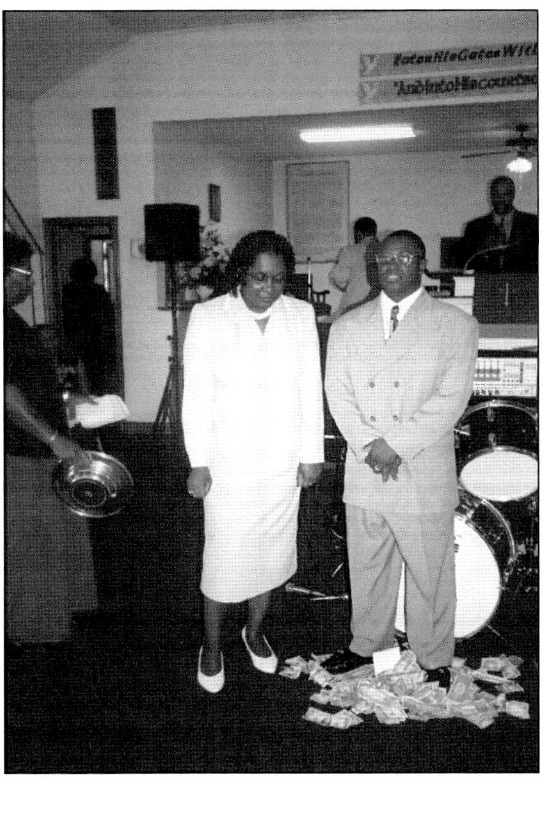

A BLESSING. Cades Chapel Missionary Baptist Church congregation and pastor "break off"—give a financial blessing—to Diana Demoss Glaze and Joe Glaze at Rev. Joe Glaze's trial sermon. Traditionally, the couple does not pick up the money. A member from the congregation blesses the offering and then gives it to the recipient. Today, Reverend Glaze is the pastor of Pole Branch Missionary Baptist Church in Tignall, Georgia. (Courtesy Diana and Joe Glaze.)

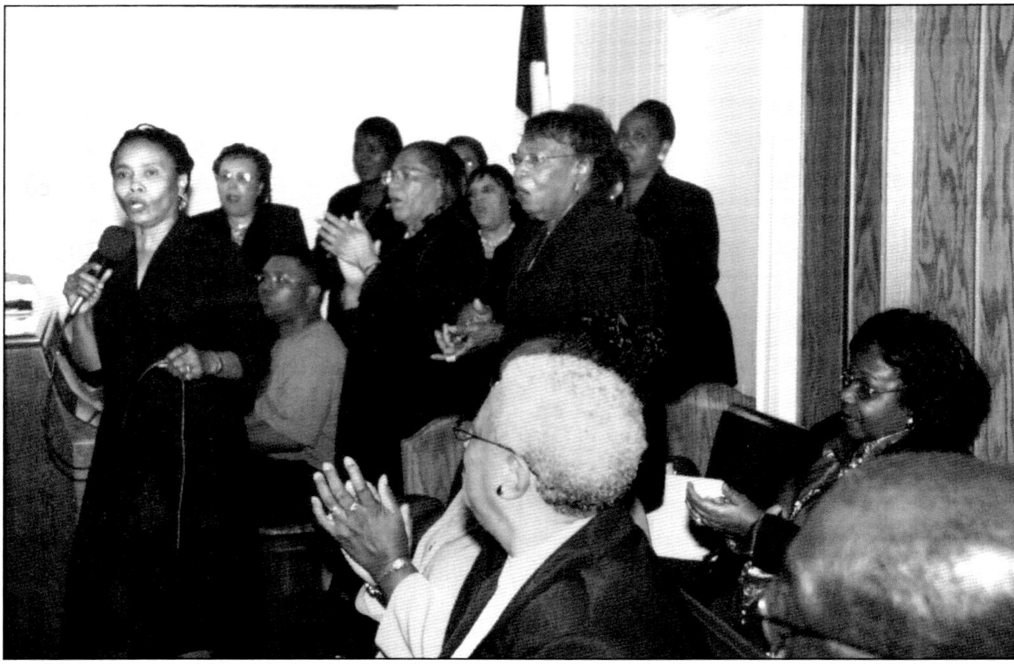

Le Ladies. The Christian singing group performs at White Chapel C.M.E. Church. (Courtesy Jimmy O. White.)

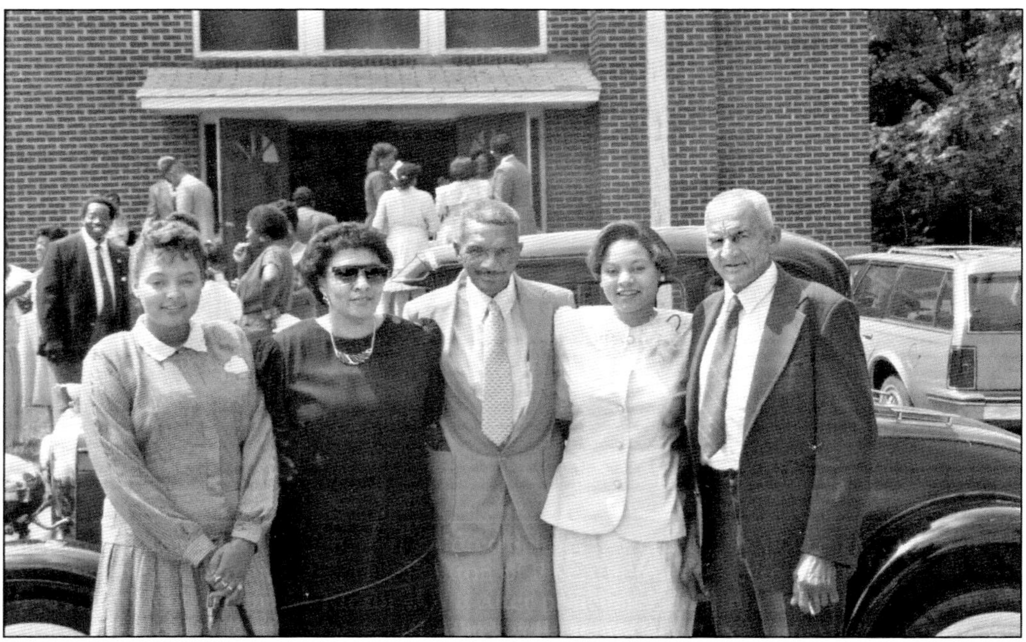

Leroy Fortson. Over a half a century after World War II had ended, Leroy Fortson received many commendations for heroic actions during the war. Pictured at St. Mary's C.M.E. Church after a wedding ceremony are Cynthia Fortson, Linda Fortson Rucker, John Neal Fortson, Rachel Rucker, and Leroy Fortson. (Courtesy Mike Fortson.)

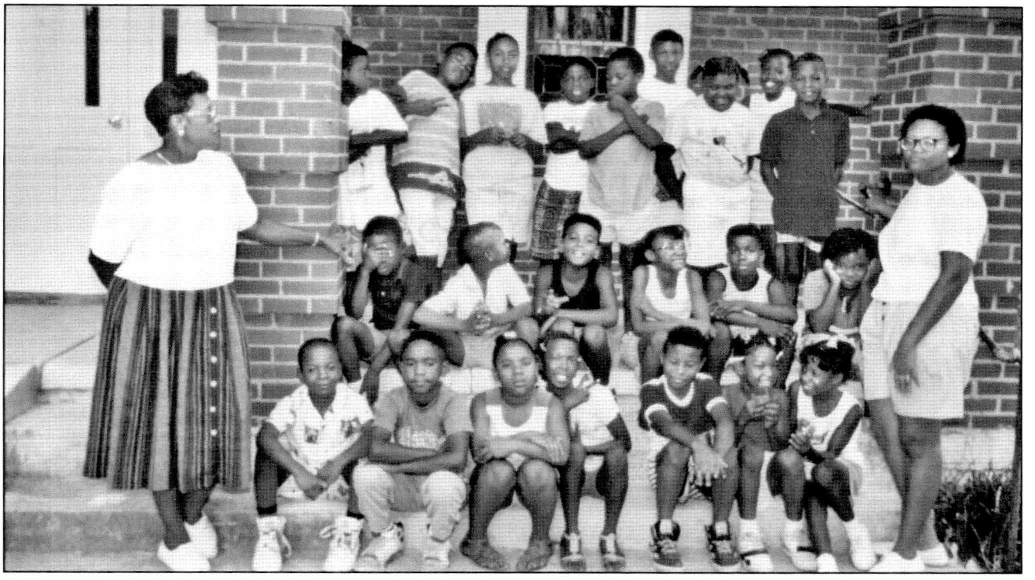

Summer Lunch Program. Adults pictured are Helen Jones (left) and Glenda Allen (right). Even though school was out for the summer, the state continued to sponsor a lunch program for any youth under 21 years of age. Youths converge at the church for their meal and pause to take a picture while they wait for the delivery of the food. (Courtesy Minnie Winston Abner.)

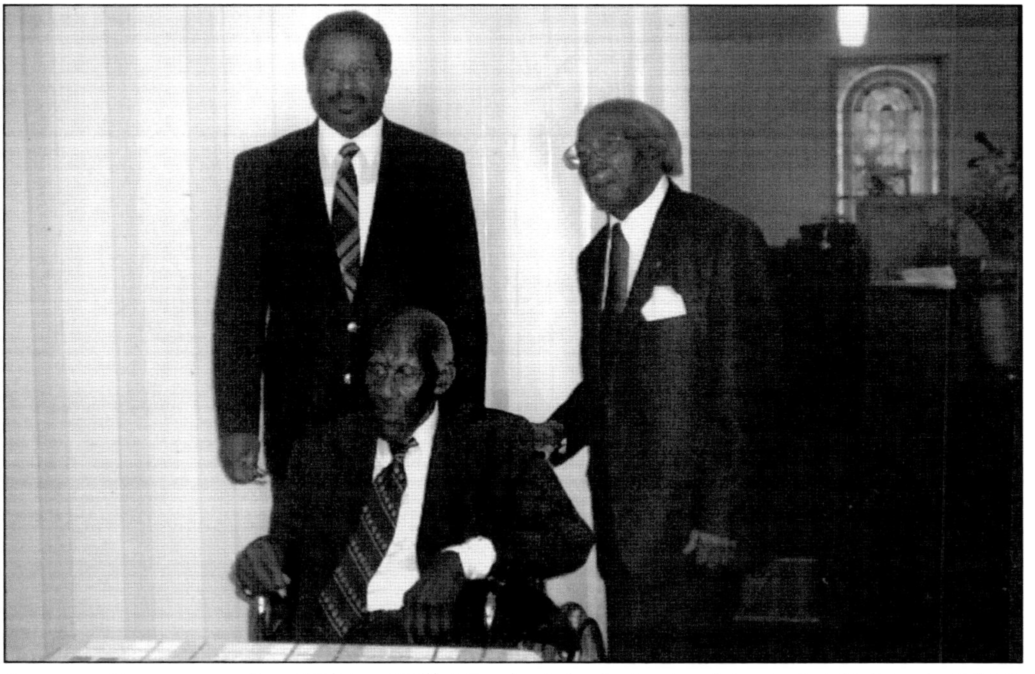

Birthday Celebration. Rev. William "Billy" Rucker's birthday is celebrated at St. Mary's C.M.E. Church. Dr. Slater is pictured on the left, Rev. Billy Rucker is seated, and Marion Davis is on the right. (Courtesy Nell Rucker.)

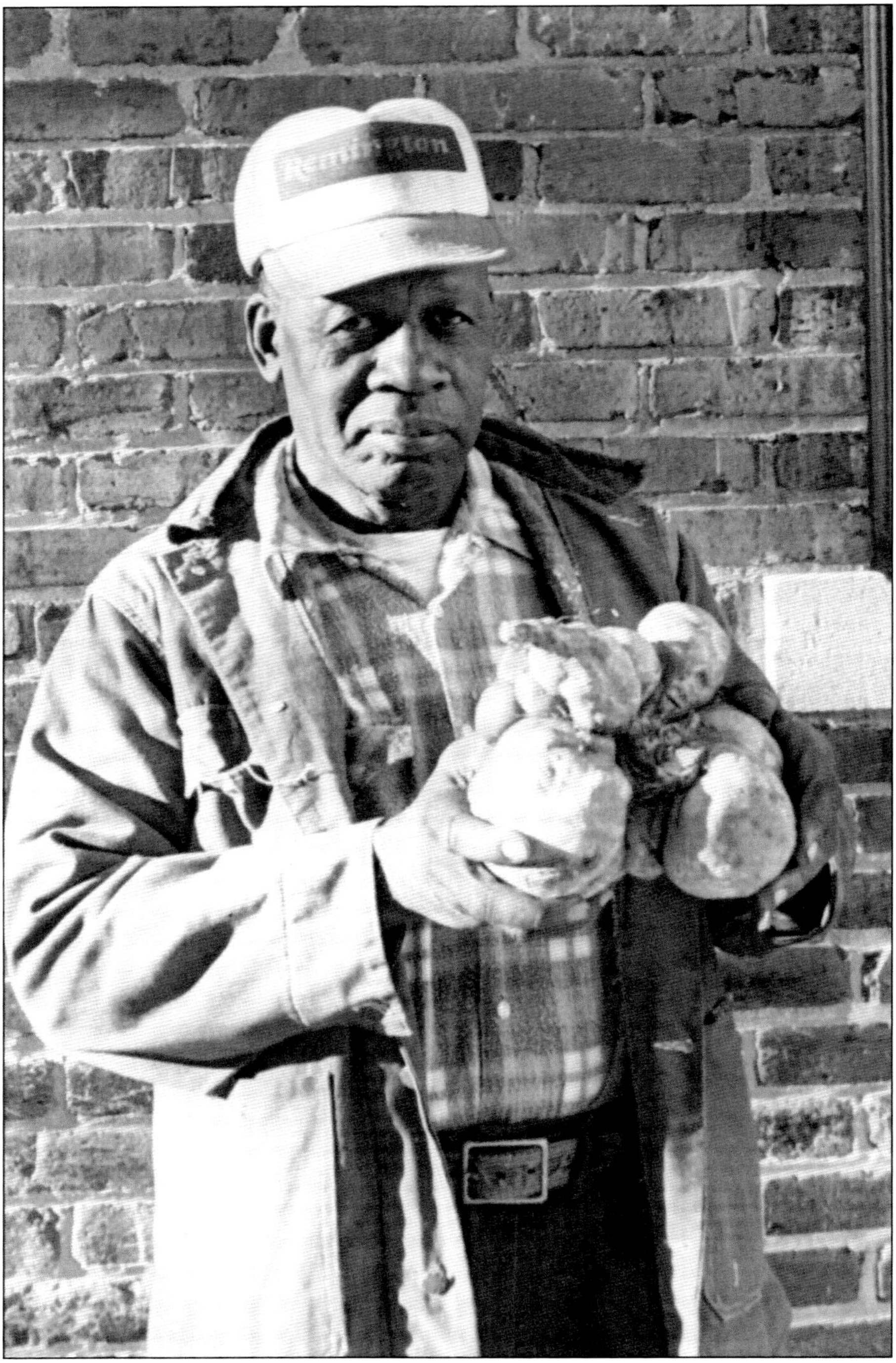

SPOTLIGHT. Then: Harry Tate shows off a tuber that he grew in his garden; today: Harry Tate is the only deacon in Cades Chapel Missionary Baptist Church's history to hold the seat of chairman of the church for so long. He has held that position for 57 years! (Courtesy Jim-Ree African American Museum, Inc. Archives.)

Three

Schools Provide Educations

Of all the civil rights the world has struggled and fought for, for 5,000 years, the right to learn is undoubtedly the most fundamental.
—W.E.B. Dubois

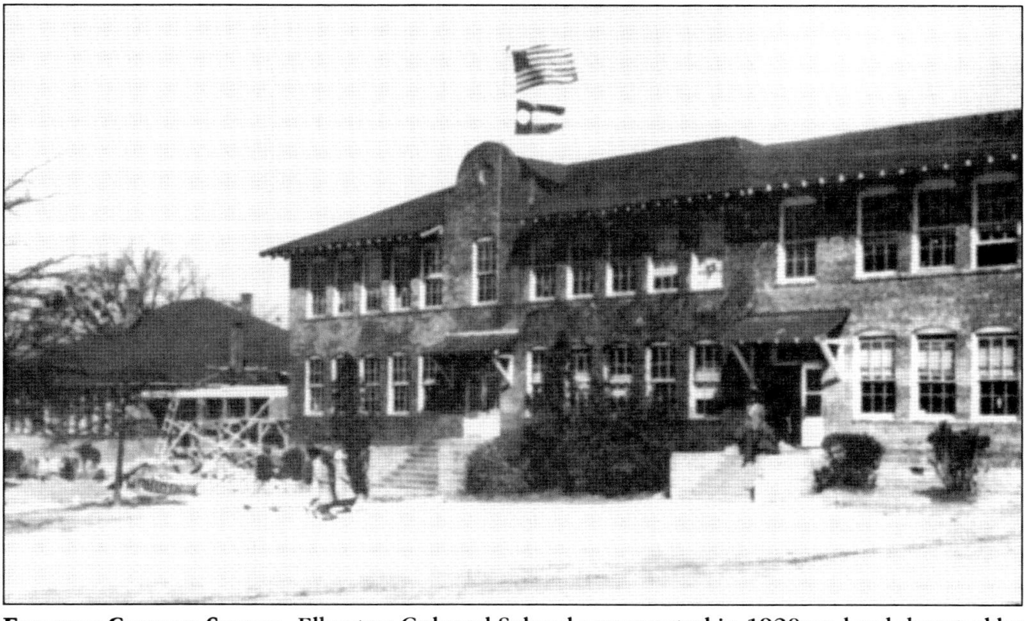

Elberton Colored School. Elberton Colored School was erected in 1920 on land donated by Miss Sarah Bowman and Mrs. Laura Lofton of Elberton to the "negro children." The school housed students in grades 1 through 11. After principal Paul J. Blackwell's death, Elberton Colored School was renamed Paul J. Blackwell Memorial School, honoring the man who gave so much of himself to his students and staff. In the picture, a breezeway was being built to connect the two buildings in 1949 so that the children would not get wet as they traveled between buildings. The school's name was later shortened to Blackwell Memorial School. (Courtesy Azalee Biggs Dye.)

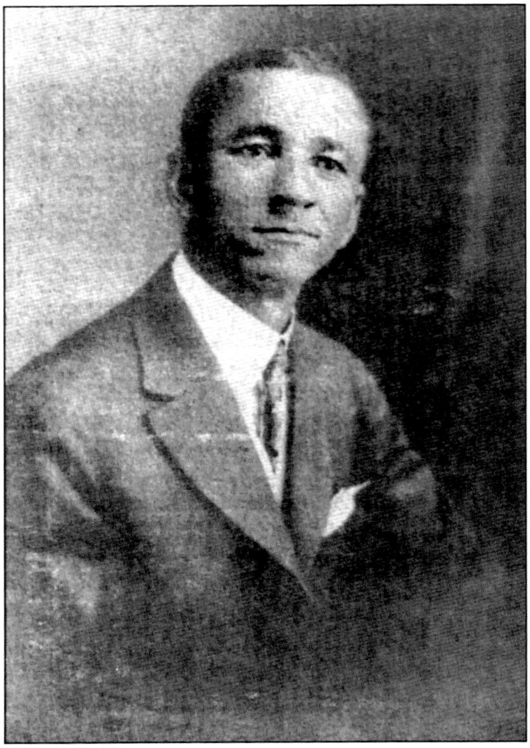

Paul Julian Blackwell, February 16, 1879–May 14, 1948. Blackwell attended preparatory school at Morris Brown University and earned his bachelor's degree from Paine College in 1902. He began teaching in Rayston and was hired as a principal of Elberton Colored School in 1908. A draft registration card placed him at Camp Wheeler in Macon on September 10, 1918, during World War I. He indicated that the Army YMCA employed him. He died while rushing to assist a teacher with an unruly student. (Courtesy Patricia Hamm Allen.)

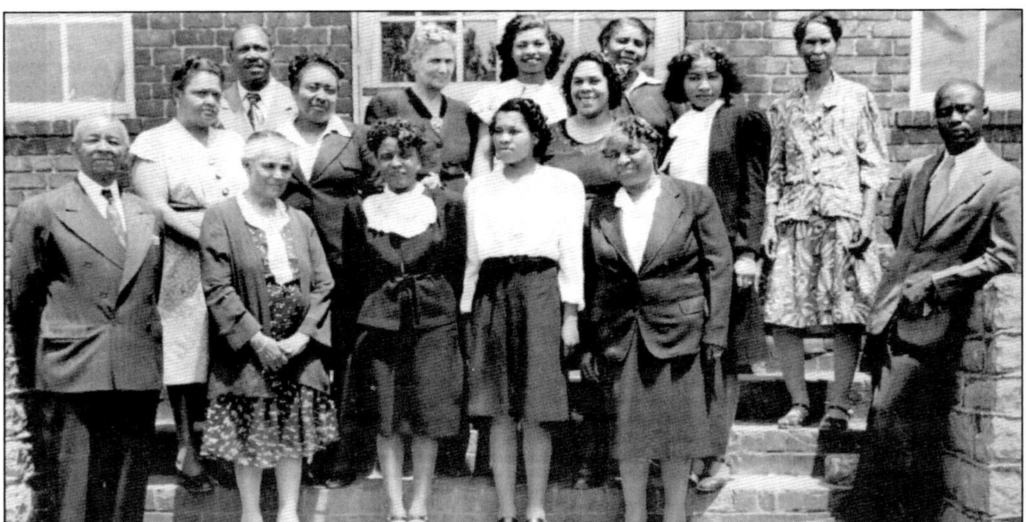

Elberton Colored School Faculty. The faculty poses for a picture around 1944. Pictured are, from left to right, (front row) "Professor" Paul J. Blackwell, Alice Pitt, two unidentified people, Mary Frances Roebuck, and Walter Z. Thomas; (middle row) Hattie Dye Johnson, Neva J. Dennis, Janesta McKinney, and unidentified; (back row) Herbert King, Martha Bessie Brewer Williams, Loraine Grippon (Smith), Miriam Keys, and Georgia Upshaw. (Courtesy Jim-Ree African American Museum, Inc. Archives.)

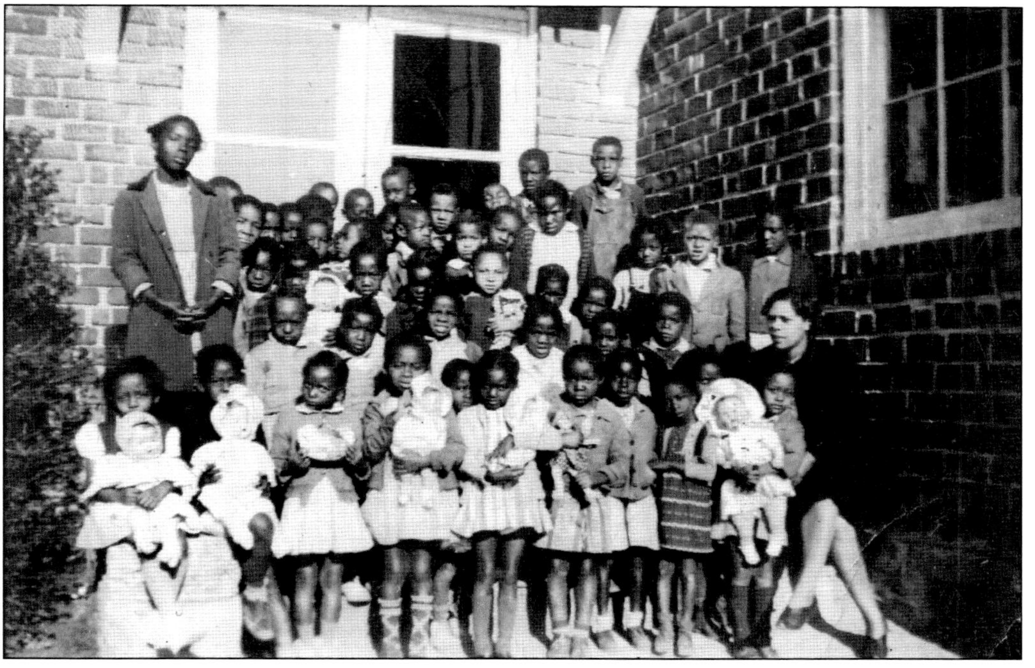

Toy Day. First-grade students show off their toys at Elberton Colored School in 1941. Mrs. Janesta McKinney poses for a picture with her students. (Courtesy Genora Hamm Biggs.)

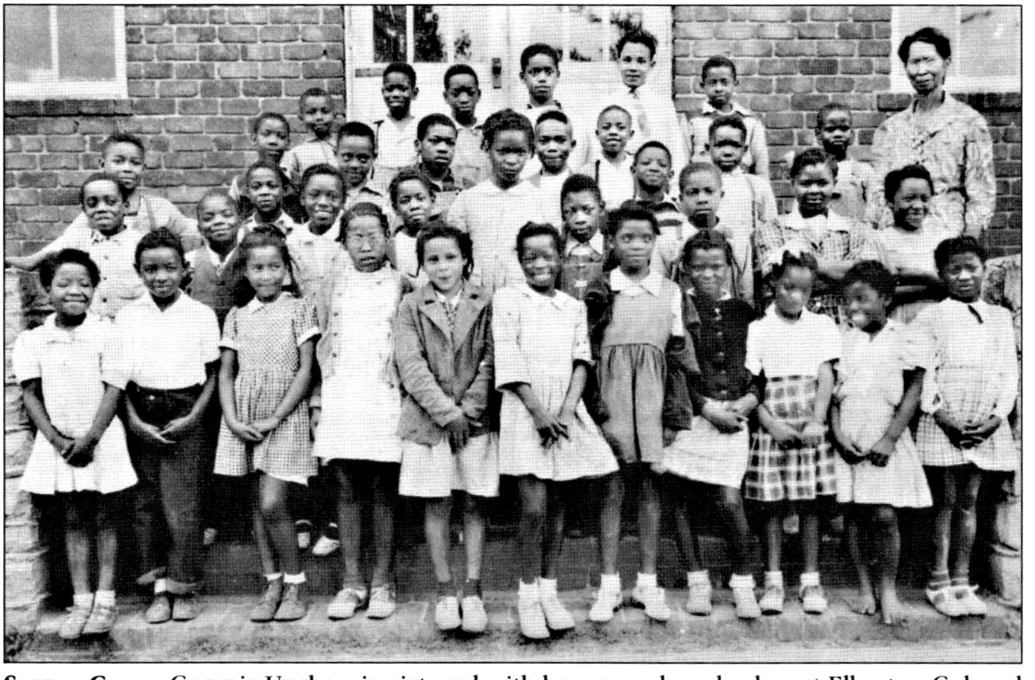

Second Grade. Georgia Upshaw is pictured with her second-grade class at Elberton Colored School. (Courtesy Jim-Ree African American Museum, Inc. Archives.)

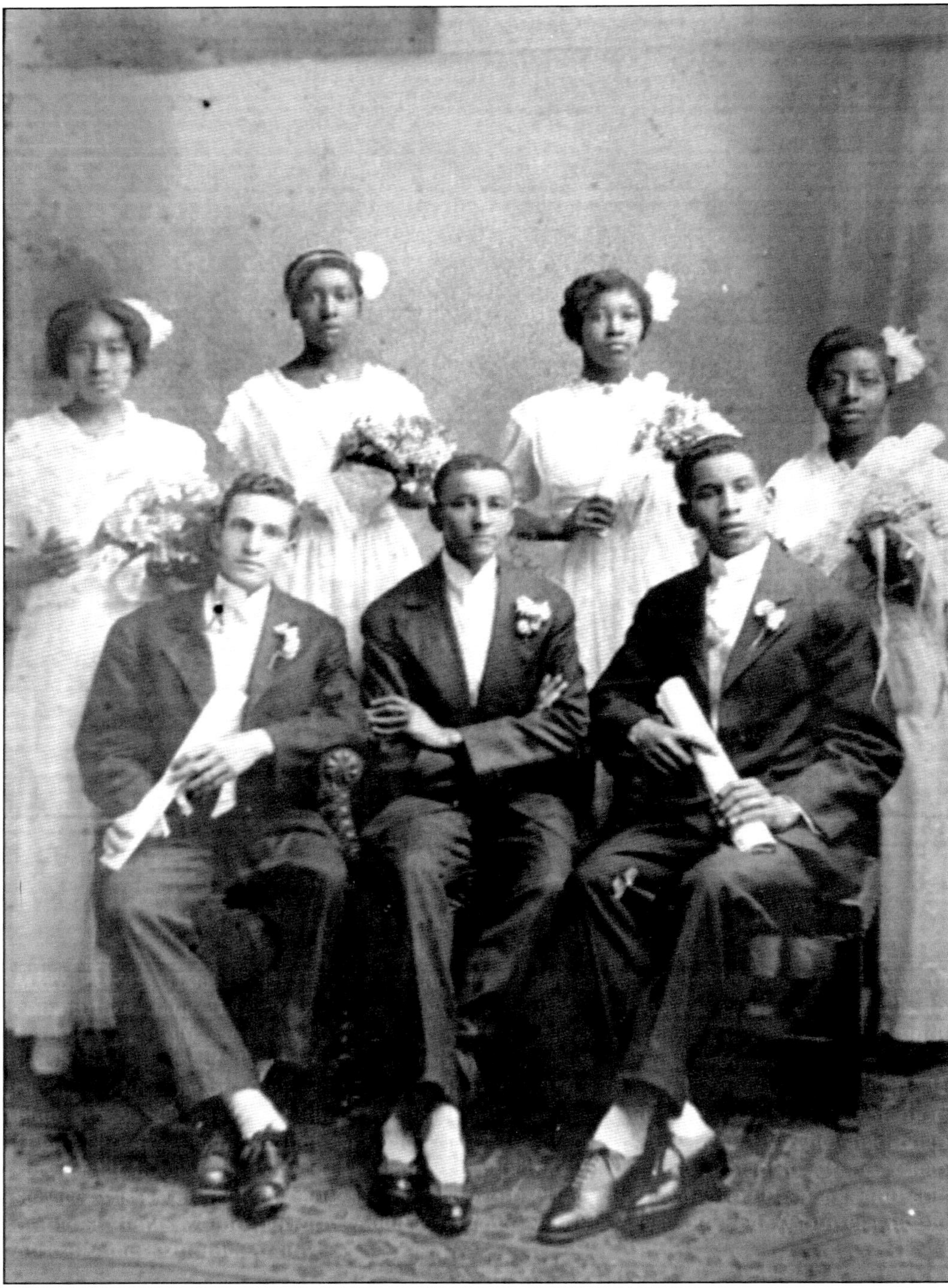

Graduation. At the end of the graduation ceremony, Paul J. Blackwell (center) posed for a picture with the recent graduates of Elberton Colored School. (Courtesy Sarah J. Willingham.)

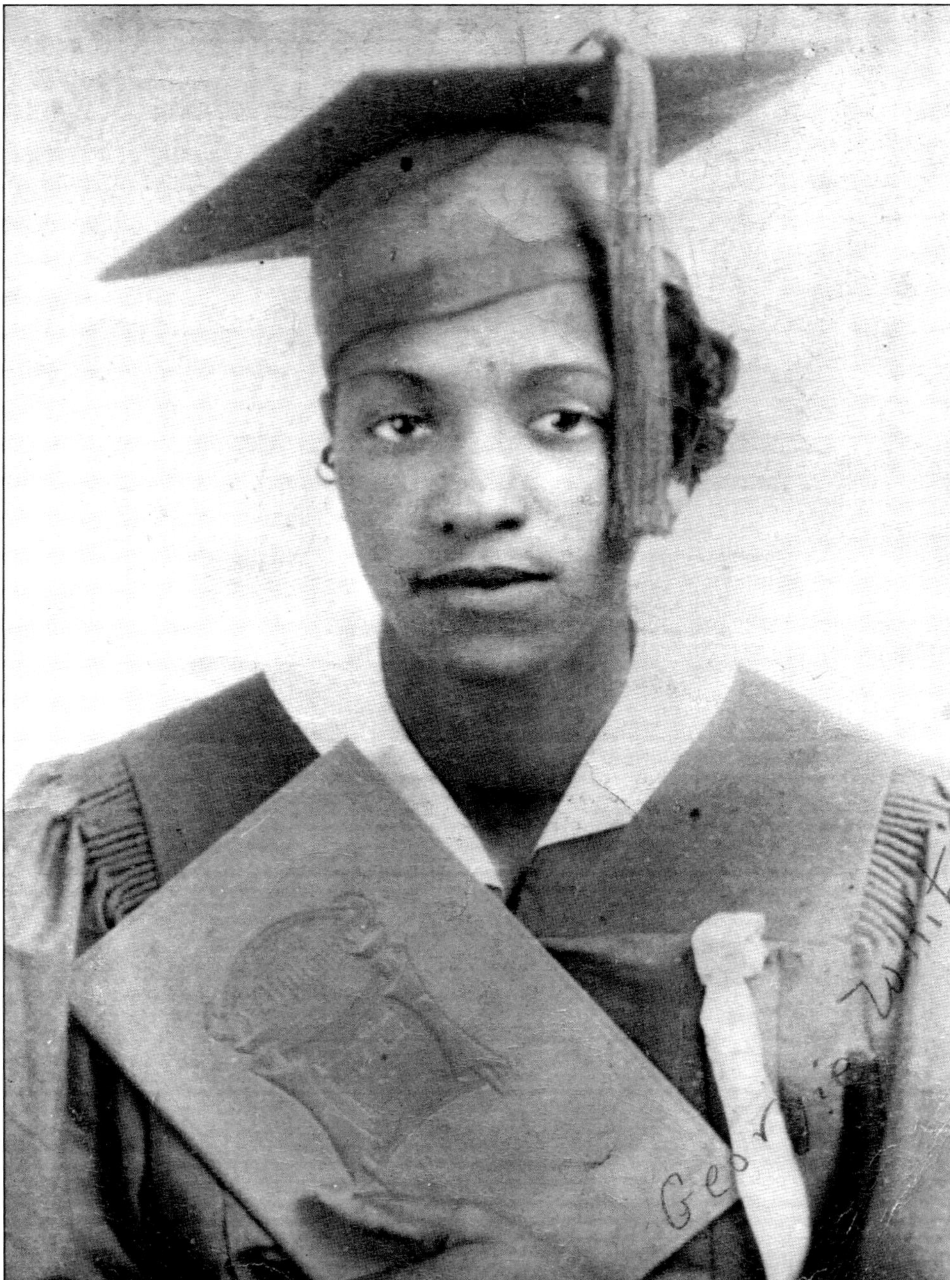

DIPLOMA IN HAND. Georgia White proudly displays her diploma after graduating from Elberton Colored High School in the 11th grade in 1938. White was 22 when she completed high school. Many students went to school on the farm schedule, and if they did not live in Elberton, many parents kept their children at home until their children were old enough to walk to school or to board with someone who lived close to the school. (Courtesy Georgia White.)

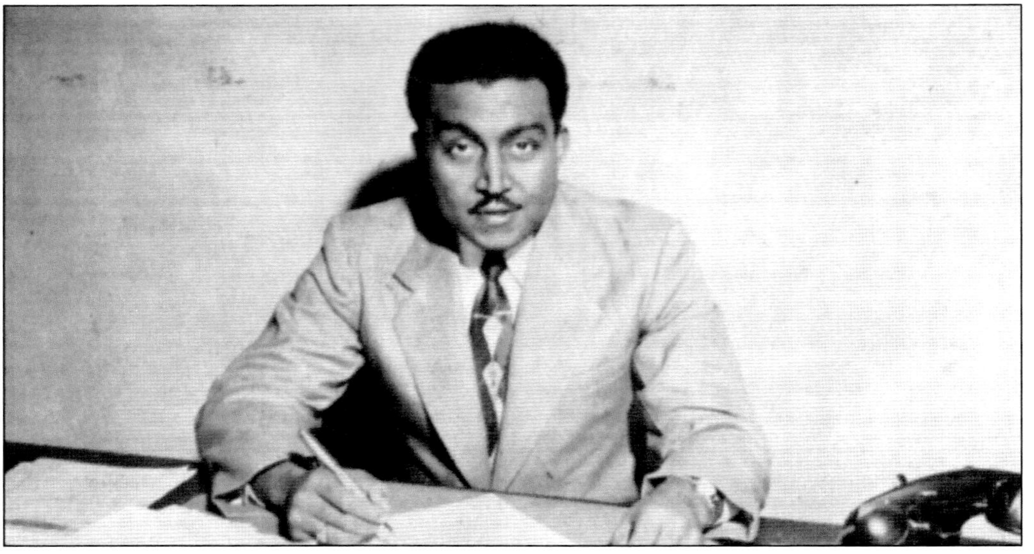

JAMES HAWES JR. Hawes took over the reigns as principal at Paul J. Blackwell Memorial School the year after Paul J. Blackwell died. He was principal until the integration of the public schools in 1970 and then became principal of Blackwell Memorial Junior High School, where he remained until his retirement in 1981. Hawes received his bachelor's degree from Fort Valley State College and his master's degree from Fisk University. He also studied at Ohio State University. (Courtesy Jimmy O. White.)

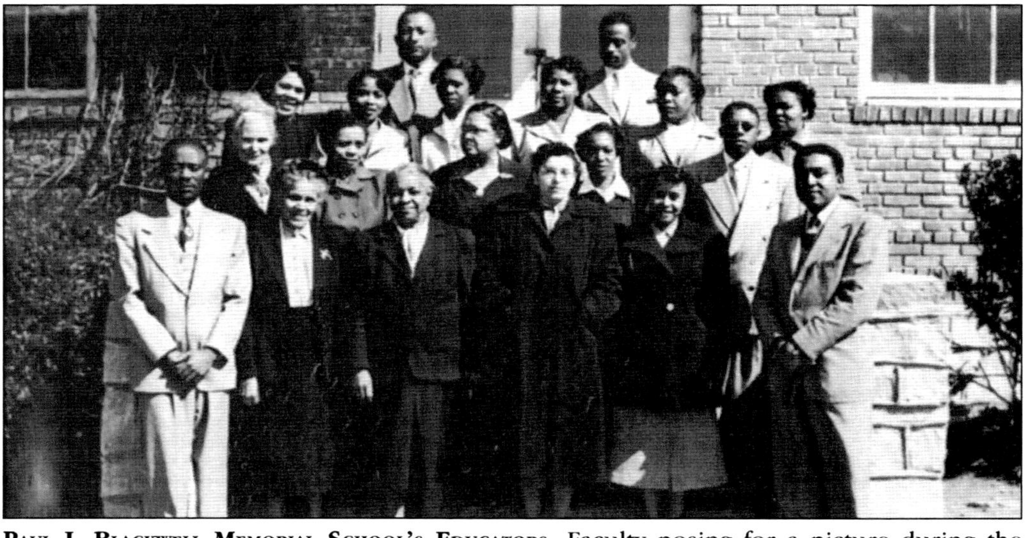

PAUL J. BLACKWELL MEMORIAL SCHOOL'S EDUCATORS. Faculty posing for a picture during the 1949–1950 year are, from left to right, (first row) Walter Z. Thomas (assistant principal), Alice Pitt, Mary Frances Roebuck, Mamie Sapp Dye (assistant principal), Geraldine Goss (Lindsey), and James Hawes Jr. (principal); (second row) Martha "Bessie" Brewer Williams, Beulah O. Hawes, Hattie Johnson, Mamie C. Epps, and Nathaniel T. Lindsey; (third row) Janesta McKinney, Constance Palms, Ruby L. Roberts (Hicks), Miriam P. Key, Cora M. Long, and Sara J. Willingham; (fourth row) Albert T. Smith and Oswald V. Hicks. (Courtesy Jim-Ree African American Museum, Inc. Archives.)

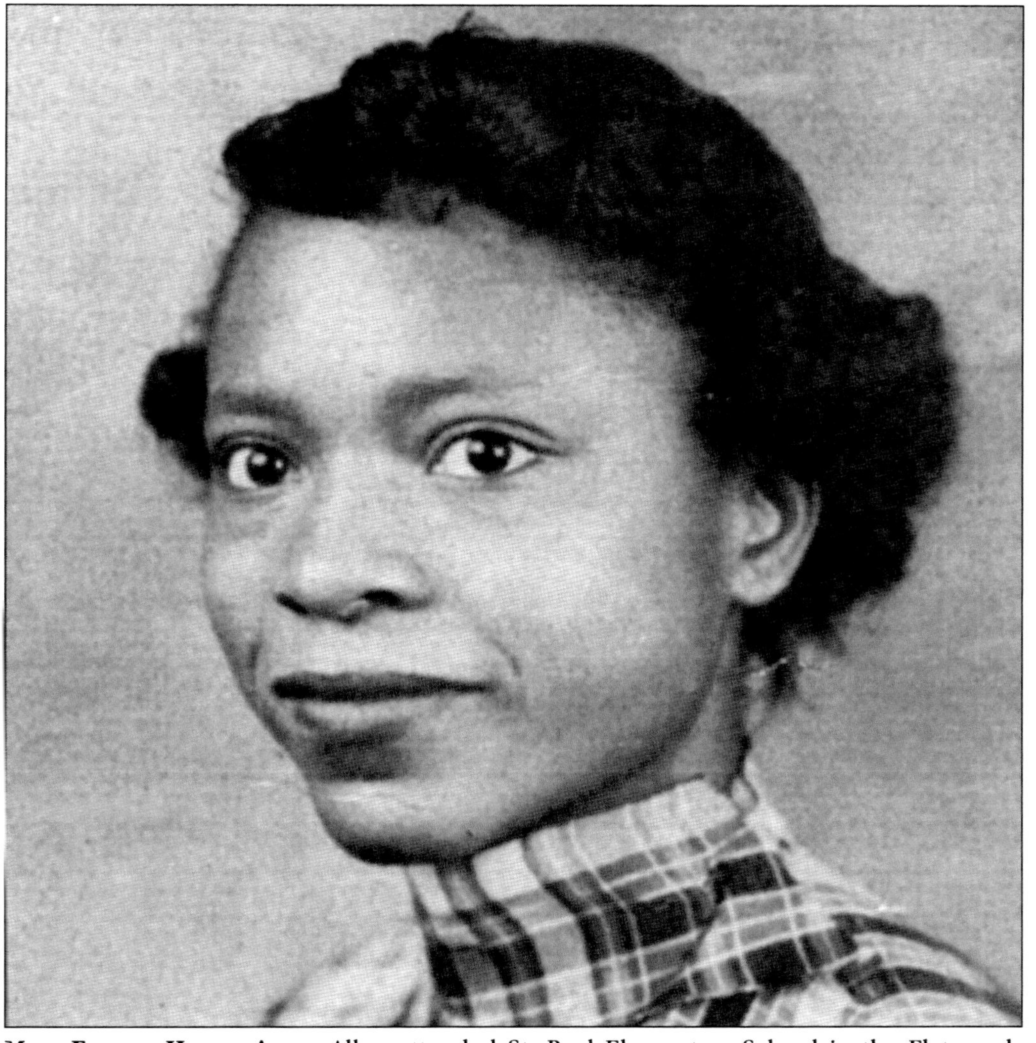

Mary Frances Harper Allen. Allen attended St. Paul Elementary School in the Flatwoods community. Lula Brewer Thompson was the teacher at the school. Allen recalls that students brought sack lunches, except on the occasions when the government funded meals. Lula Brewer Thompson would prepare the meals and bring the food to school on her mule wagon. When Allen's family moved to Rose Hill, she attended Rose Hill Elementary School under the direction of Lillian Byrd Rucker. At Blackwell Memorial High School, a peanut-butter sandwich cost 5¢ and a fish sandwich 10¢. They had chapel services at Blackwell every Friday, and every person in the school had to attend. Chapel service was a very solemn and sacred occasion. Principal Hawes would speak, and some of the students would perform. Allen graduated with the class of 1954. (Courtesy Jim-Ree African American, Inc. Archives.)

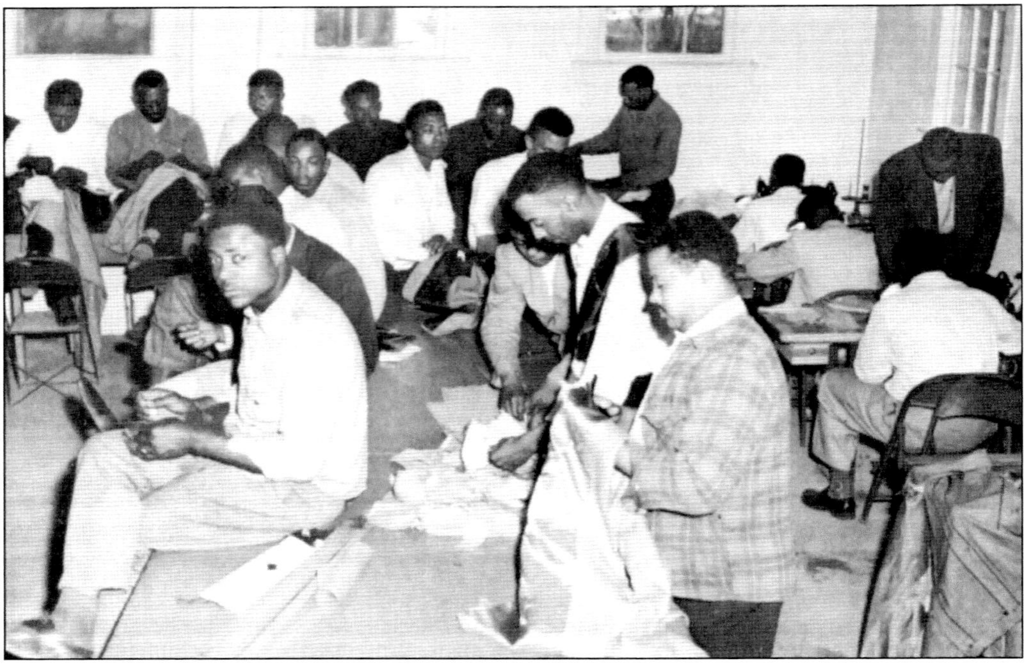

Night School. Veterans attend night school at Blackwell Memorial School to learn a trade in 1949. (Courtesy Azalee Dye.)

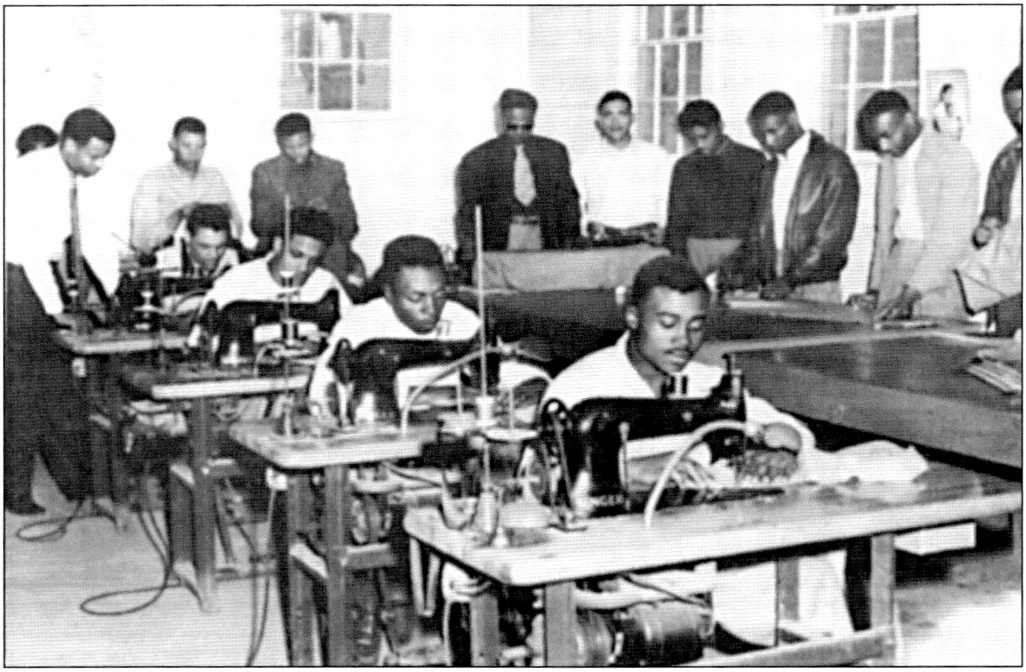

Tailoring Class. Veterans use sewing machines to make jackets in their tailoring class at night school in 1949. (Courtesy Azalee Dye.)

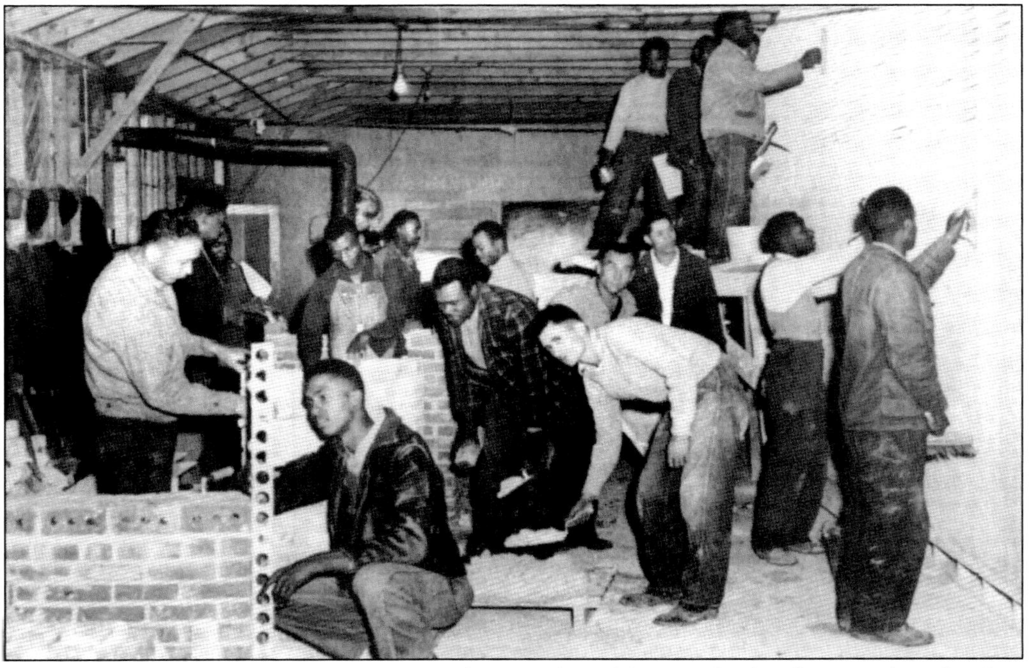

Masonry. Veterans learn how to plaster sheet rock and how to lay bricks at night school in 1949. (Courtesy Azalee Dye.)

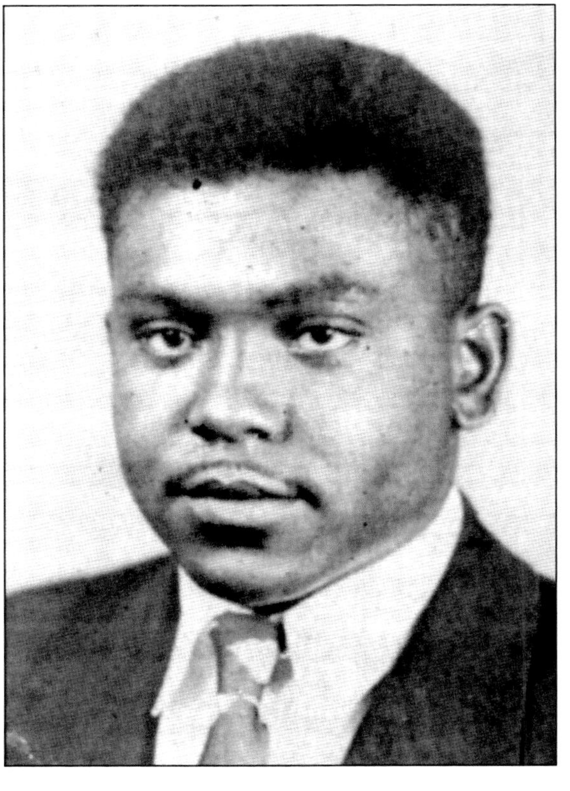

Joe Allen Harper. A veteran of the Korean War, Joe Allen Harper attended Adult Academic Class at Blackwell Memorial High School in the 1950s to earn his high-school diploma. He had attended elementary school in the Flatwoods community and had dropped out of school after he completed the sixth grade. (Courtesy Jim-Ree African American Museum, Inc. Archives.)

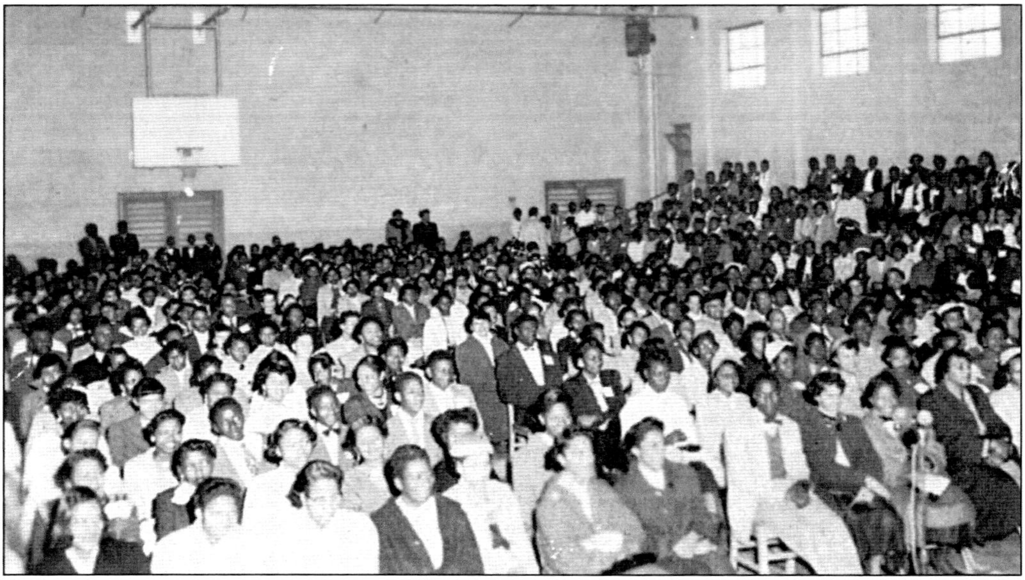

Conference in Toccoa, Georgia. Hi-Y and Tri-Hi-Y members from Blackwell Memorial School attend the regional conference in Toccoa. The clubs, affiliated with the Young Men's Christian Association (YMCA), promotes Christian values. (Courtesy Jim-Ree African American Museum, Inc. Archives.)

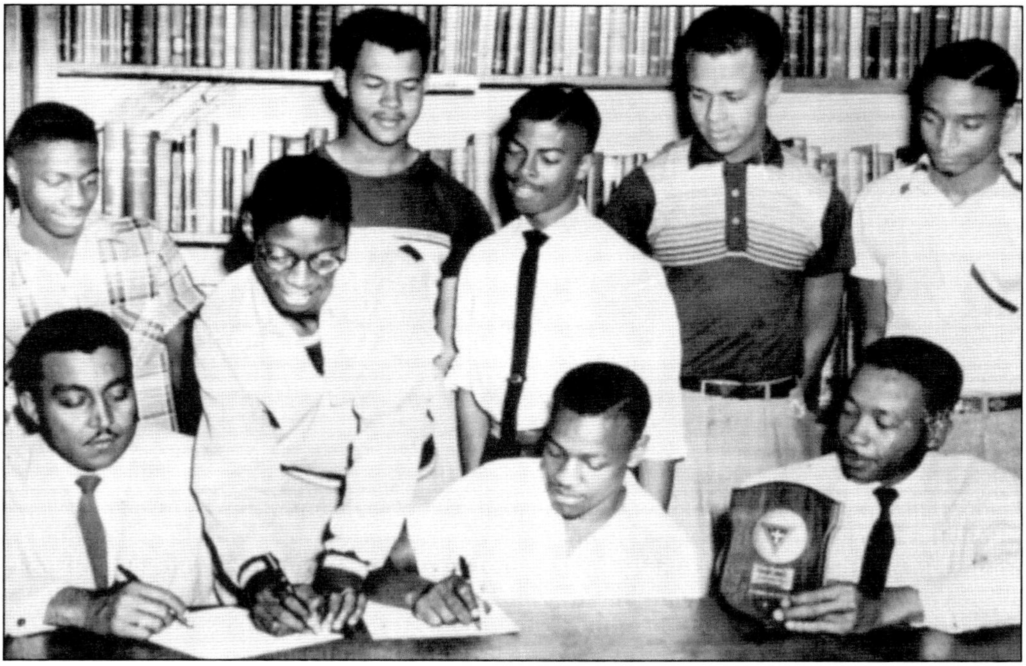

Hi-Y. Members of the Hi-Y are enthused about the club's rank as an AA club in 1954. Pictured are, from left to right, (front row) James Hawes Jr., Judge Jefferson Cleveland, Bobby G. Hunt, and C.H. Harris; (back row) Morris Hunt, William Calhoun, Henry Johnson, John C. Calhoun, and Samuel Phelps. (Courtesy Jim-Ree African American Museum, Inc. Archives.)

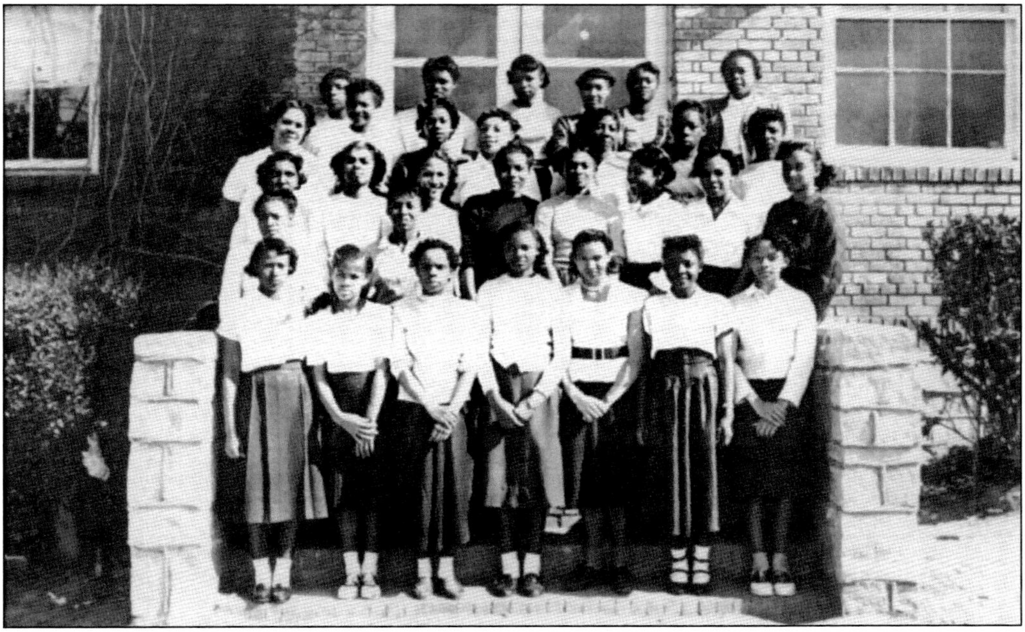

Tri-Hi-Y. High School girls in the Tri-Hi-Y club pose on the steps of Blackwell Memorial High School in 1950. (Courtesy Azalee Biggs Dye.)

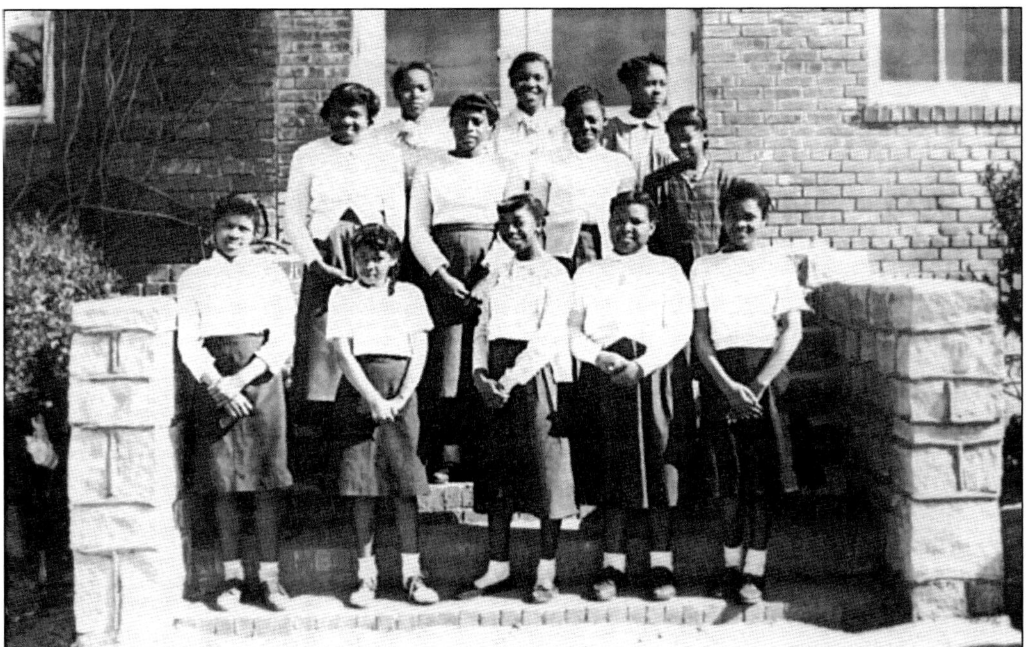

Junior Tri-Hi-Y. Grade school girls were also members of the Tri-Hi-Y club. (Courtesy Azalee Biggs Dye.)

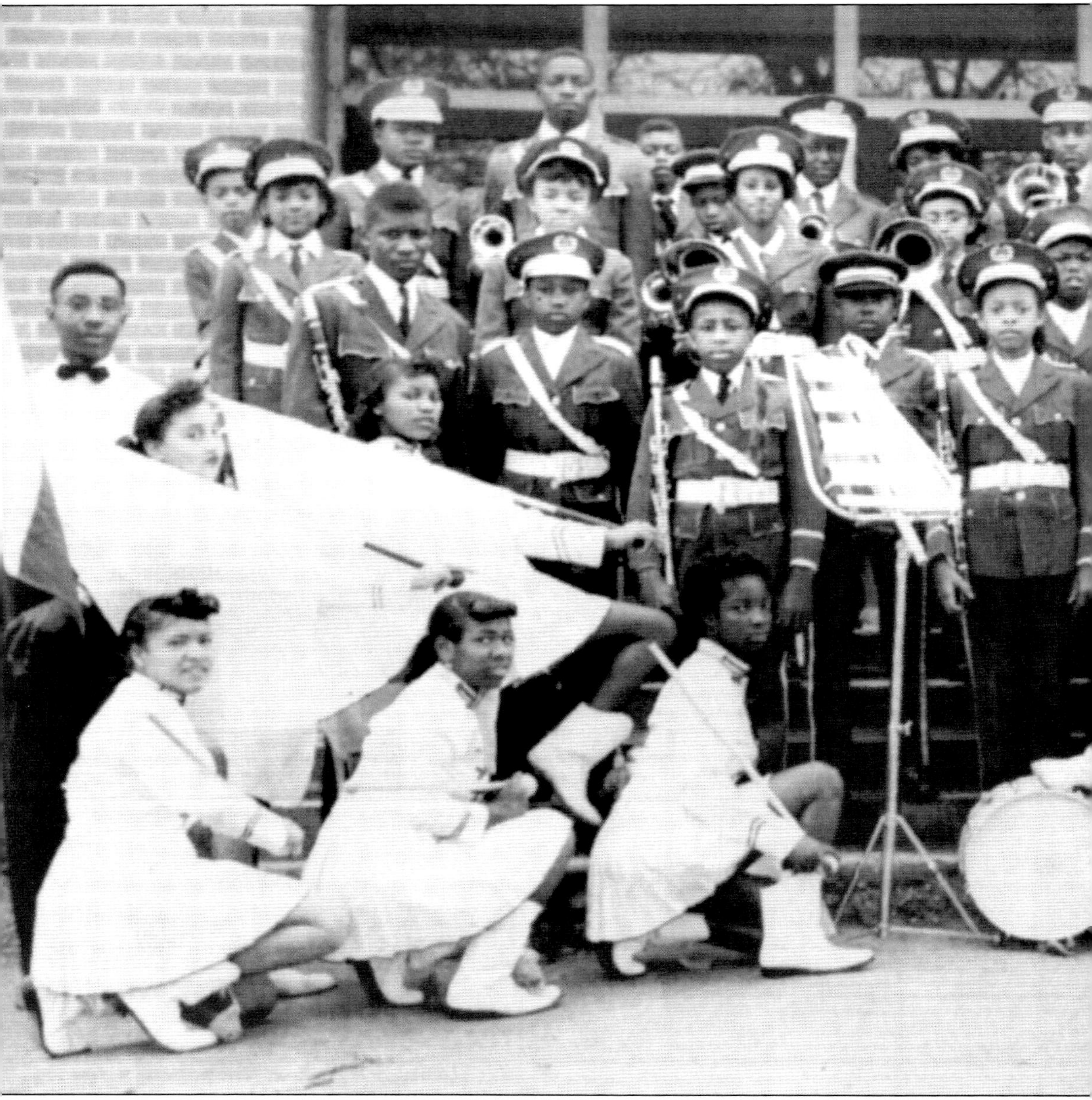

Rams Marching Band, 1956. Wearing hand-me-down band uniforms from Elbert County High School, band students in 7th through 12th grades pose for a portrait. The school acquired its first band teacher, Carl Reeves, in 1954. Pictured are, from left to right, (first row) Ruth Haynie, Charlene Herndon, Lula Bolton, Emma Moon, Myrtle Walton, Lucinda Thompson, and Dorothy Burton; (second row) Mary Harris, Doris Anderson, Yvonne Cade, and Bernice Winn; (third row) Cartrell Harper, James White, Lawyer Fortson, Henry Settles, Allen Jones, Theodosia Tharps, Annie Jones, Janice Hamm, Francis Eberhardt, Billie Brown, and George

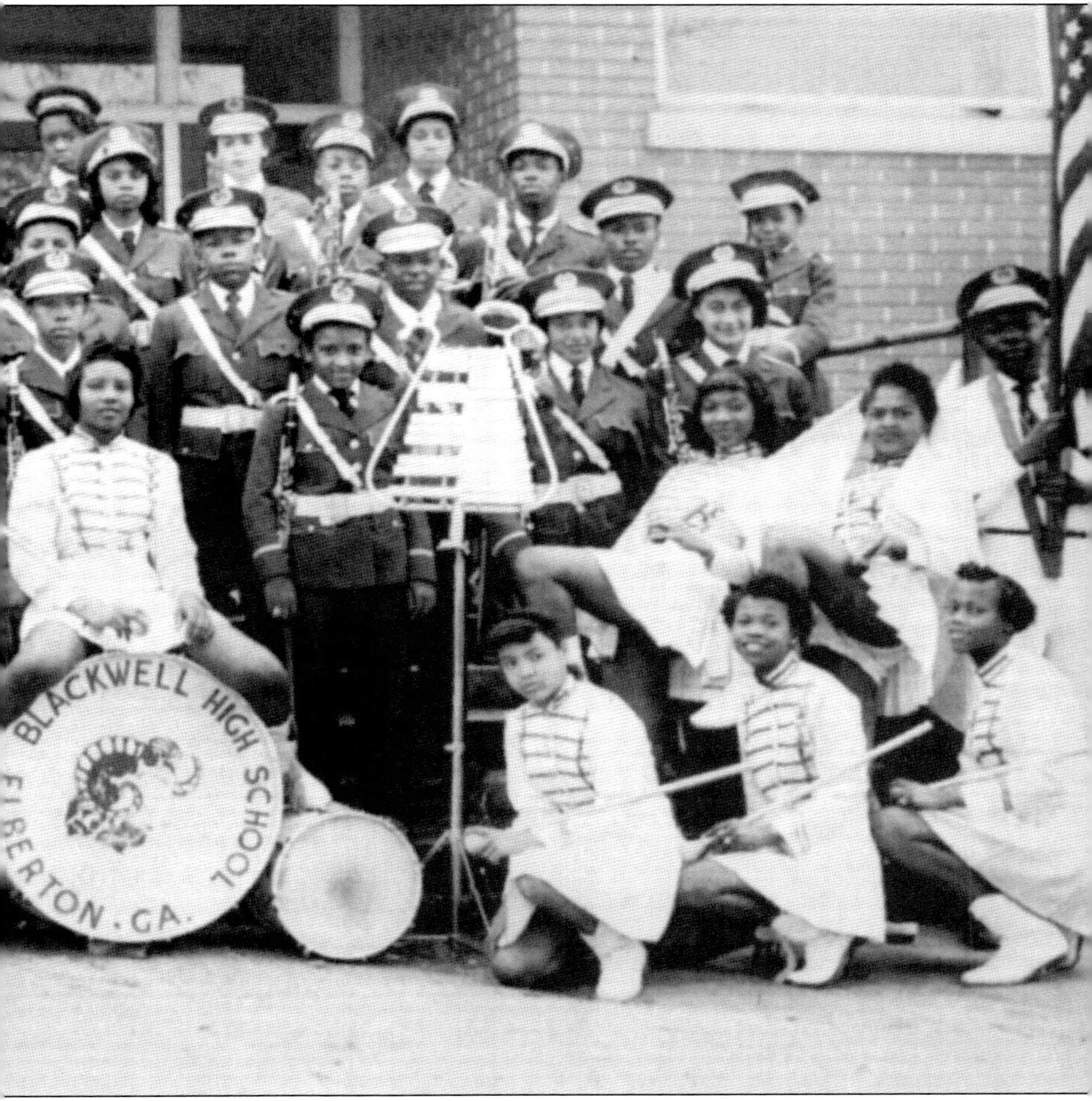

Carter; (fourth row) Johnnie Mae Robinson, Johnnie Mae McCalla, Jo Ann Fortson, Francine Smith, Alex Odister, George Mattox, Claude Smith, Horace Highsmith, Vandebilt Martin, Ronald Dye, and Kirkteena Blackwell; (fifth row) Jones Tate, James Huff, Charlie McLendon, William Logan, John Ford, Sarah Perlotte, Sara Welbon, Jimmy White, Louise Davis, Dorothy Tenant, Barbara Richard, Marion Davis, Virginia Smith, and Eugene Harper. (Courtesy Jim-Ree African American Museum, Inc. Archives.)

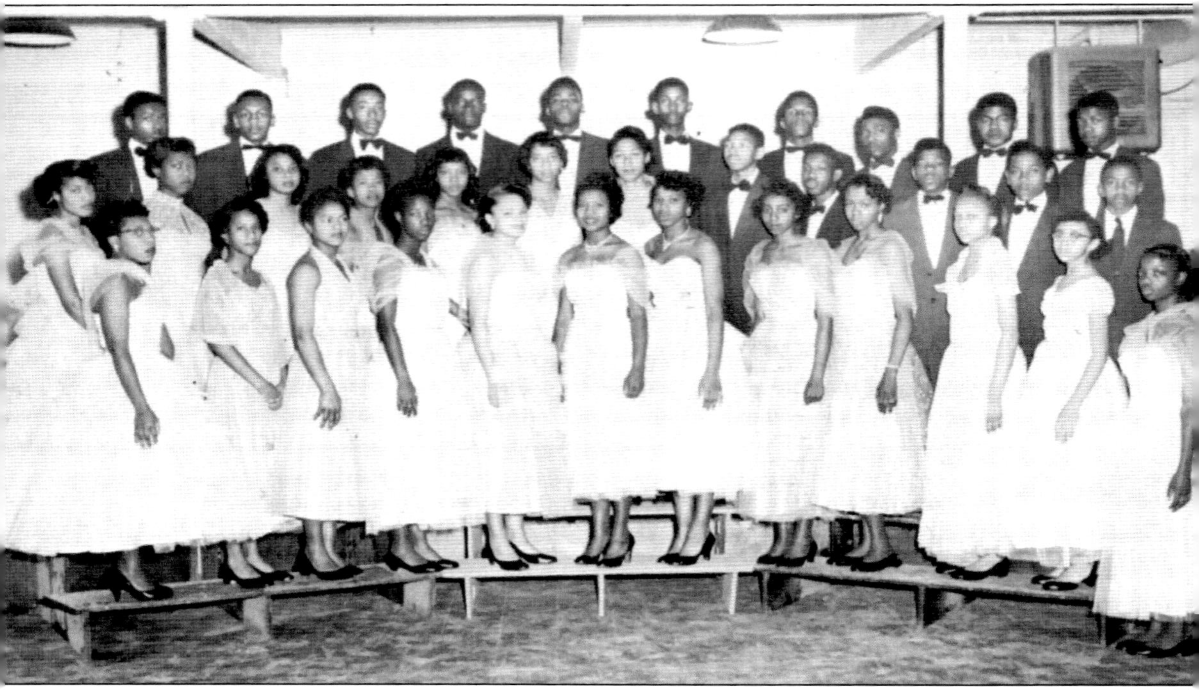

Blackwell Memorial High School's Chorus, 1956. The Blackwell Memorial High School Chorus performs in formal attire at the graduation ceremony, one of their biggest performances of the year. Pictured are, from left to right, (front row) Mildred Watson, Jo Ann Fortson, Bernice Winn, Lula Bolton, Ethelda Bolton, Emma Moon, Helen Tate, Janie Turman, Louise Davis, Doris Willis, Francine Smith, and Barbara Bolton; (middle row) Francis Eberhardt, Charlie Mae Allen, Dorothy Tenant, Lucinda Thompson, Yvonne Cade, Virginia Smith, Barbara Bowman, Herbert Clark, Eugene Harper, Horace Highsmith, Arthur Jones, and Bennie Ed Willis; (back row) Ronald Dye, Jimmy White, Cartrell Harper, Charlie McLendon, Bobby Blackwell, Lazurus Alexander, Herman Carter, Morris Hunt, James Huff, and Cornelius Winn. (Courtesy Jim-Ree African American Museum, Inc. Archives.)

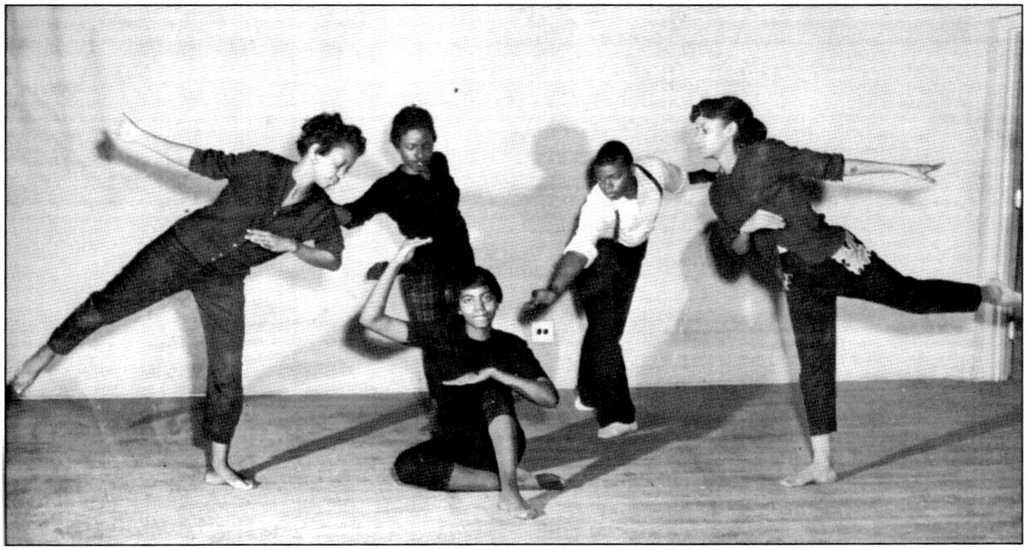

Modern Dance Club. Students in the modern dance club from Blackwell Memorial High School performed at locations throughout the county. One of the club's goals was to increase the students' and the general community's appreciation of creative dance. (Courtesy Jim-Ree African American Museum, Inc. Archives.)

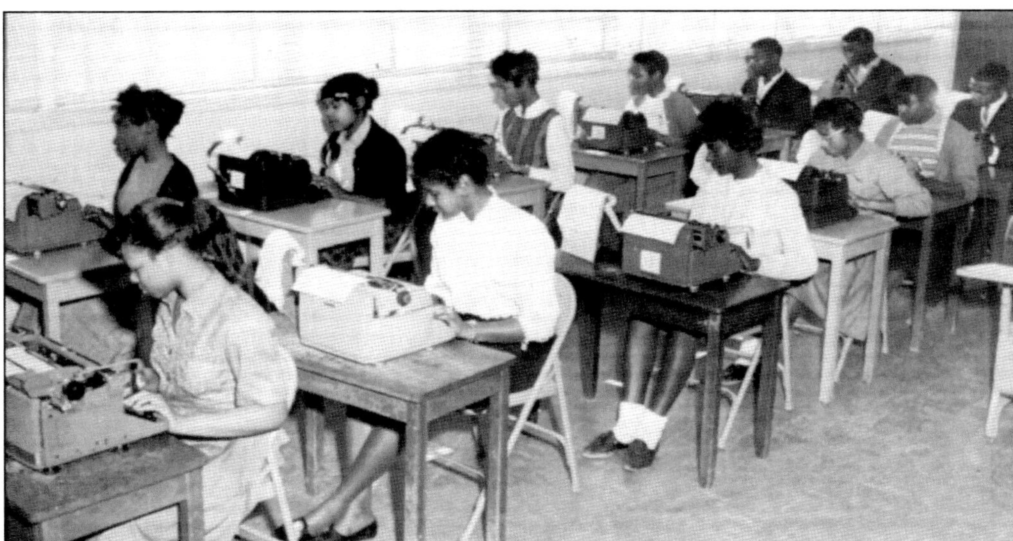

Technology. Students at Blackwell use manual typewriters in 1961. The students received their first classroom set of typewriters in 1960. (Courtesy Jim-Ree African American, Inc. Archives.)

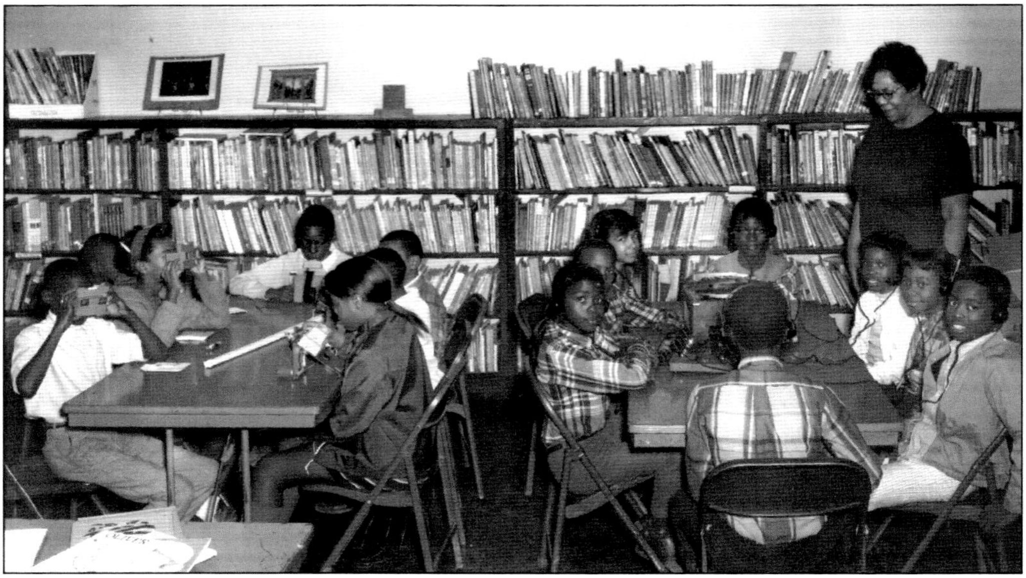

Blackwell Memorial Elementary Library. Students use visual and listening aids under the supervision of principal Janesta Lyons McKinney in the 1960s. When Jones Street Elementary School closed, McKinney became the principal of Blackwell Memorial Elementary School until her retirement. (Courtesy Jim-Ree African American Museum, Inc. Archives.)

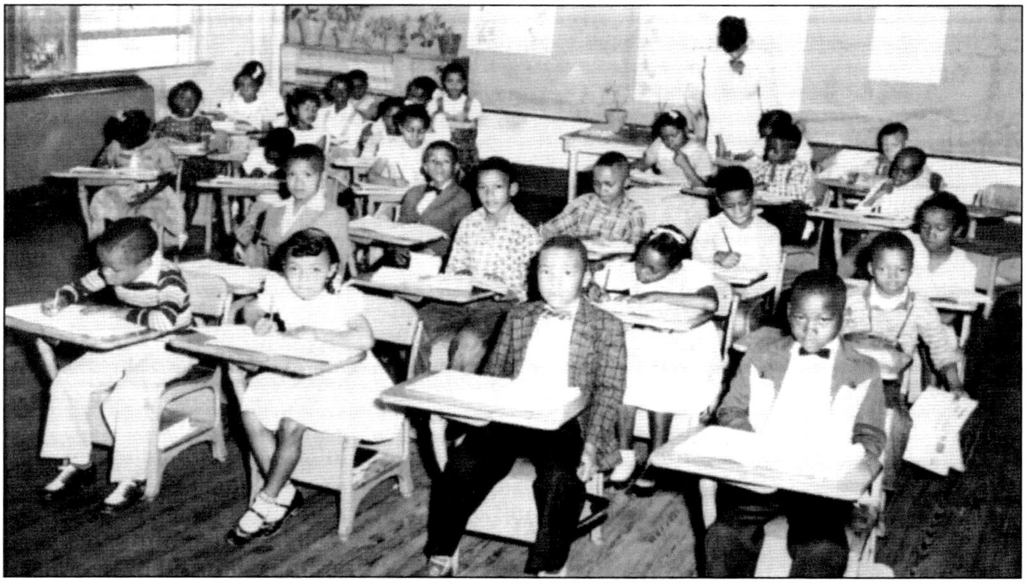

Mandatory Dresses for Girls. Before 1966, girls had to wear dresses to school. (Courtesy Jim-Ree African-American Museum, Inc. Archives.)

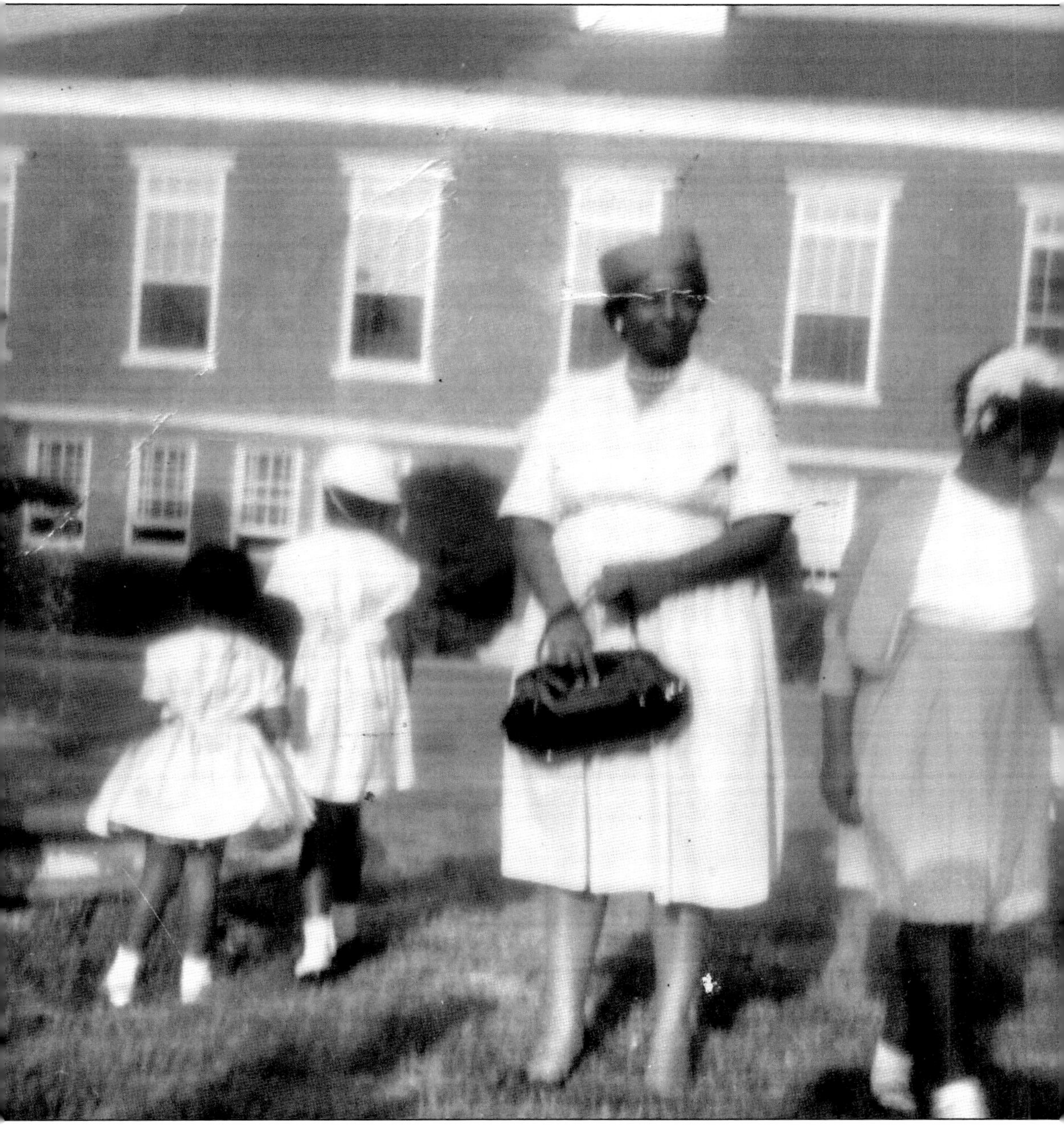

CLARK COLLEGE. Clark College—now Clark Atlanta University—a historically black college and university (HBCU) in Atlanta, was one of the few colleges matriculating African-American students. Blackwell Memorial High School students pursuing post-secondary education were usually limited to HBCUs. (Courtesy Barbara Lois Hamm.)

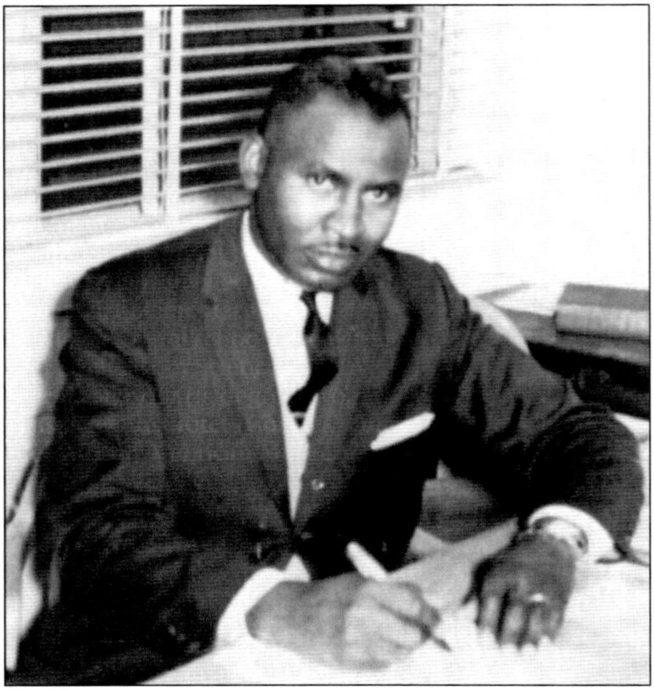

Reverend Luther Randall Neal. Neal was the principal of Northwest Bowman Elementary School and the pastor of St. Mary's C.M.E. Church. He was a graduate of Paine College in Augustus, Georgia. (Courtesy Jim-Ree African American Museum, Inc. Archives.)

Board Work. A Northwest Bowman Elementary student reviews a subtraction problem with the class. (Courtesy Genora Hamm Biggs.)

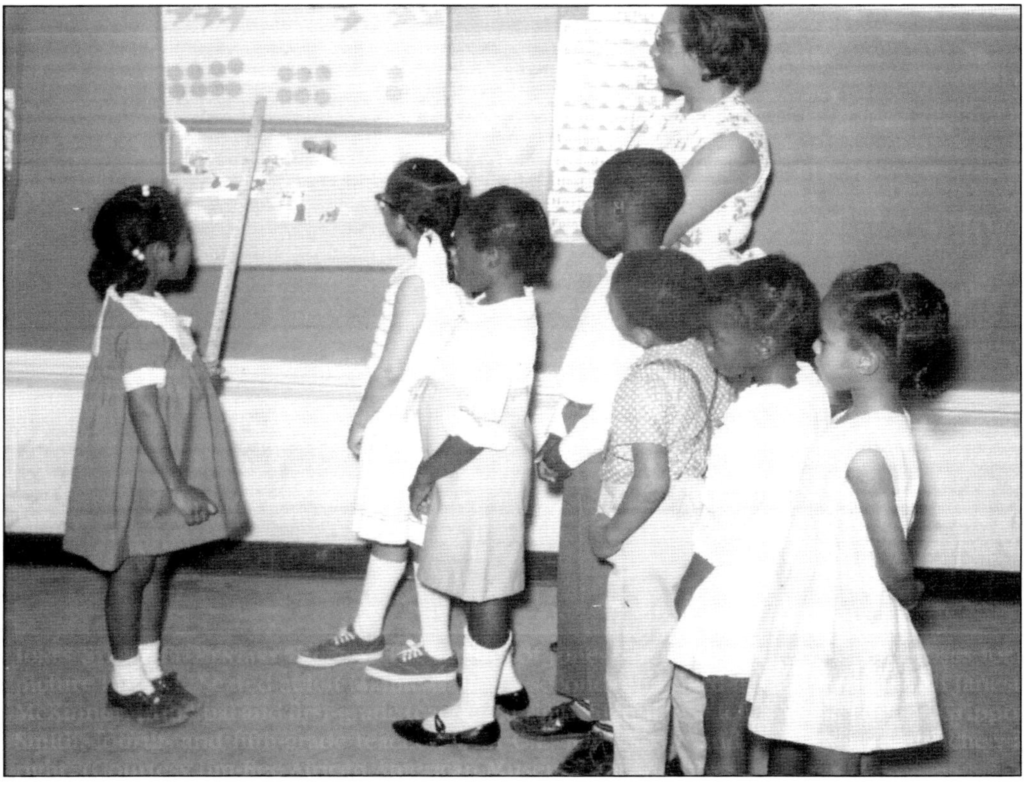

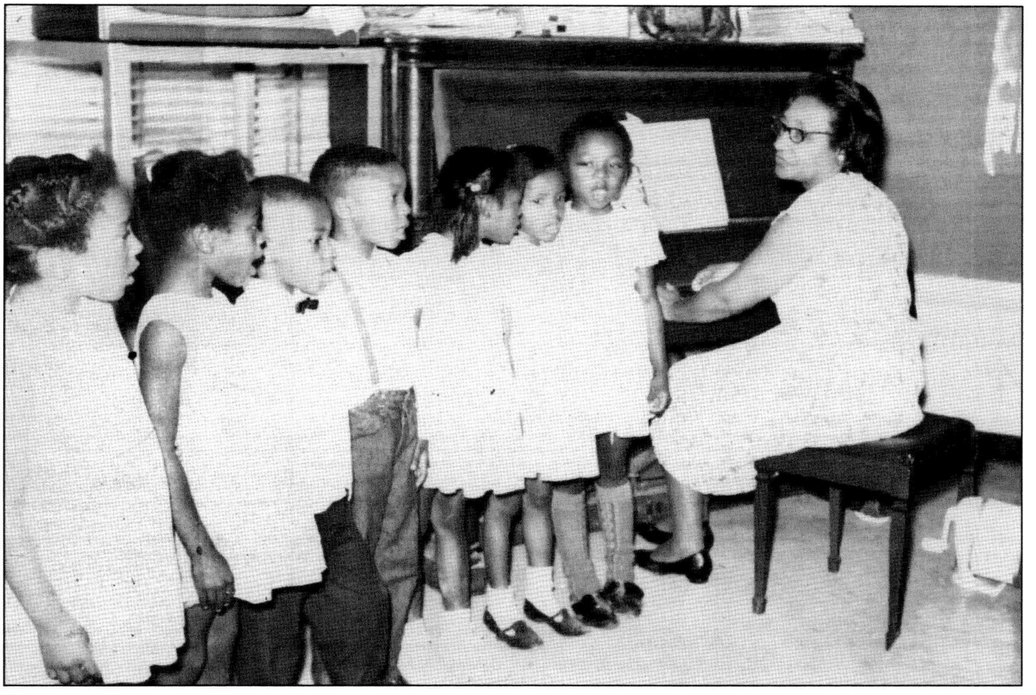

MORNING DEVOTION. Every morning, after the students recited the Pledge of Allegiance, they recited the Lord's Prayer and sang a hymn. Here, Genora Hamm Biggs plays the piano while her first-grade students at Northwest Bowman Elementary sing "Jesus Loves Me." (Courtesy Genora Hamm Biggs.)

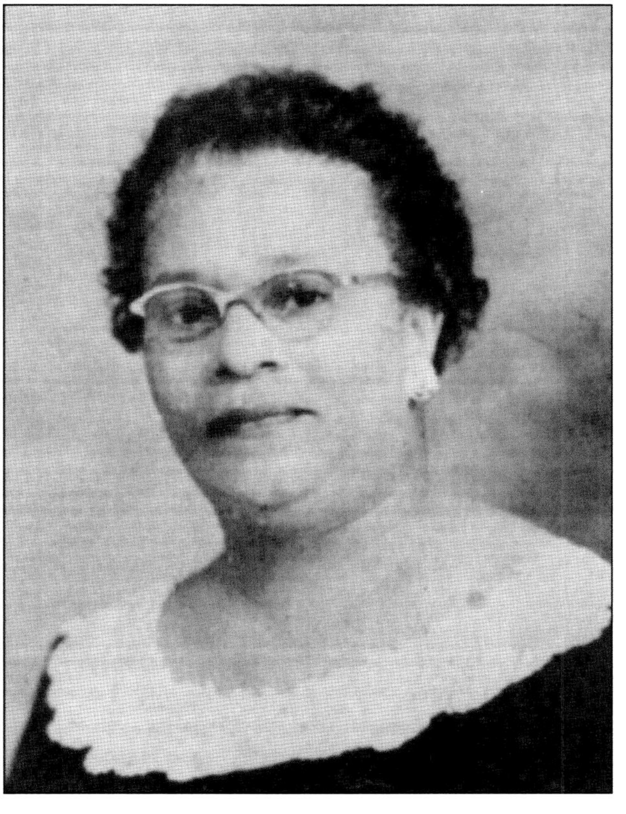

LILLIAN WATKINS EVANS. Evans was a supervisor of the African-American feeder elementary schools in Elbert County. After the consolidation of the many community elementary schools, Watkins became classified as the curriculum director. Evans was a graduate of Morris Brown College and did advance study at Atlanta University and the University of Boston. (Courtesy Jim-Ree African American Museum, Inc. Archives.)

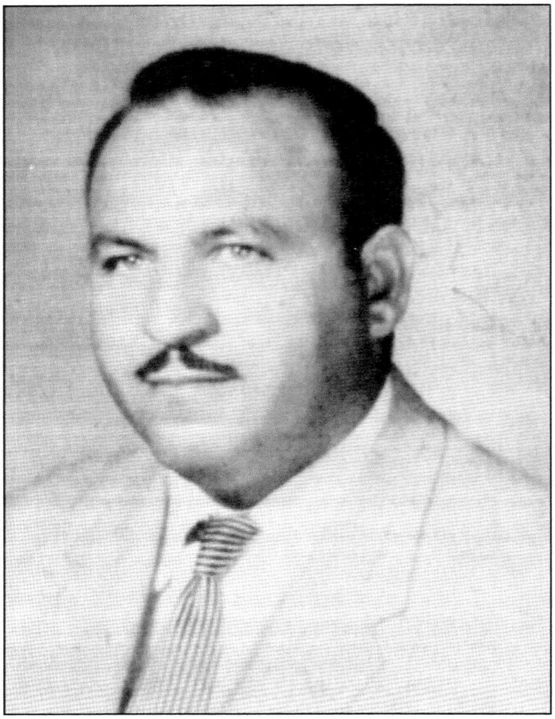

Edward H. Brownlee, October 20, 1916–February 26, 1989. Brownlee was educated in Elbert County schools. He received his bachelor's degree from South Carolina State College and his master's from Columbia University in New York. He was a principal at Bethel Grove Elementary School and at Heard's Grove Elementary School. He was a World War II veteran and was actively involved in his church and community. (Courtesy Jim-Ree African American Museum, Inc. Archives.)

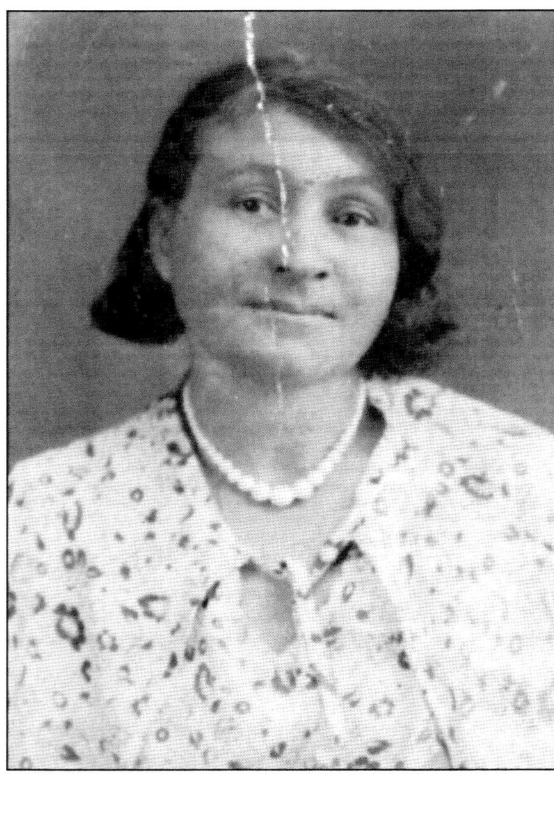

Mamie Banks. Heard's Grove Elementary's name was later changed to Banks Elementary. The new name of the school was a tribute to a teacher, Mamie Banks, for her dedicated service to the school. (Courtesy Jim-Ree African American Museum, Inc. Archives.)

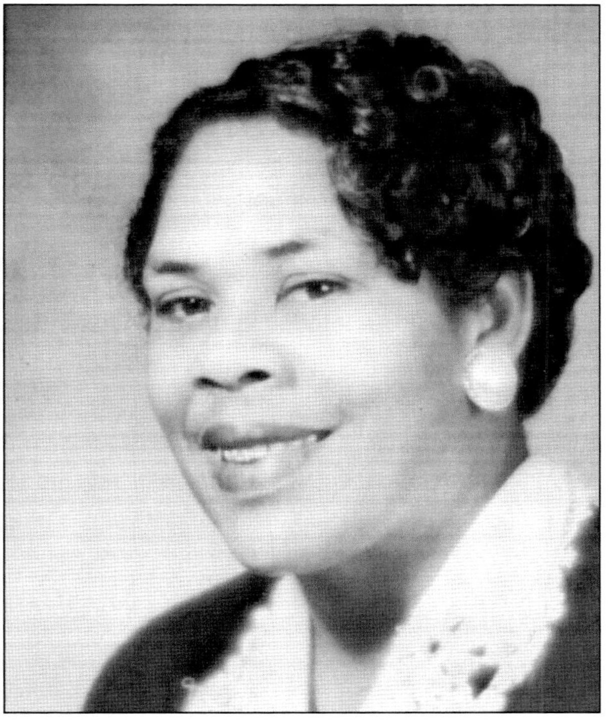

JANESTA LYONS MCKINNEY. McKinney's career began in 1935 at Elberton Colored School as a first-grade teacher. McKinney left Blackwell Memorial School to become a principal and an instructor at Jones Street Elementary School in 1950. With the closing of Jones Street School, she returned to Blackwell Memorial Elementary as the principal of the school. She earned her Bachelor of Science and her Master of Arts degrees from Tuskegee Institute. (Courtesy Jim-Ree African American Museum, Inc. Archives.)

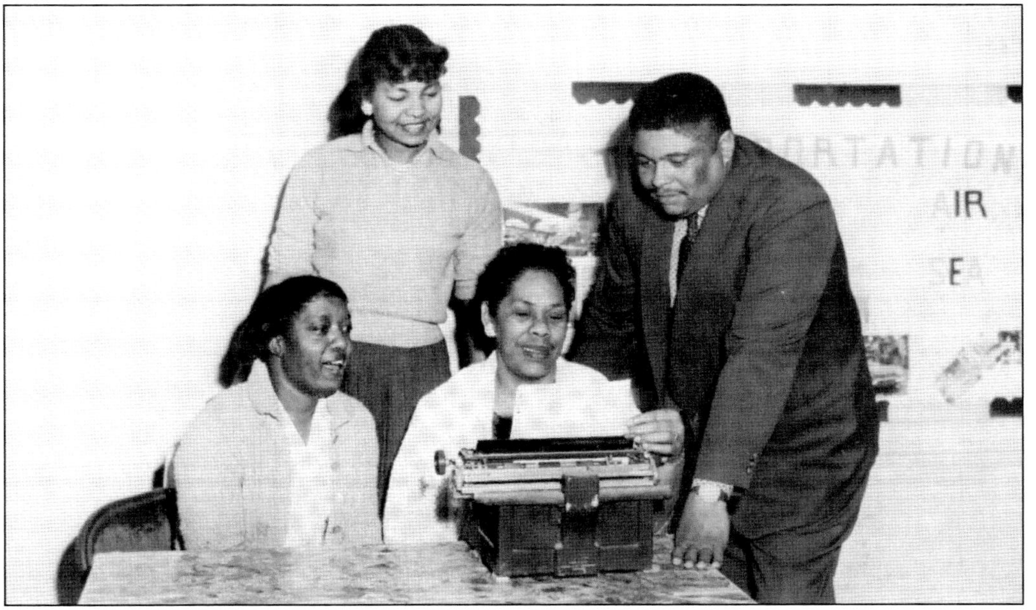

JONES STREET ELEMENTARY FACULTY. The faculty of Jones Street Elementary School poses for a picture in 1961. Seated at left Mamie C. Epps, second- and third-grade teacher, with Janesta McKinney, principal and first-grade teacher, at right. Standing at left is Willie Loraine Grippon Smith, fourth- and fifth-grade teacher, with C.L. Reid, sixth- and seventh-grade teacher, at right. (Courtesy Jim-Ree African American Museum, Inc. Archives.)

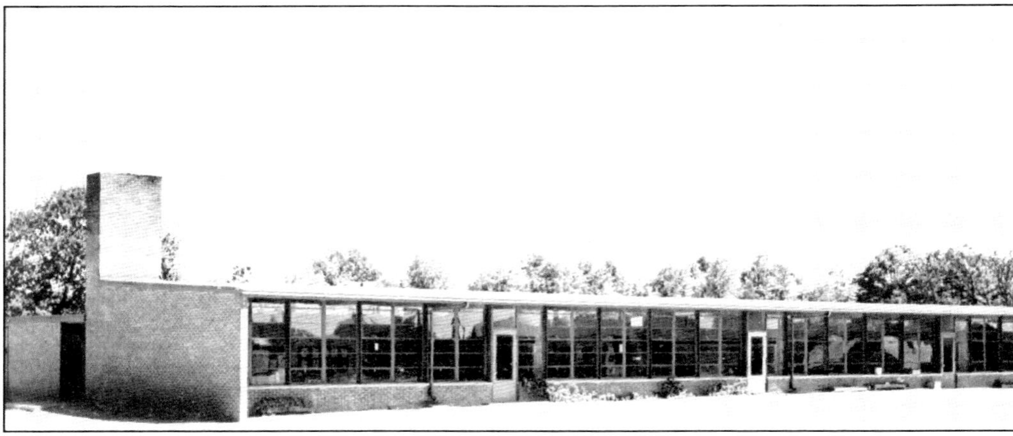

Jones Street School. Jones Street Elementary School was a feeder school to Blackwell Memorial High School. It closed when it consolidated with Blackwell Memorial Elementary School in the late 1960s. (Courtesy Jim-Ree African American, Inc. Archives.)

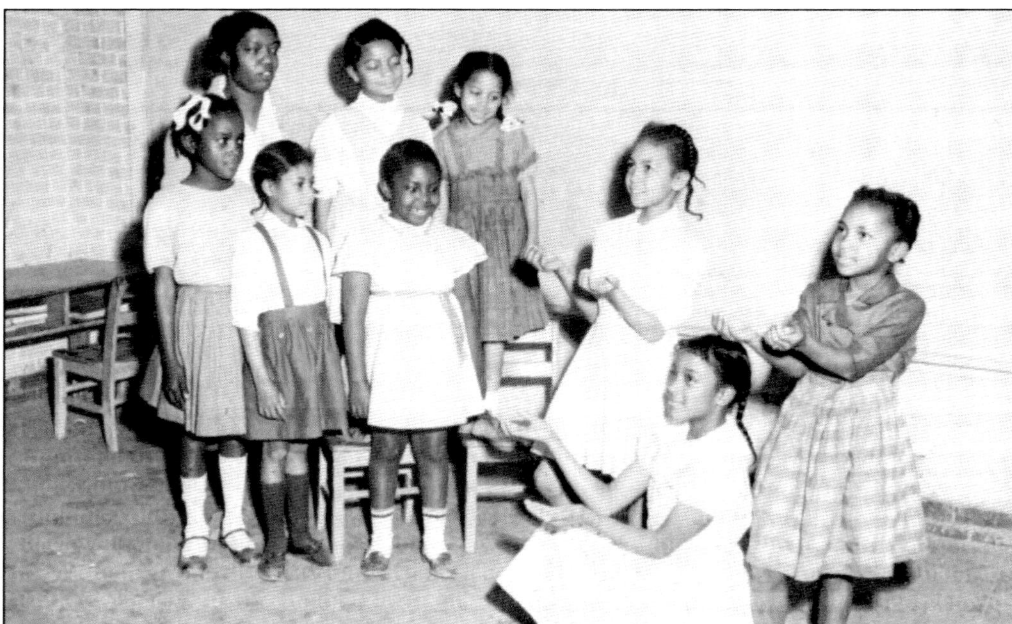

Jones Street Dance Group. The students at Jones Street Elementary School appreciate the fine arts. Mamie C. Epps sponsored the after-school dance group. (Courtesy Jim-Ree African American, Inc. Archives.)

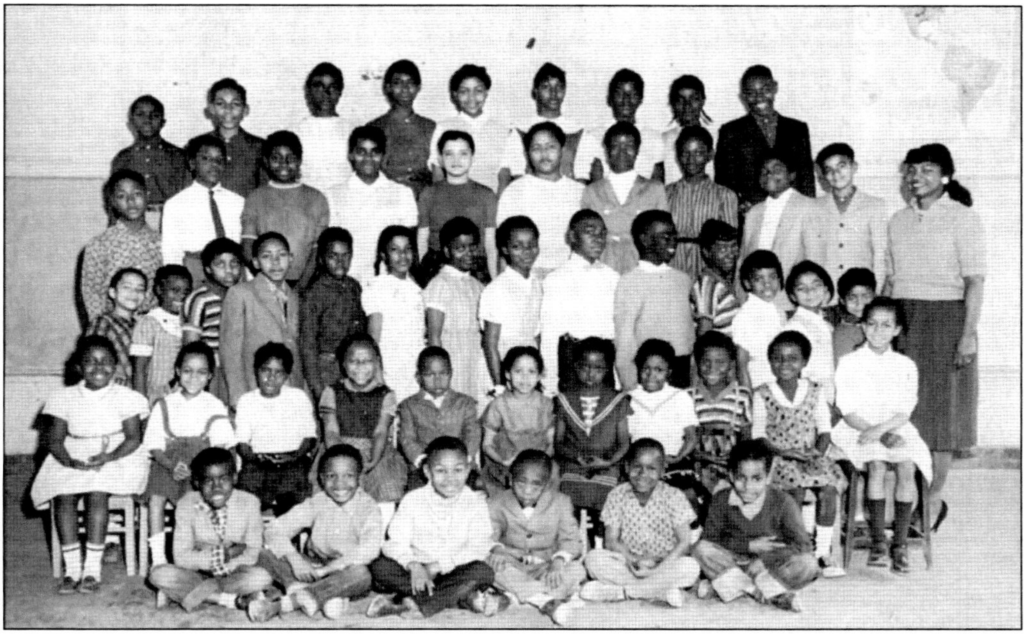

Jones Street Choir. Not having risers did not hinder Willie Loraine Grippon Smith. With the aid of chairs and tables from the classroom, the students arranged themselves so that they appear to be standing on risers. (Courtesy Jim-Ree African American, Inc. Archives.)

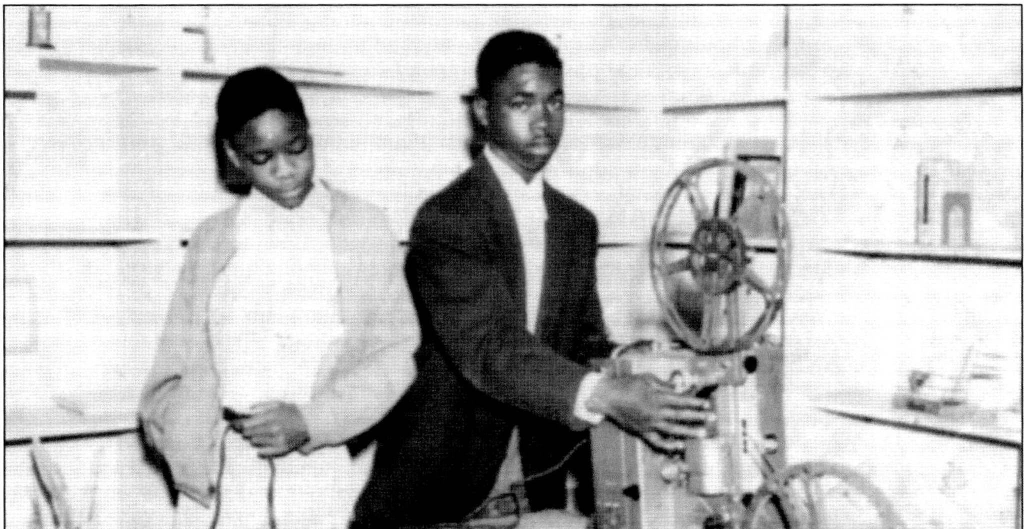

Visual Aid. Two students set up the projector for their teacher so that the class can view a film. (Courtesy Jim-Ree African American, Inc. Archives.)

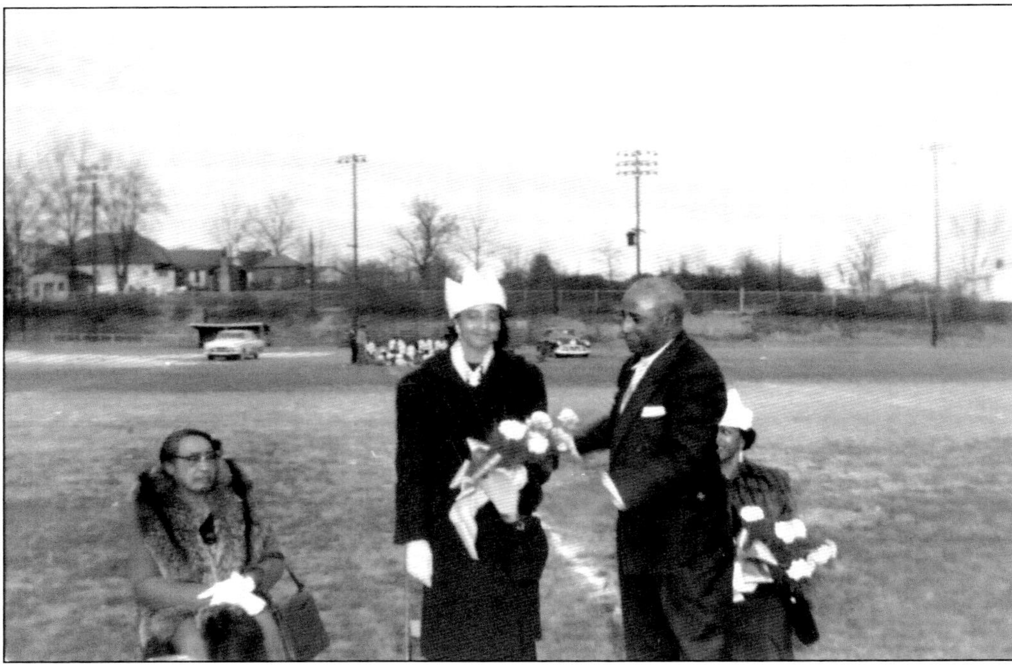

Blackwell Memorial High School's Football Field. A social club is shown using the Rams' Football Field. The field was located on Mill Street. (Courtesy Georgia White.)

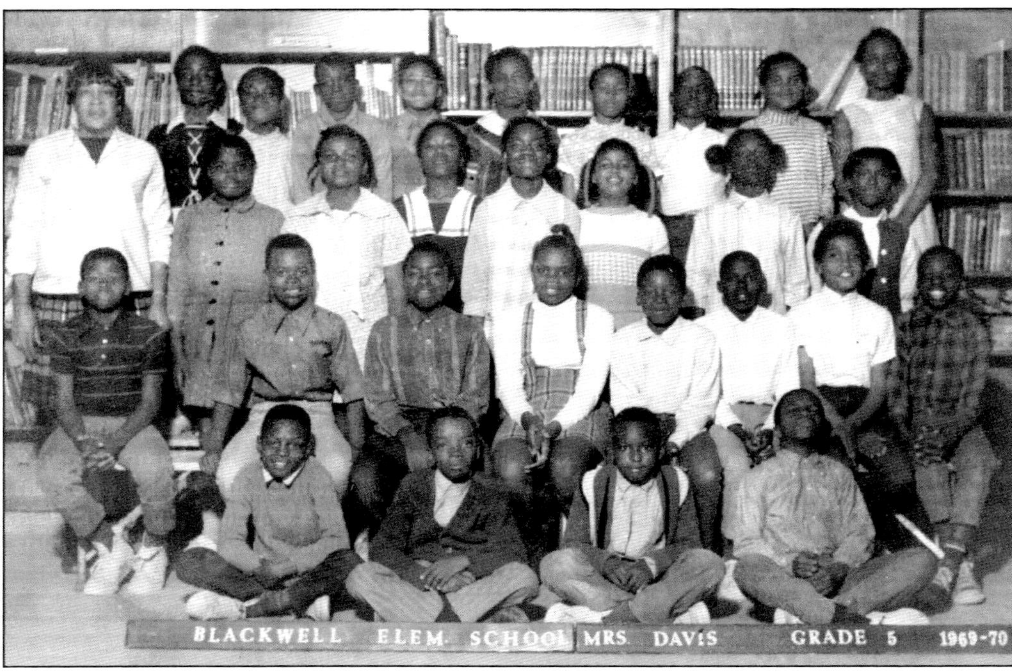

Segregation. The segregation of schools in Elbert County came to an end in 1970. Lozzie Martin Davis poses for a picture with her fifth-grade class at Blackwell Memorial Elementary School. (Courtesy Marie and Charles Hamm Collection.)

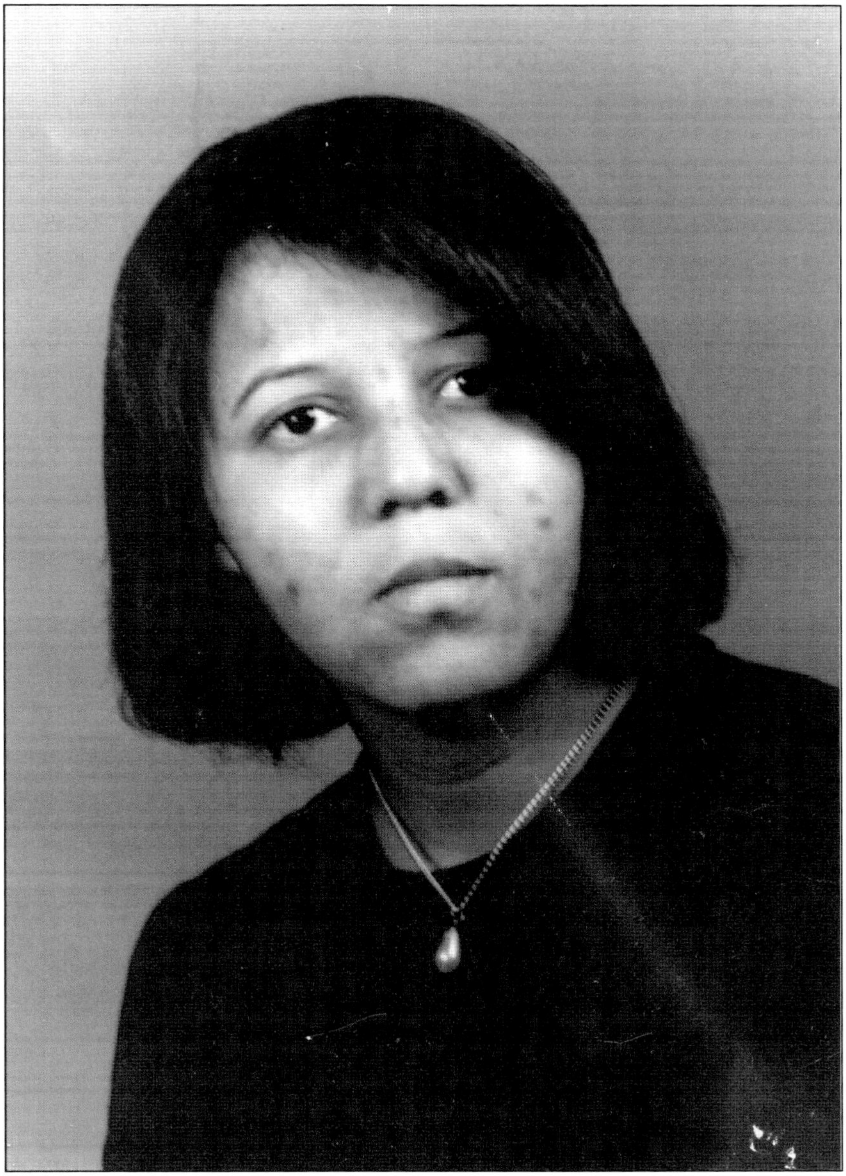

Freedom of Choice Act. Deborah Rucker was one of the first African-American students to attend Elbert County High School, the then–all-white school, on the Freedom of Choice Act. She volunteered to attend her senior year, 1965 through 1966. Two other African-American students volunteered to attend that year as well. However, unlike Rucker, they returned to Blackwell Memorial High School after a few days. Rucker became the first African American to graduate from Elbert County High School in 1966. Rucker went on to graduate from Paine College with a bachelor's degree in Biology and from the University of Georgia with a master's degree in Education. After working as an educator in Gainesville, Georgia, and as a manager at Sears and Roebuck as a manager, Rucker enrolled at North Carolina Central University School of Law, graduating in 1983. (Courtesy Deborah Lucinda Rucker.)

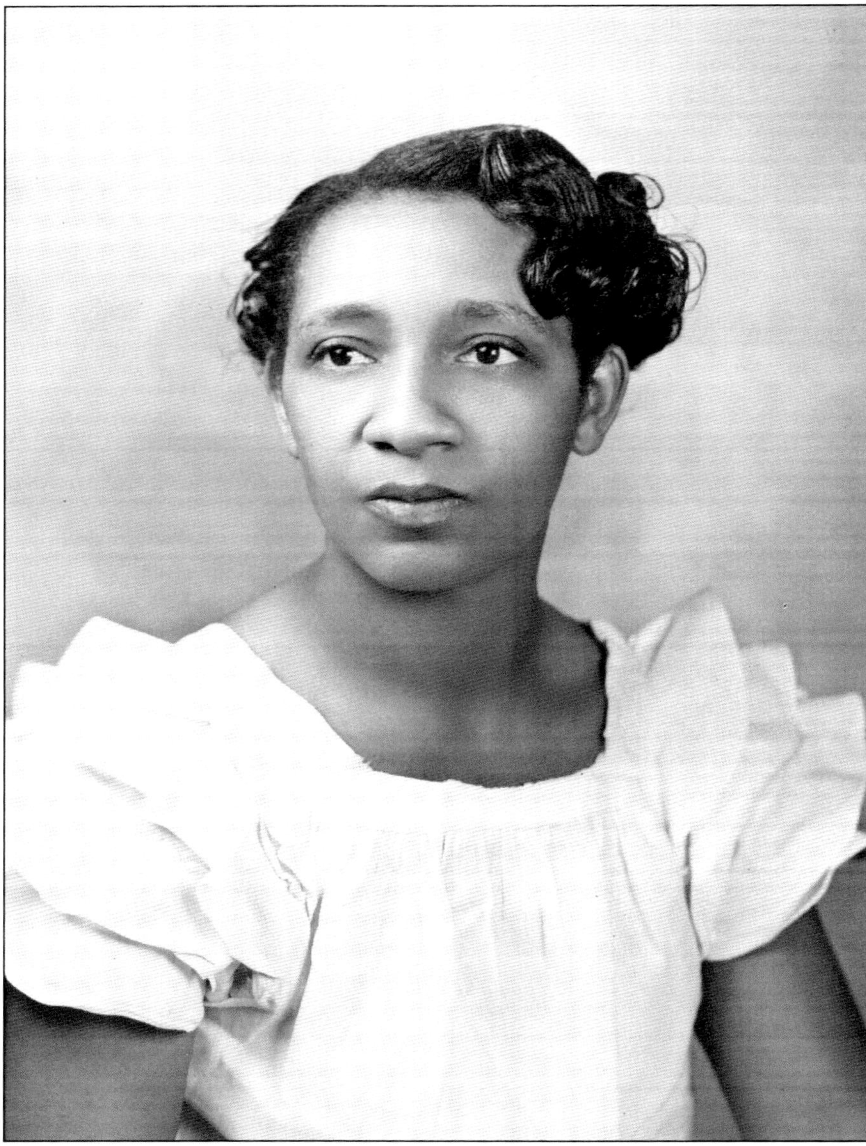

Genora Hamm Biggs. Biggs was the daughter of Luther and Mary Wall Hamm. She grew up in the Wyche district of Elbert County and attended Friendship Elementary School on Jones Ferry Road. After elementary school, her parents sent her to Shiloh High School in Washington, Georgia. Shiloh was a private school affiliated with the Baptist Church. Biggs's parents paid about $10 a month for tuition and room and board. She graduated in 1930. Later, Biggs became an educator in Elbert County. She taught at Friendship, Oliver Grove, Man Grove, Bell's Grove, Piney Grove, White's Chapel, Northwest Bowman, Blackwell Memorial, and Beaverdam schools. She recalls walking to the first few schools from home. For convenience, every community had at least one school. There was little transportation. She obtained her college degree from Fort Valley State College in 1964 and was an educator for 40 years. (Courtesy Genora Hamm Biggs.)

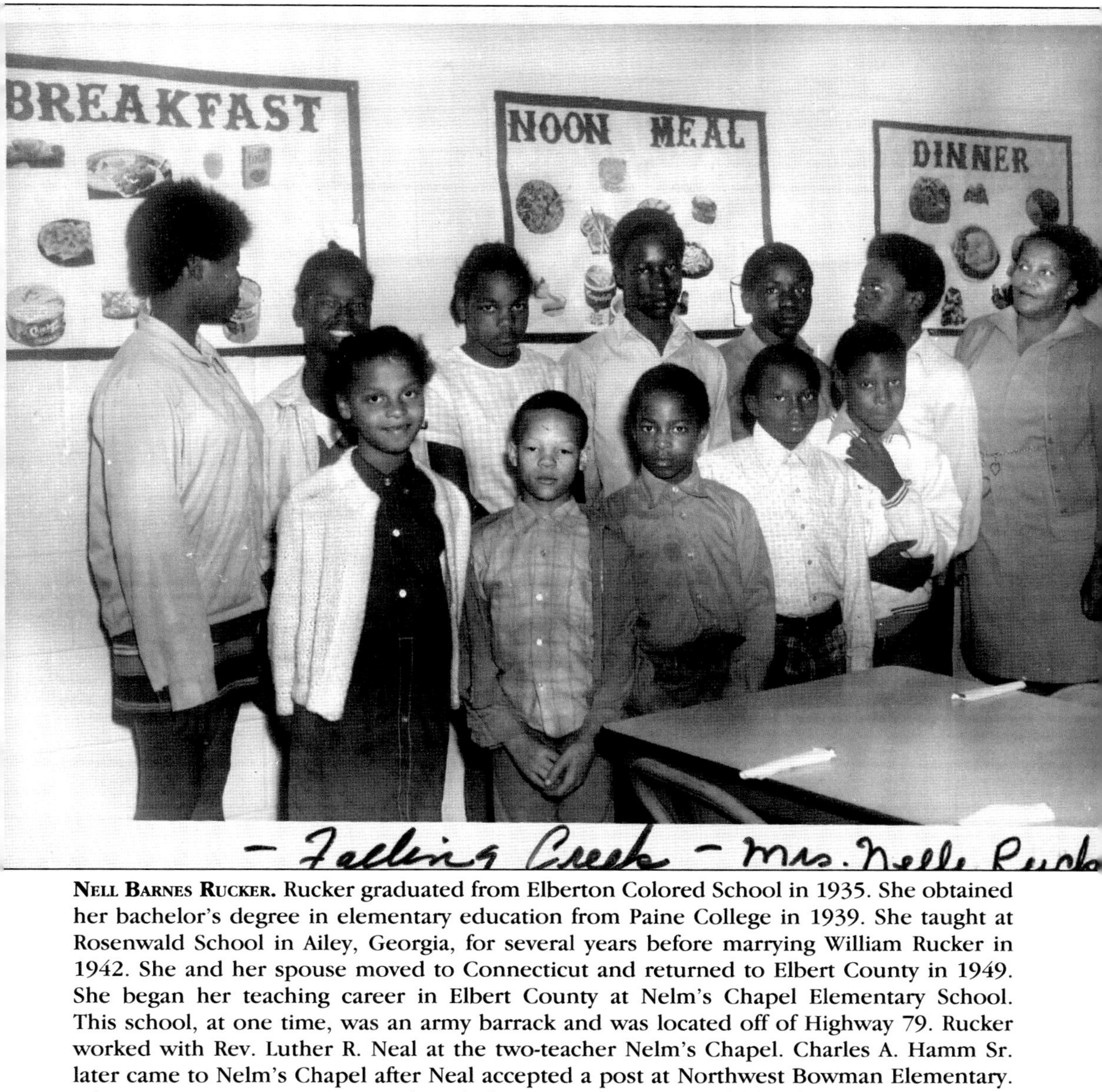

Nell Barnes Rucker. Rucker graduated from Elberton Colored School in 1935. She obtained her bachelor's degree in elementary education from Paine College in 1939. She taught at Rosenwald School in Ailey, Georgia, for several years before marrying William Rucker in 1942. She and her spouse moved to Connecticut and returned to Elbert County in 1949. She began her teaching career in Elbert County at Nelm's Chapel Elementary School. This school, at one time, was an army barrack and was located off of Highway 79. Rucker worked with Rev. Luther R. Neal at the two-teacher Nelm's Chapel. Charles A. Hamm Sr. later came to Nelm's Chapel after Neal accepted a post at Northwest Bowman Elementary. When an opening at Morrison Chapel Elementary became available, she taught there until the consolidation of schools. With the merging of schools, she taught at Heard's Grove Elementary until the integration of schools in 1970. Rucker is pictured with some of her students at Falling Creek Elementary. (Courtesy Jim-Ree African American Museum, Inc.)

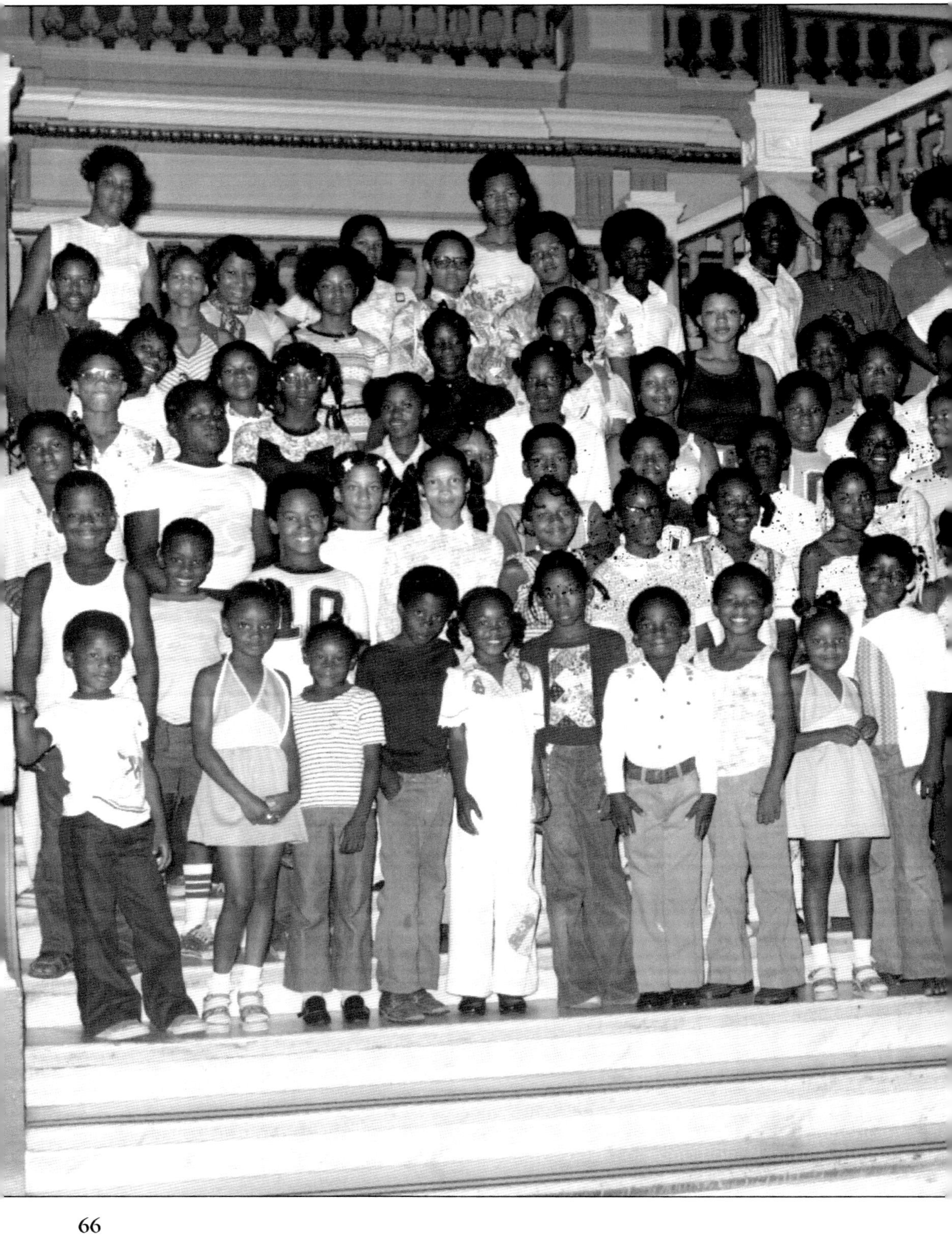

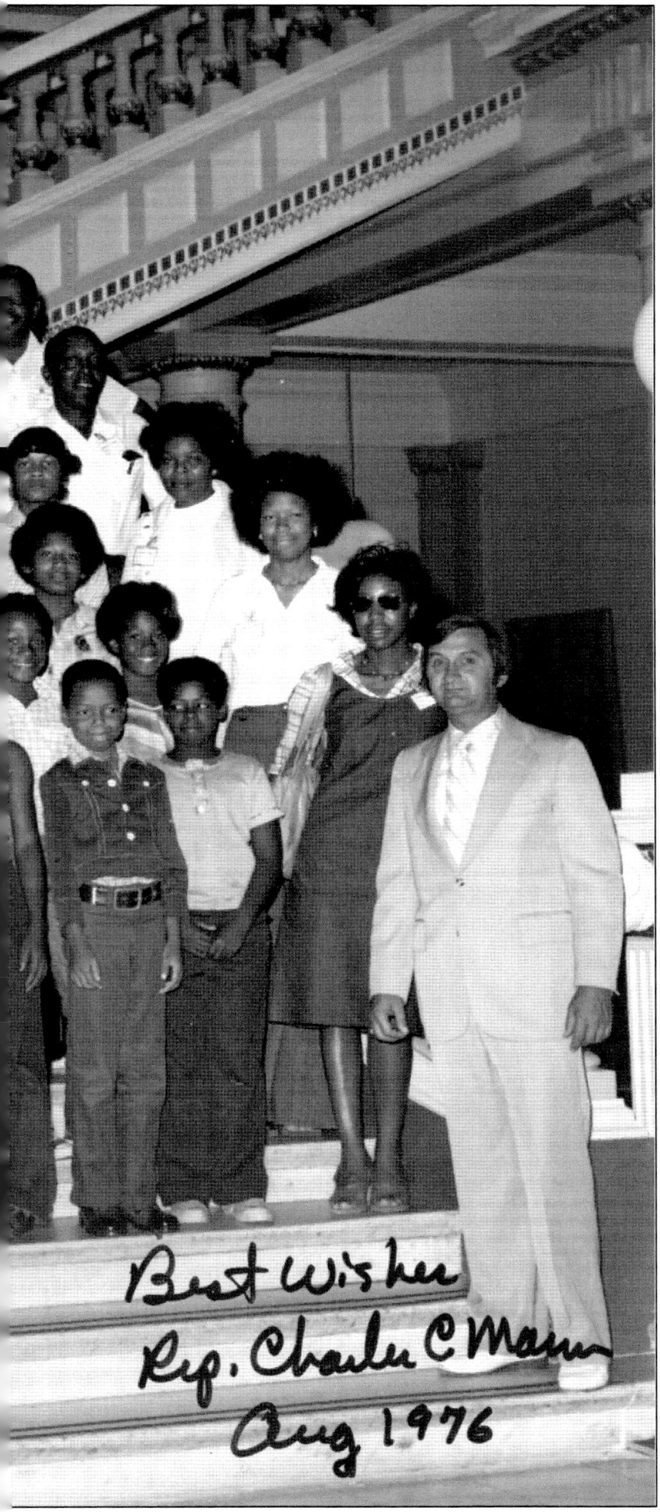

State Capitol. Local youths visit the Georgia State Capitol in the summer of 1976. Rep. Charles C. Mann greets them. (Courtesy Minnie Winston Abner.)

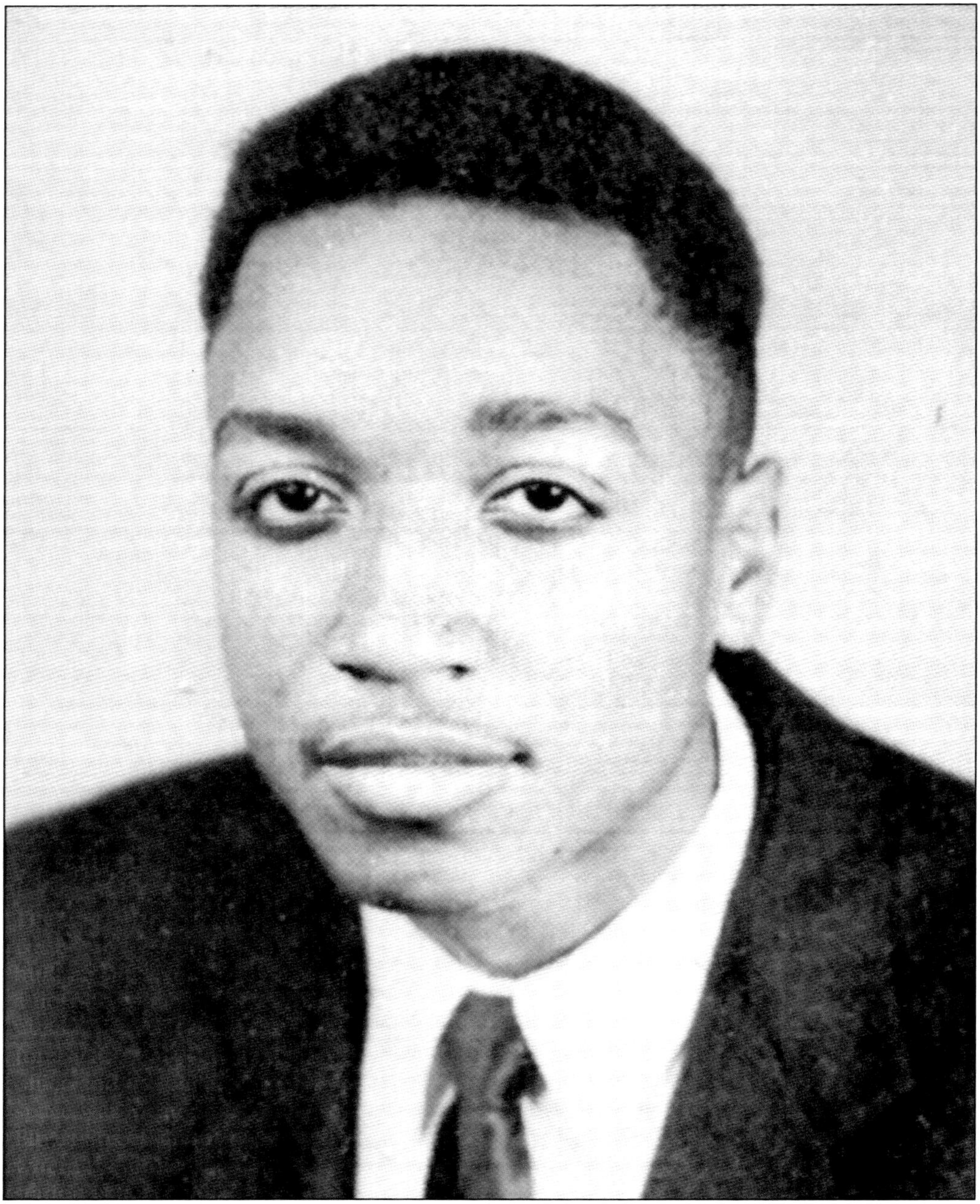

ABE PLUMMER. While students at Friendship Junior College in Rock Hill, South Carolina, Abe Plummer and Arthur Hamm, both of Elbert County, helped to stage South Carolina's first sit-ins at Woolworth's and McCrory's stores on February 12, 1960. Plummer went on to become a teacher, a principal, and an associate superintendent of the Elbert County School System.

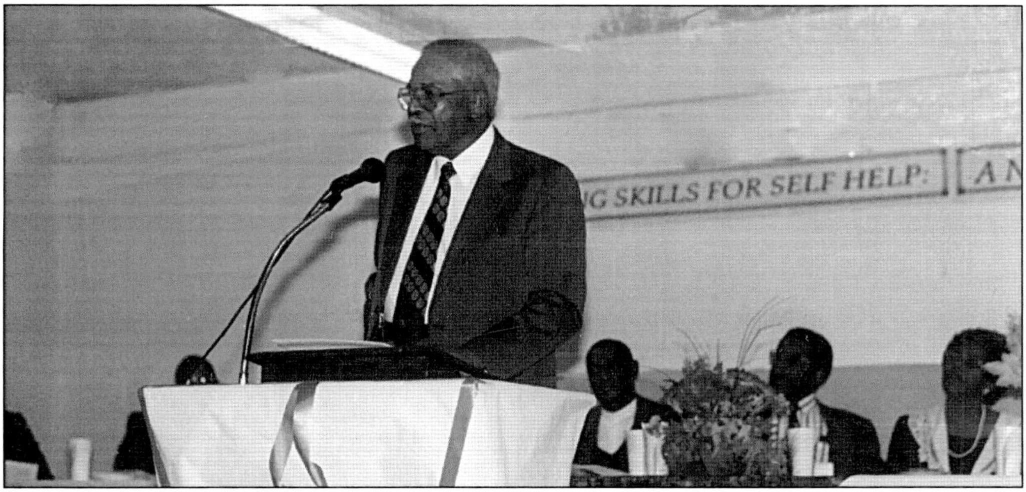

Welchel Long. A retired educator of Elbert County School System, Welchel Long became the first African American to serve on the board of education. Long was an active member of many community organizations including, but not limited to, the NAACP and the Coalition of Concerned Citizens. As the president of the local branch of the NAACP, in *c.* 1985 Long presented the county government with plans to change the at-large system of voting for county commissioners and board of education members to a district system. (Courtesy Jimmy O. White.)

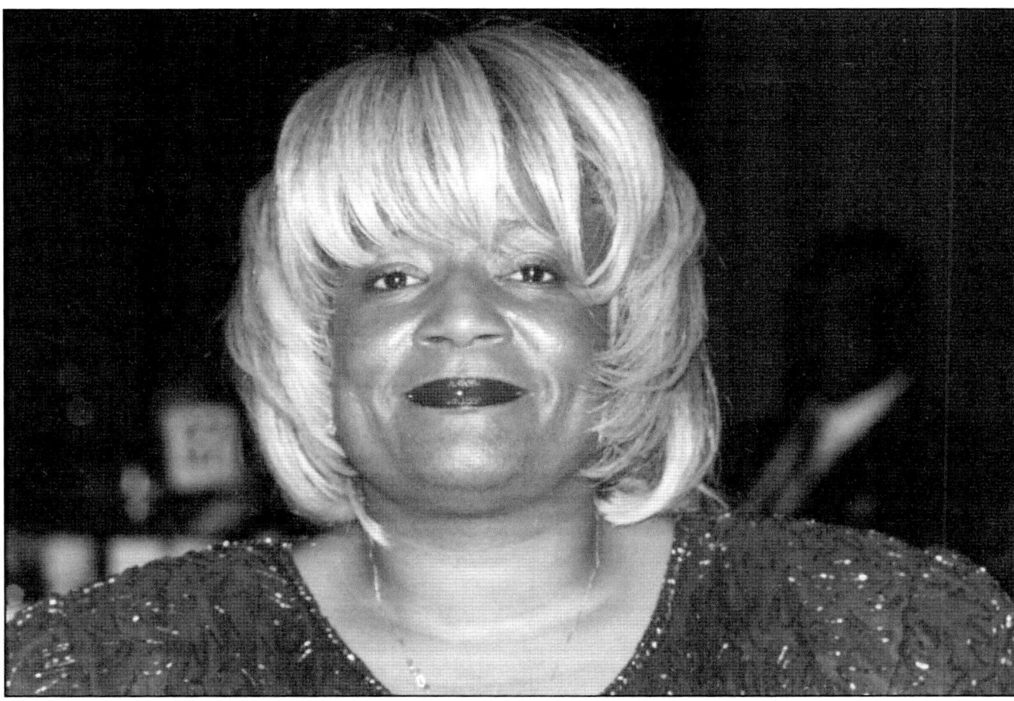

Bobbie Paulk. A former local business owner, Paulk became the second African American and the first African-American woman to serve on the board of education. (Courtesy Jimmy O. White.)

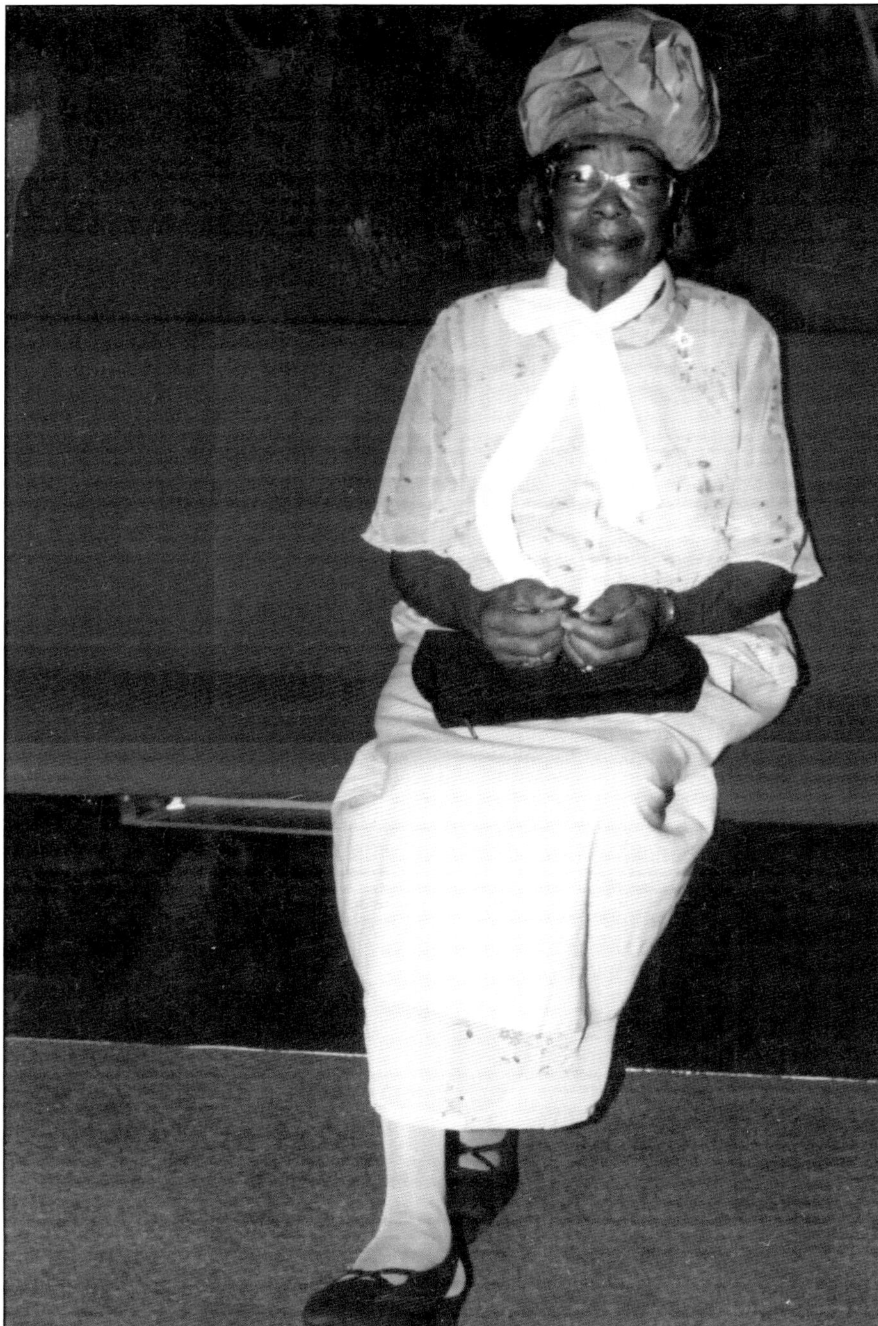

Spotlight. Evangelist Lula Estelle Hughes is the oldest citizen in the record of Elbert County's History to return to school and earn her GED, at the age of 76 years. Hughes grew up in the Dewey Rose community and dropped out of school after completing grade school. Hughes loved doing missionary work and talking to people about God. She was born on January 9, 1920, and died February 9, 2002. (Courtesy Brenda Hughes Trimble.)

Four

People Serve Communities

A sure way for one to lift himself up is by helping to lift someone else.
—Booker T. Washington

The Jones Hospital. Dr. Rembert C. Jones built an office and a hospital wing that was known as the Jones Hospital. The office and hospital space was located on Elbert Street, about where the police station is today. When urban renewal brought changes to Elbert Street, Dr. Jones decided to move his office to his home on Locklin Street. (Courtesy Jimmy O. White.)

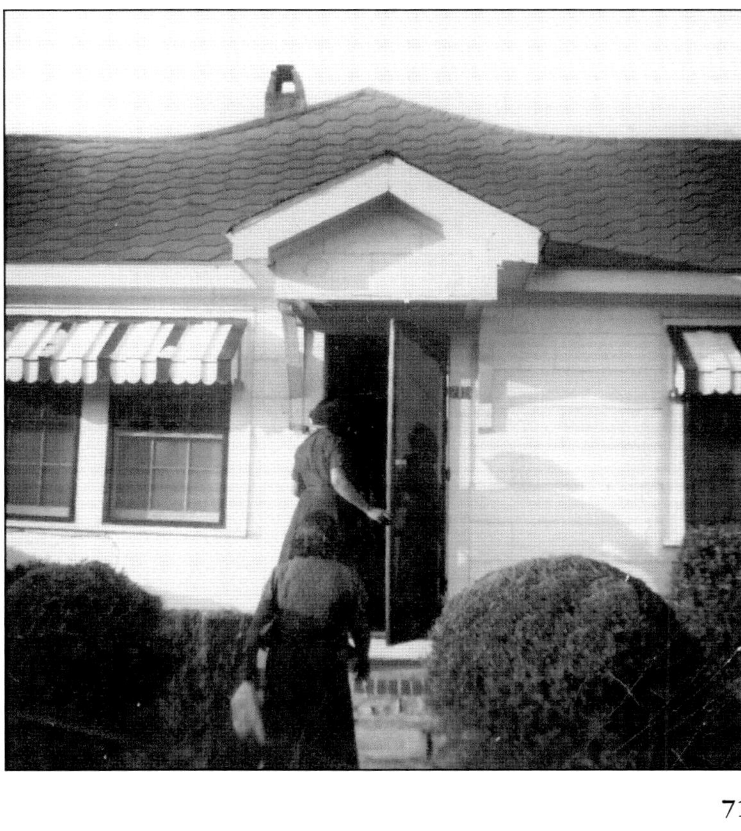

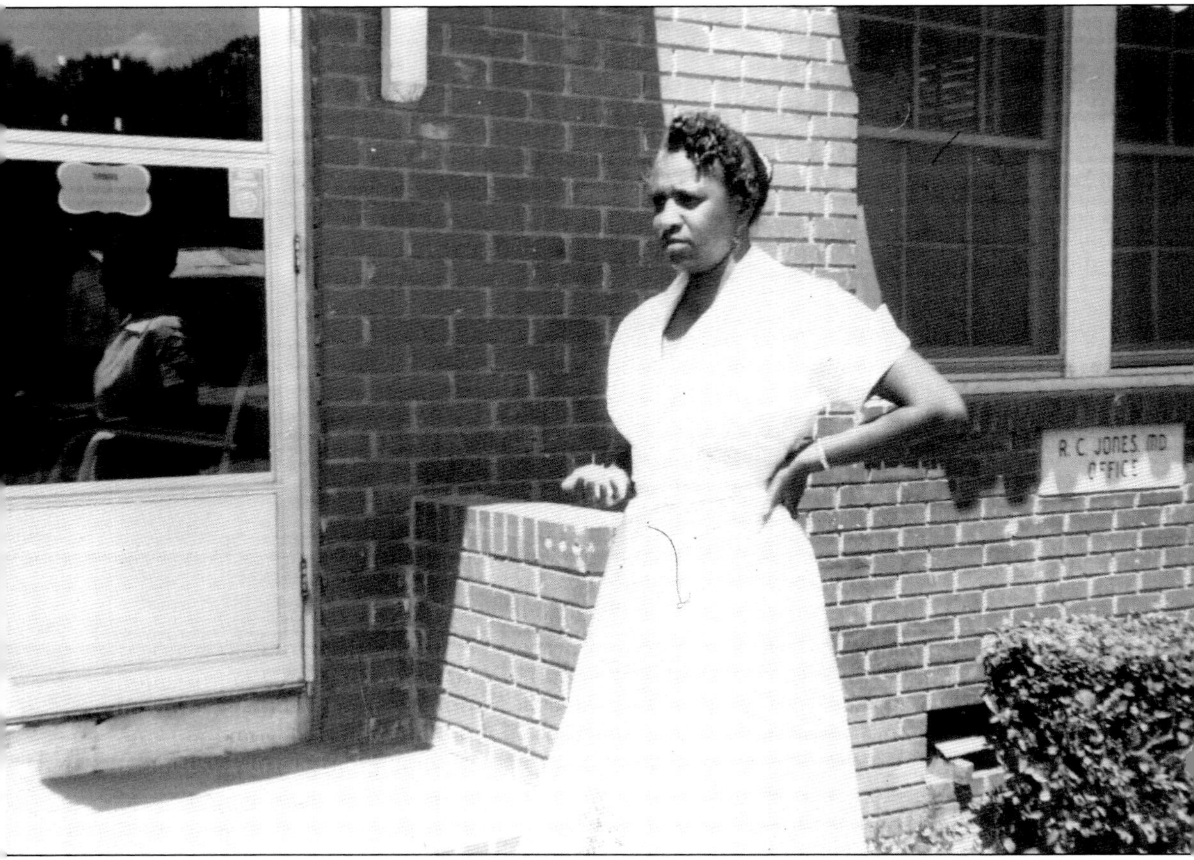

DR. JONES'S LOCKLIN STREET OFFICE. Dr. Rembert C. Jones remodeled his home, adding a side entrance and altering rooms in his residence to accommodate his patients. Georgia White, one of Dr. Jones's nurses, poses for a picture. (Courtesy Georgia White.)

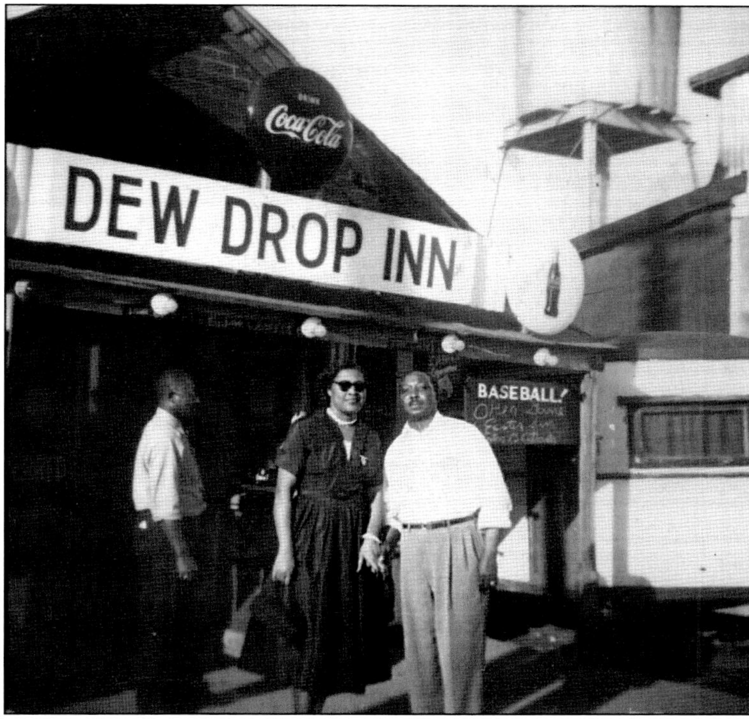

Dew Drop Inn. Before urban renewal in the 1960s, Elbert Street was lined with businesses owned by African Americans. Dew Drop Inn was a café. Pictured are Lois Strickland Fleming and Marion Davis. (Courtesy Jimmy O. White.)

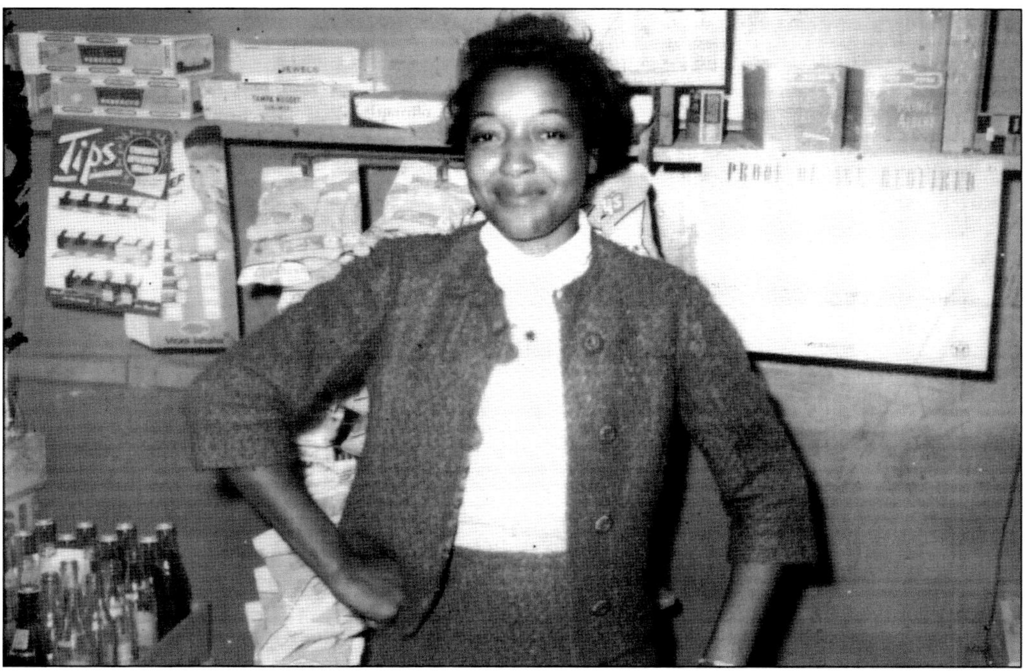

Dooley. Leroy and Alive Dooley were the owner of the Dew Drop Inn. It went out of business after the urban renewal in the mid-1960s. Emma Bradford Heard, a cashier at the café, is pictured. (Courtesy Emma Bradford Heard.)

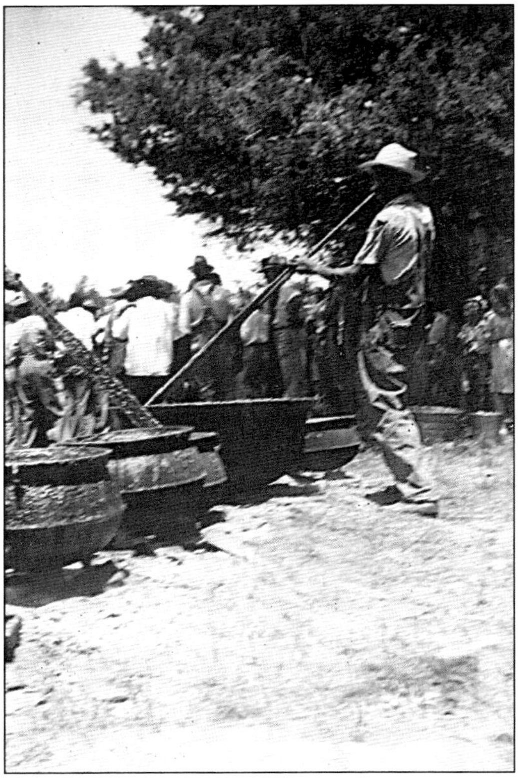

Cookout. A granite-shed owner sponsored a cookout for his employees. The owner purchased all the ingredients, and the employees organized and prepared the food for the cookout. Here a man makes Brunswick stew. (Courtesy Jimmy O. White.)

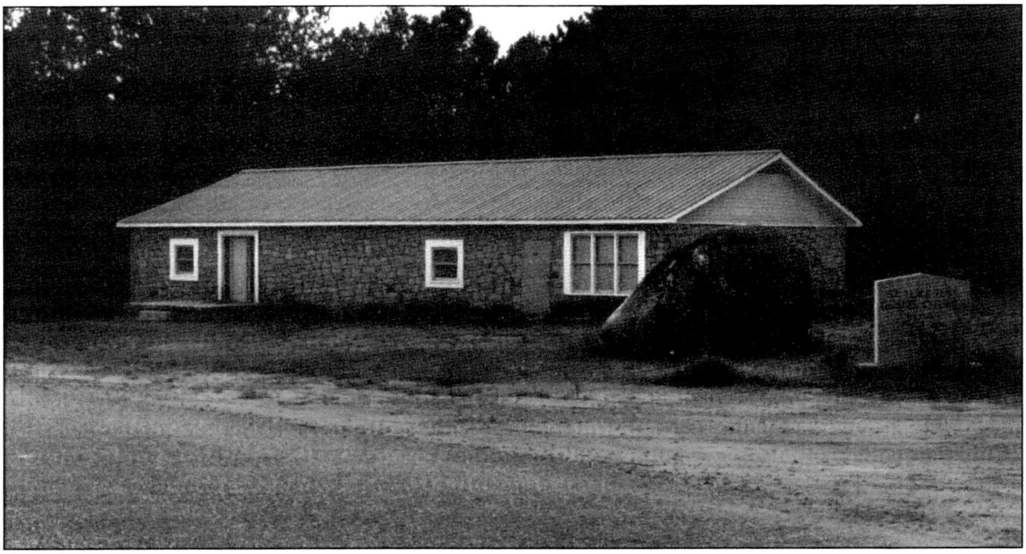

Granite Building. Mike Fortson designed and built this building in the Sweet City community. Originally, he thought to possibly use it for a grocery store. Today, it is a site for a church. (Courtesy Marie and Charles Hamm Collection.)

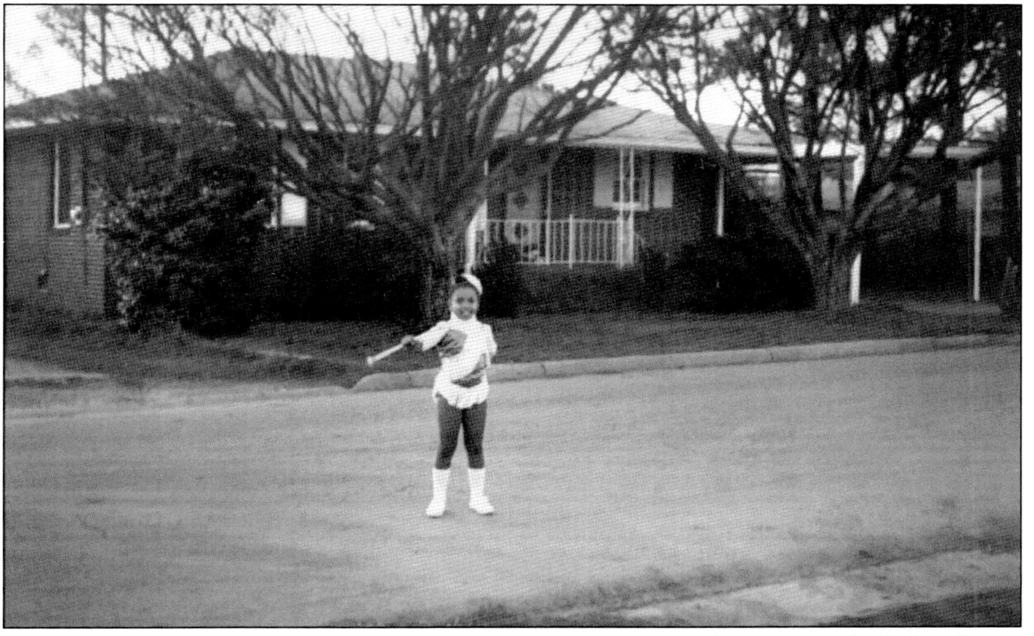

Hershel Thornton's Home. Hershel Thornton, a contractor and carpenter, built his dream home in the late 1950s on Almond Street. By today's standards, it is a modest brick home; however, at the time it was built, it was quite impressive. In the 1950s, the majority of African-American homes built in Elbert County were wooden or made with asbestos siding. (Courtesy Patricia Hamm Allen.)

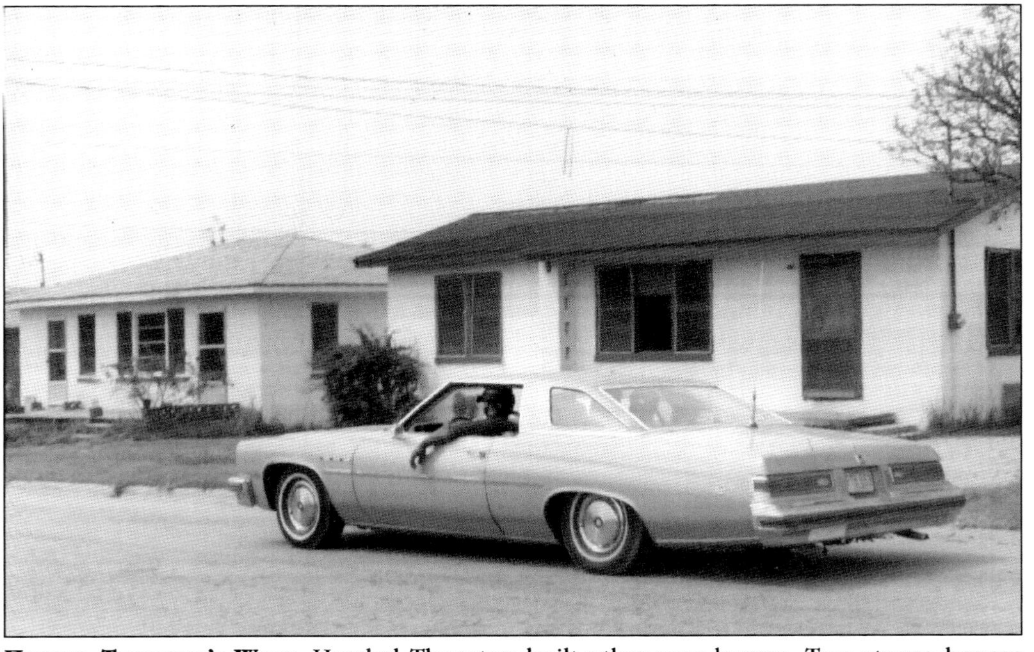

Hershel Thornton's Work. Hershel Thornton built other area homes. Two stucco houses that he built are pictured. (Courtesy Marie and Charles Hamm Collection.)

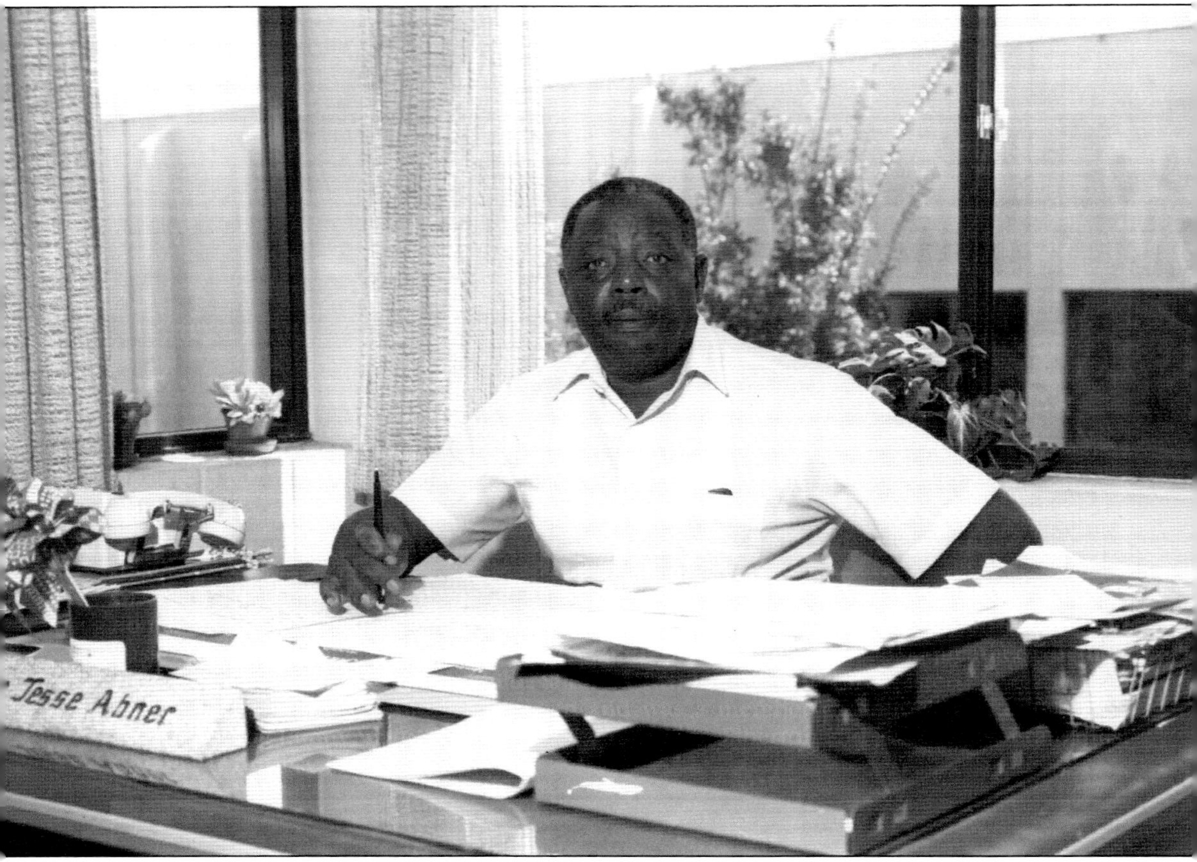

JESSE ABNER JR., MARCH 11, 1930–FEBRUARY 9, 1986. Jesse Abner was born in Lafayette, Alabama to Jesse Abner Sr. and Susie Holloway Abner. He graduated from the East Tenth Street High School in West Point, Georgia, in 1950. He received his B.A. from Clark College in history education and his M.A. in guidance and counseling from Atlanta University. His career with public education began in Jones County High School in Gray, Georgia. He worked as a guidance counselor in the Elbert County School System for 20 years. He was a member of many service groups, including the NAACP and the Coalition of Concerned Citizens, and he was president of the Burke Street Recreation Center Advisory Board. After his death, his wife, Minnie Kate Winston Abner, and six children initiated the Jesse Abner Scholarship as a tribute. (Courtesy Minnie Winston Abner.)

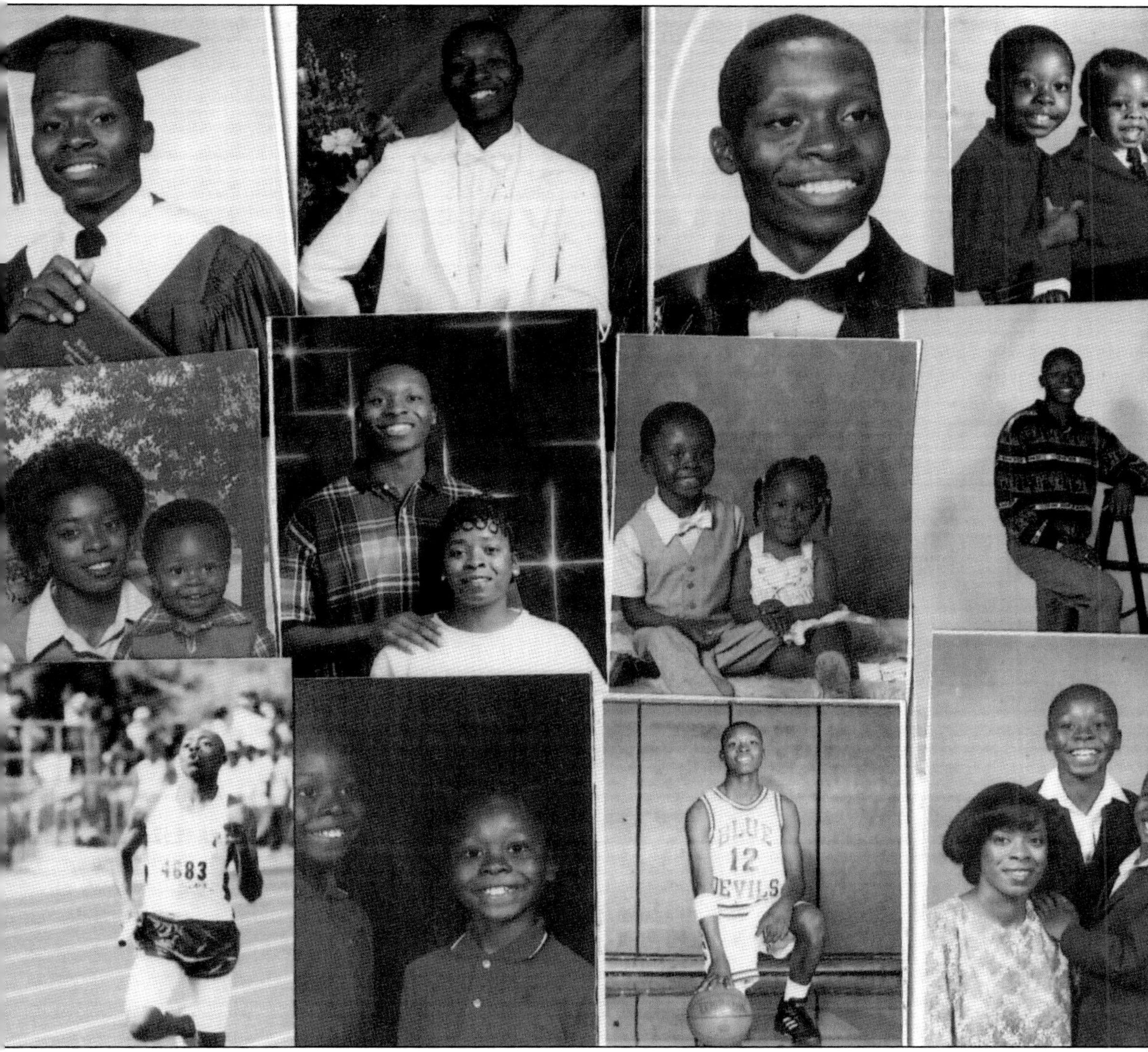

Tamileo Kinté Odister, April 29, 1977–March 25, 1996. Gary Jarvis, a teacher at Elbert County Comprehensive High School; John Wayne Strong, the pastor at Lofton Grove Baptist Church; and Project Redeem of Lofton Grove Baptist Church initiated the Tamileo Kinté Odister Scholarship after Tamileo Kinté Odister was murdered in Atlanta, Georgia, by a car hijacker while visiting one of his aunts during spring break from Savannah State University. In May 1996, the first recipient at Elbert County Comprehensive High School was awarded the scholarship. Since then, Bettina Odister Allen, mother of Tamileo Kinté Odister, and her mother, Janie Odister Sanders, have continued the Tamileo Kinté Odister Scholarship by doing yearly fund-raisers. (Courtesy Bettina Odister.)

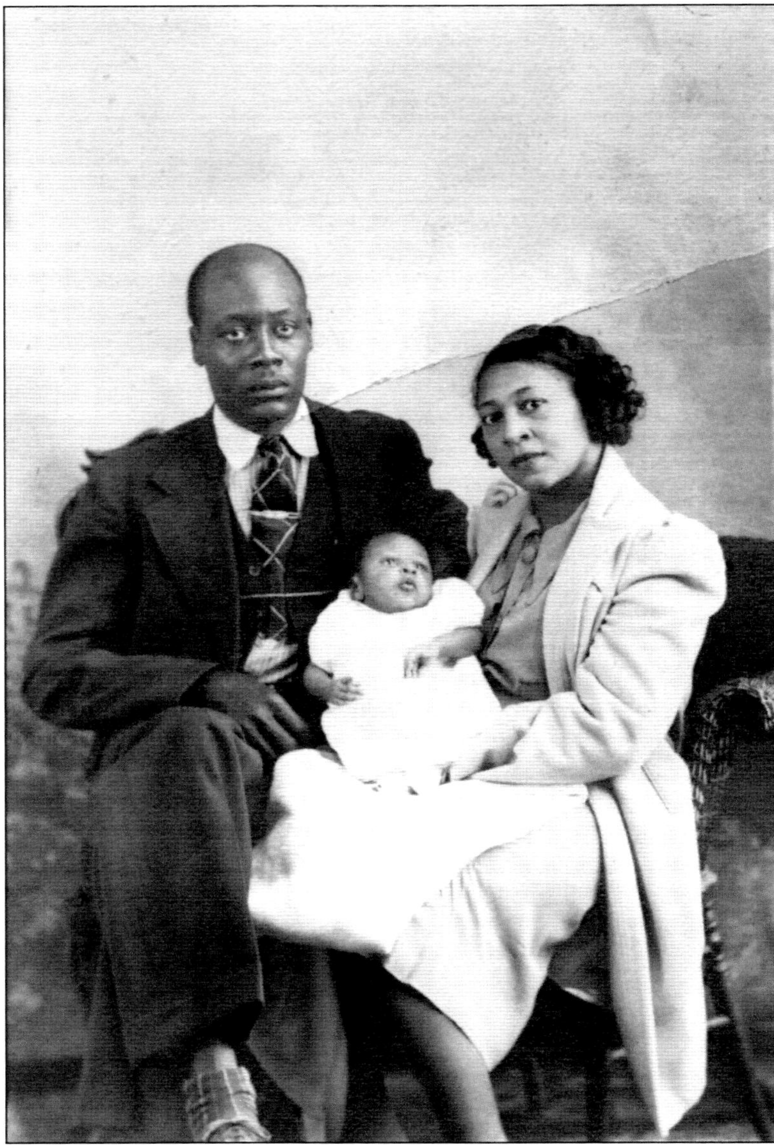

Jim-Ree African-American Museum, Inc. Jimmy O. White was inspired to start Jim-Ree African-American Museum, Inc. from historical documents and artifacts left to him by his parents, Gladys "Delree" Strickland White and Jimmy White Sr. Brenda Harper Sarkodie and Bobby G. Hunt helped to conceptualize the ideas of the museum. The museum is open to the public during the month of February. Since its first display in 1996, the museum has been shown at the Blackwell Memorial Cultural Center. The first board of directors were Jimmy O. White, president; Brenda Sarkodie; Bobby G. Hunt, public relations; Sara J. Willingham, secretary; Pamela Allen, assistant secretary and youth advisor; Carolyn Bolton, treasurer; and Imogene Holland. The mission of the Jim-Ree African-American Museum is to preserve, renew, and identify Elbert County's African-American history. Pictured are Jimmy White Sr., Gladys "Delree" Strickland White, and Jimmy Oscar White Jr. (Courtesy Jimmy O. White.)

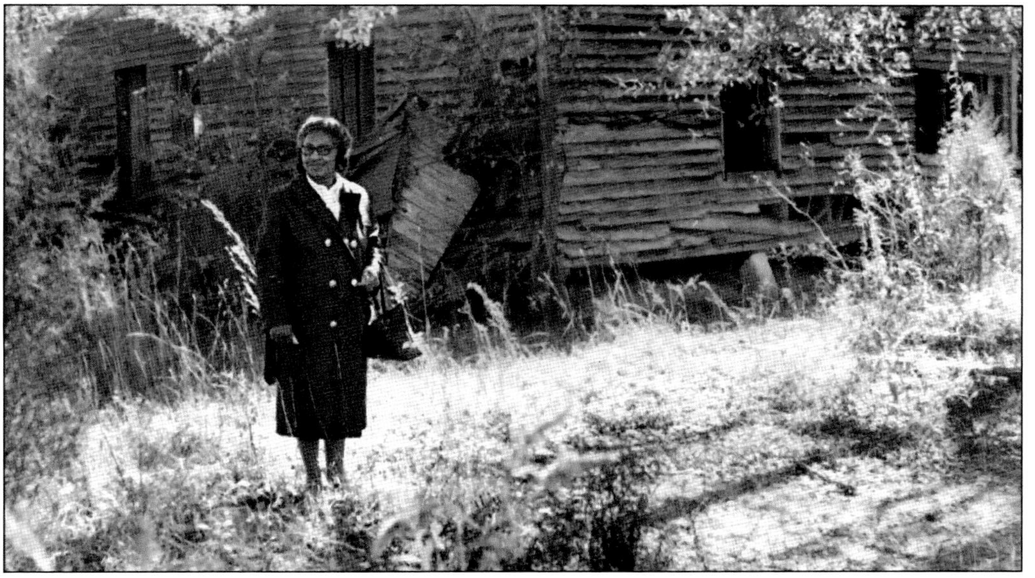

Gladys "Delree" Strickland White, April 25, 1910–May 17, 1995. White visits the old homestead in Dewy Rose, Georgia, where she grew up. Her parents, John Strickland and Susie Spurlock Strickland, owned a farm of 125 acres, which was bequeathed to their children. White was the fourth child. She had two brothers and five sisters. She attended primary school through the grade seven and was a member of Antioch Baptist Church. After marrying Jimmy White Sr. in 1933, she moved to Elberton and joined New Era Baptist Church. (Courtesy Jimmy O. White.)

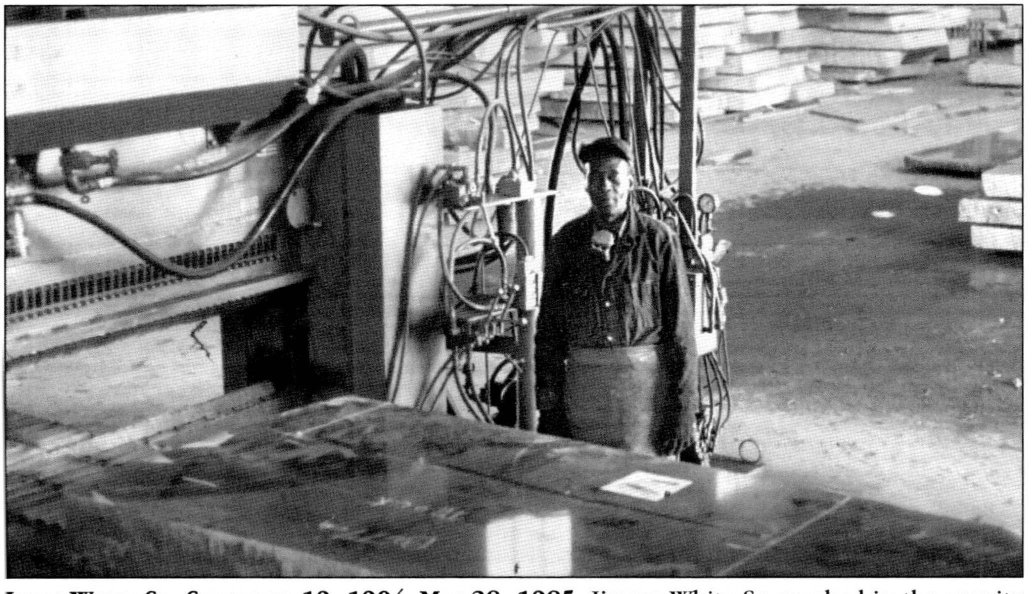

Jimmy White Sr. September 19, 1904–May 28, 1985. Jimmy White Sr. worked in the granite industry for 48 years. He attended White's Chapel Primary School through the second grade. He was a member of the Prince Hall Masonic Lodge and White's Chapel C.M.E. Church. (Courtesy Jimmy O. White.)

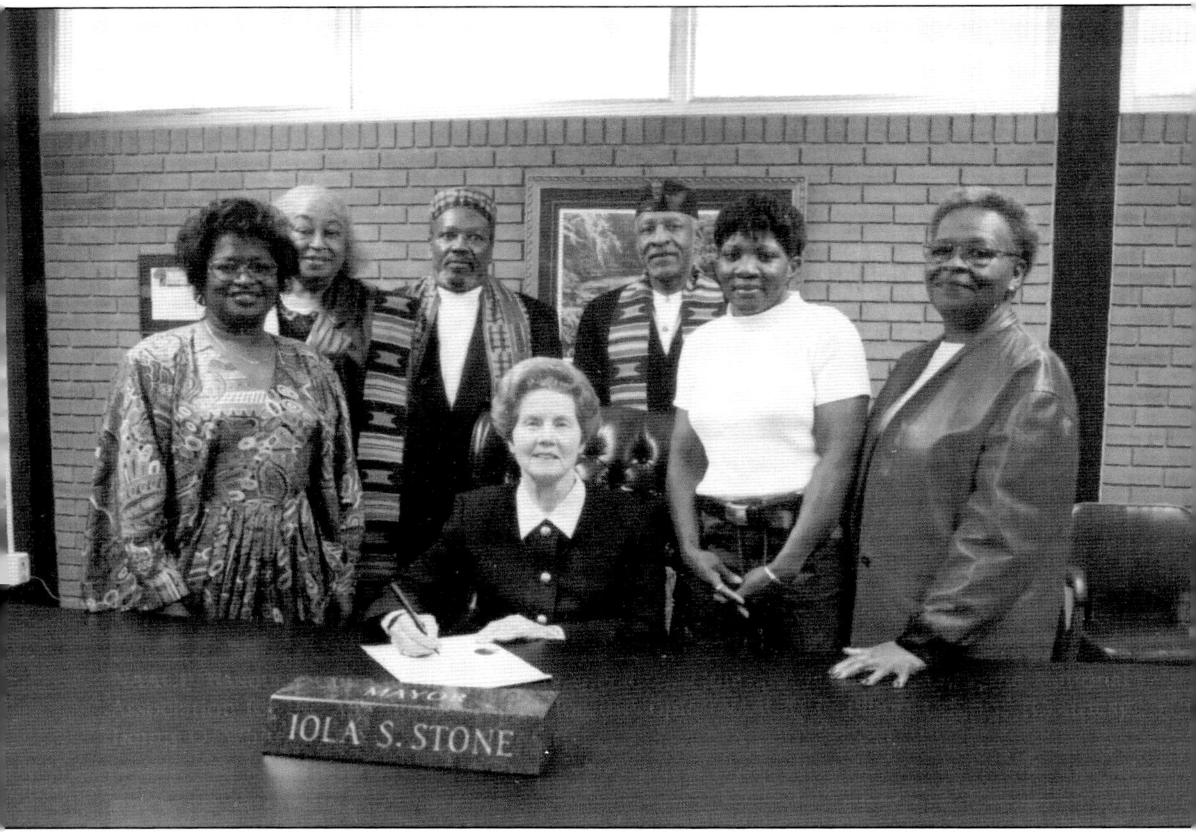

Black History Month. The mayor of Elberton, Iola S. Stone, signs an annual proclamation to honor Black History Month during the month of February. Mayor Stone presents the proclamation to the board of the Jim-Ree African Museum, Inc. Pictured are, from left to right, (front row) Carolyn Bolton, Mayor Iola S. Stone, Pam Bradford Allen, and Sara J. Willingham; (back row) Imogene Willis, Bobby Hunt, and Jimmy O. White. Not pictured is Brenda Harper Sarkodie. (Courtesy Jimmy O. White.)

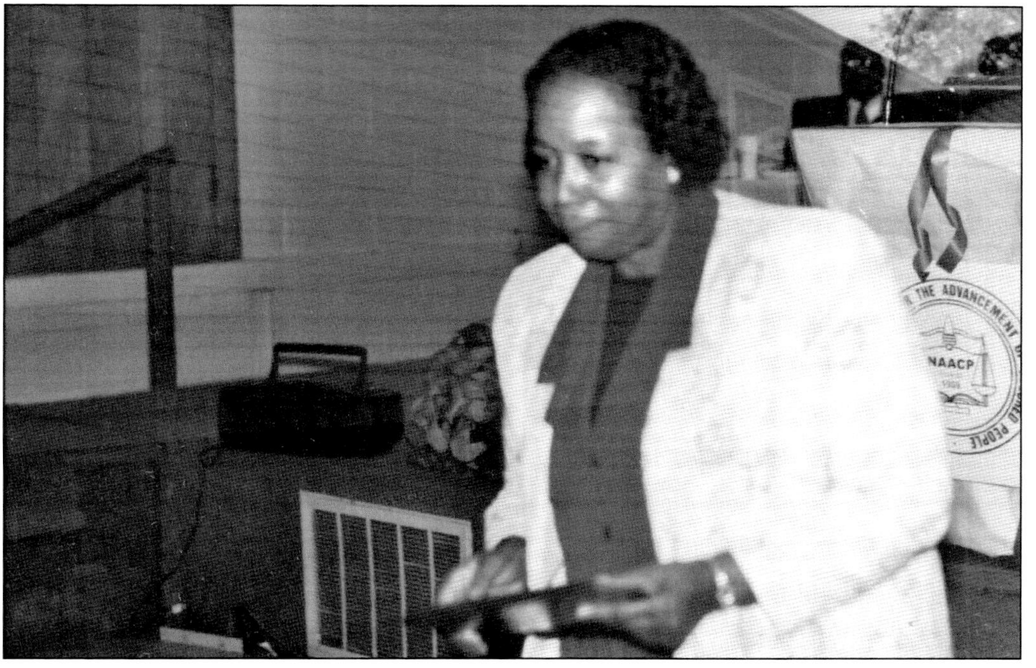

Thursday Night Family Program. Evangelist Frankie Norman initiated the Thursday Night Family Program during Black History Month. Norman is recognized at a NAACP banquet for her work in the community. (Courtesy Jimmy O. White.)

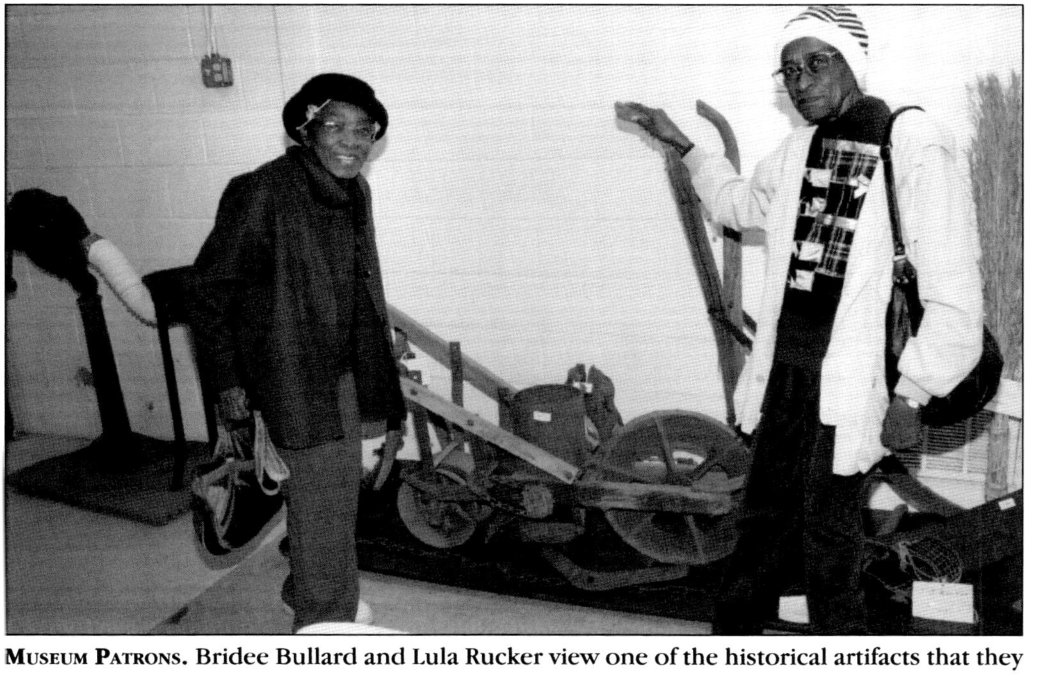

Museum Patrons. Bridee Bullard and Lula Rucker view one of the historical artifacts that they lent for display in the Jim-Ree African-American Museum, Inc. exhibition for Black History Month. (Courtesy Jimmy O. White.)

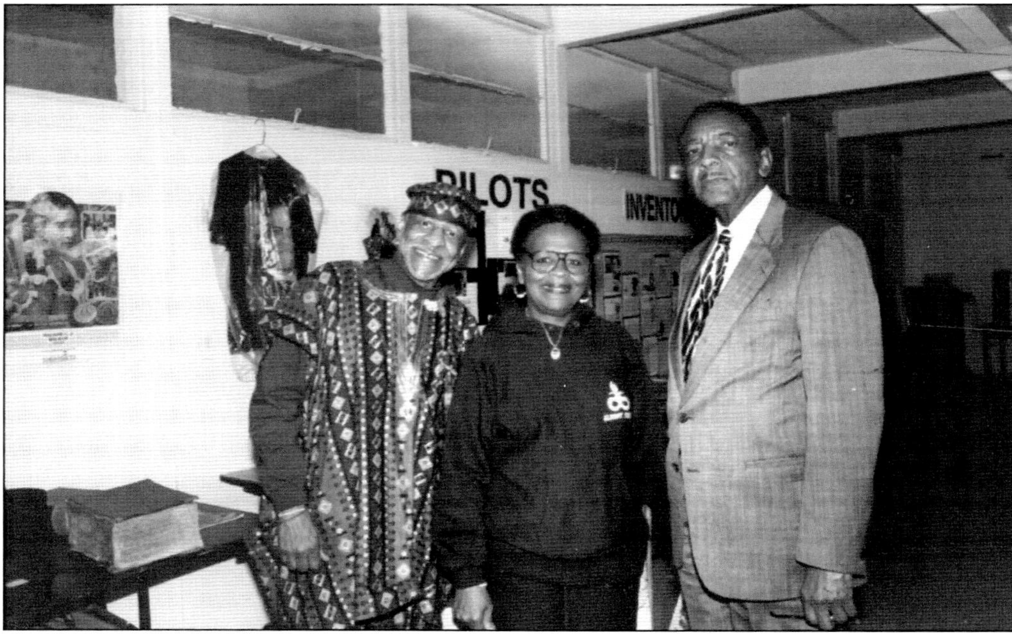

Visit from a Former Georgia State Representative. Horace Tate visits the Jim-Ree African-American Museum, Inc. Pictured from left to right are Jimmy O. White, Sara J. Willingham, and Horace Tate. (Courtesy Sara J. Willingham.)

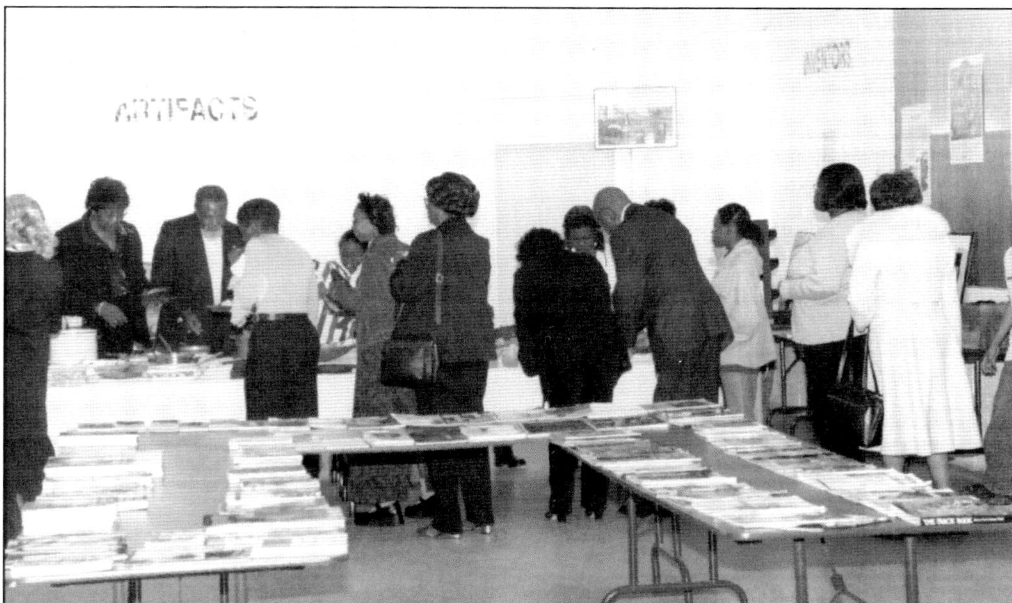

Museum Tour. Community members tour the Jim-Ree African-American Museum, Inc., during Black History Month, the sole opportunity to view exhibitions due to the lack of a host site. To date, the museum has not been able to locate a permanent site for its exhibitions. (Courtesy Jimmy O. White.)

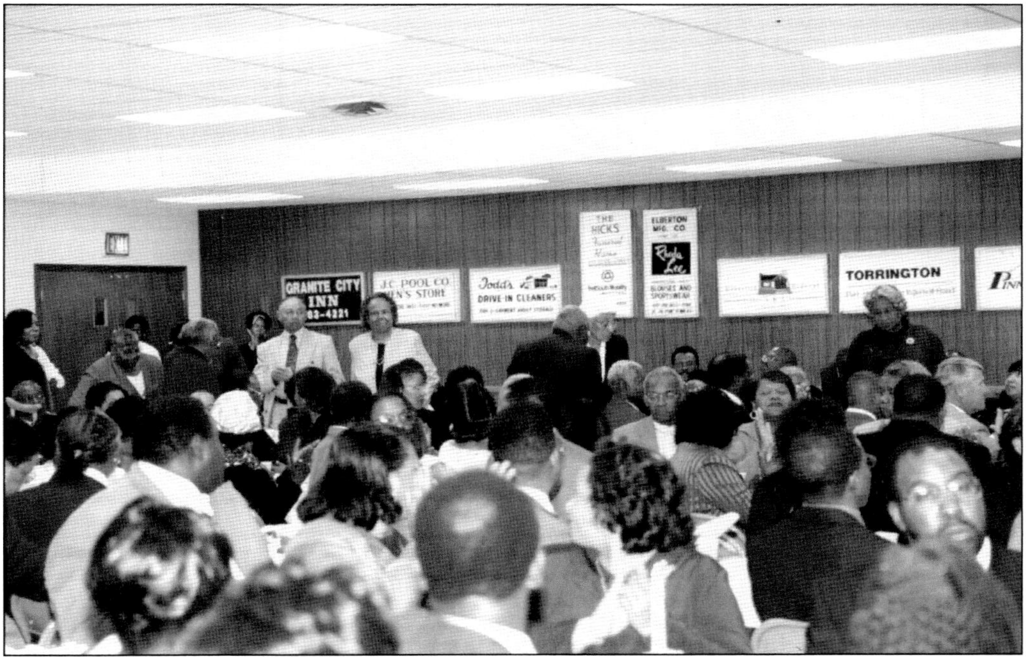

NAACP BANQUET. Community members socialize at the annual banquet for the National Association for the Advancement of Colored People (NAACP) in Elbert County. (Courtesy Jimmy O. White.)

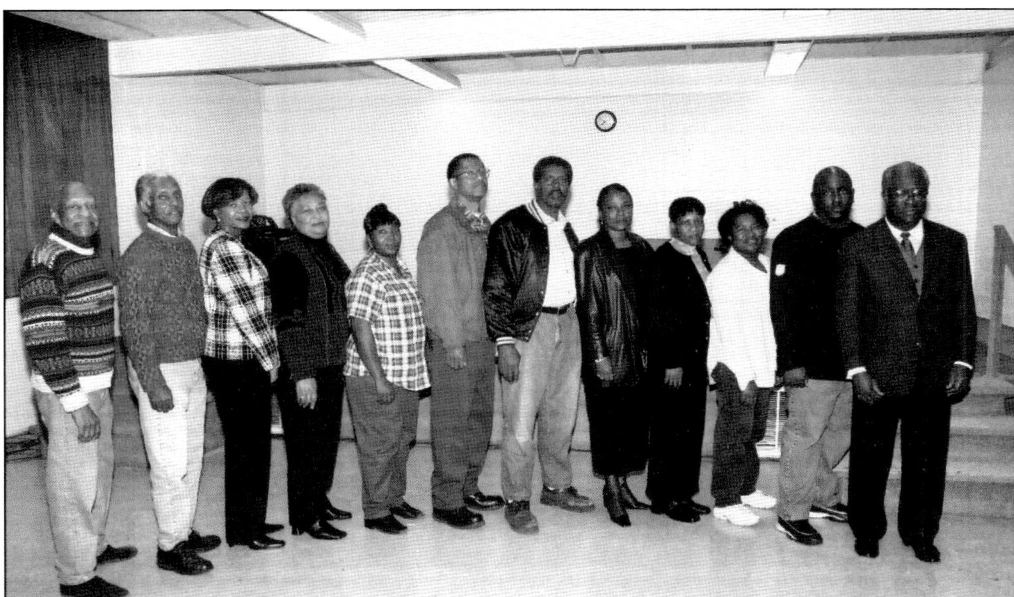

NAACP. The NAACP continues to monitor and protect the civil rights of African Americans and other minorities. Some of the members and officers of the NAACP branch in Elbert County pose for a picture in about 2002. (Courtesy Jimmy O. White.)

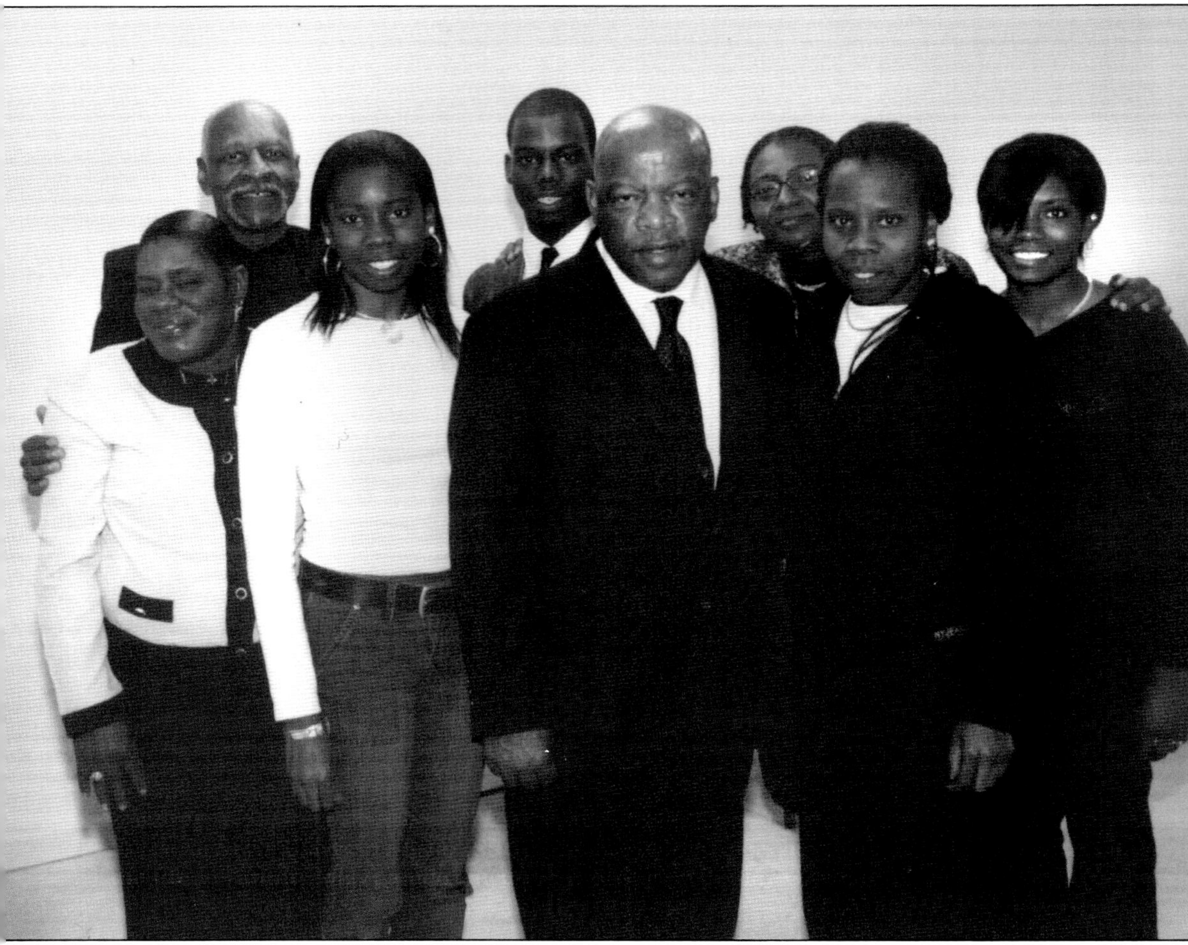

Congressman John Lewis. Congressman John Lewis, third from the left, posed for a picture with some of the people from the community at Blackwell Cultural Center in 2003. Congressman Lewis was the guest speaker later that evening at the NAACP banquet. (Courtesy Jimmy O. White.)

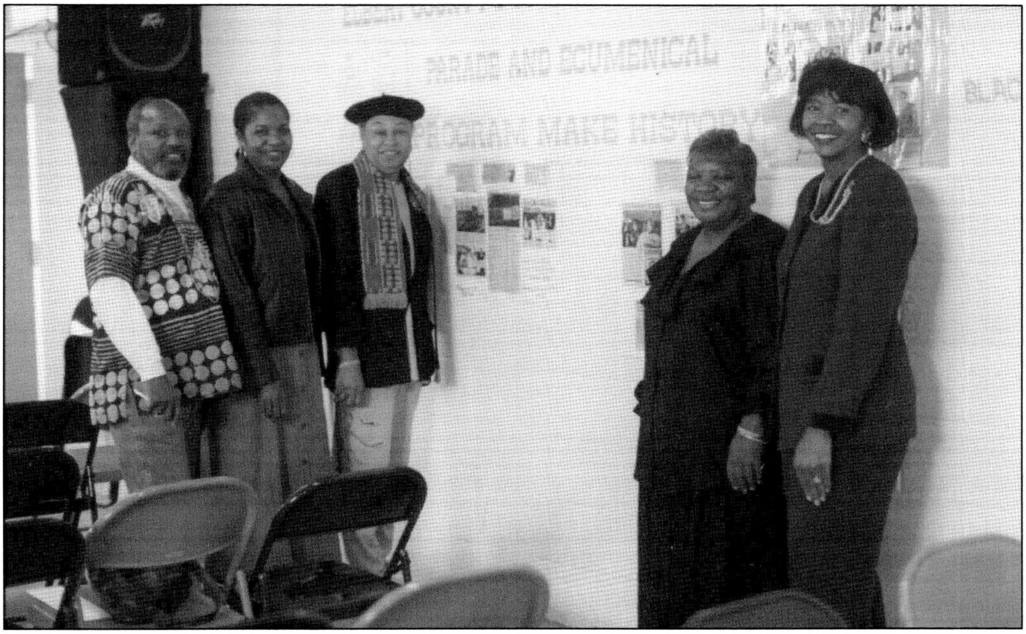

MLK Commemoration. Mary Morrison Clark conceived the concept of having a Martin Luther King (MLK) Parade and Ecumenical Program in October 1993. The idea was supported by the NAACP branch lead by the late Welchel Long. January 16, 1994, marked Elbert County's first MLK Parade and Ecumenical Service. The history of the MLK Parade and Ecumenical Service is displayed at the exhibition of the Jim-Ree African-American Museum, Inc. (Courtesy Jimmy O. White.)

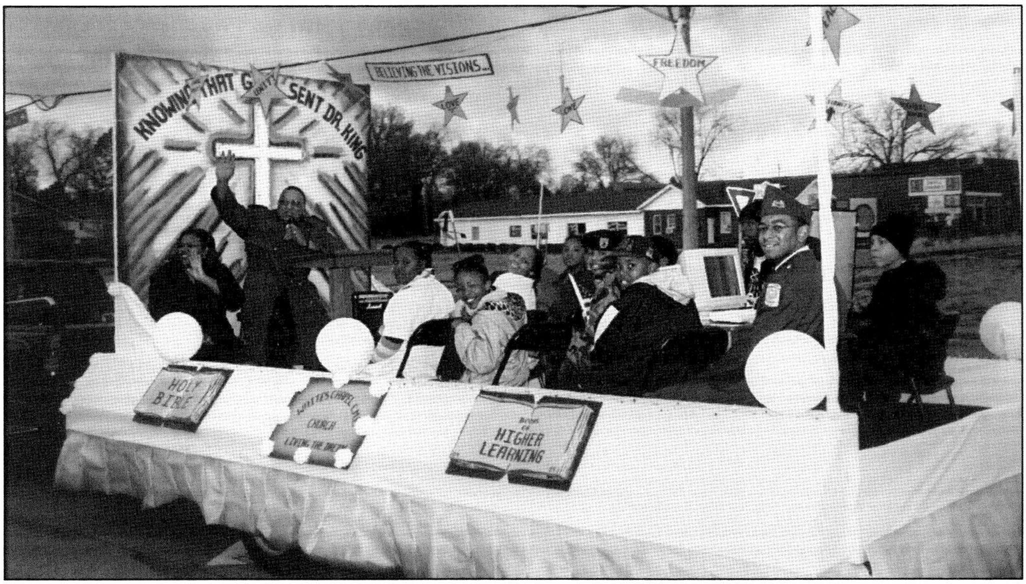

MLK Parade Float. Each year, a new theme for the MLK parade is chosen. The theme is chosen from suggestions submitted by Elbert County School children to the MLK Parade Committee. (Courtesy Jimmy O. White.)

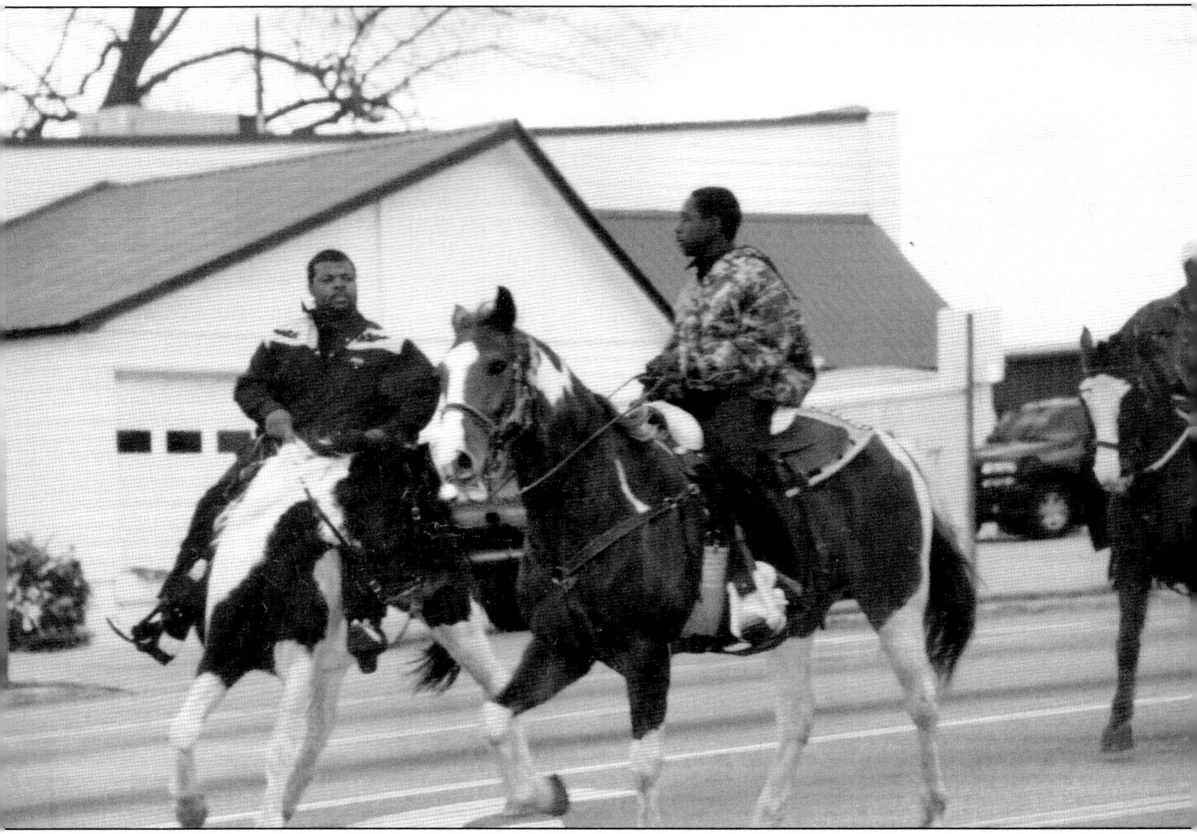

Horse Club. The local African-American horse club participates in the MLK parade, entertaining spectators with the antics of their horses. (Courtesy Jimmy O. White.)

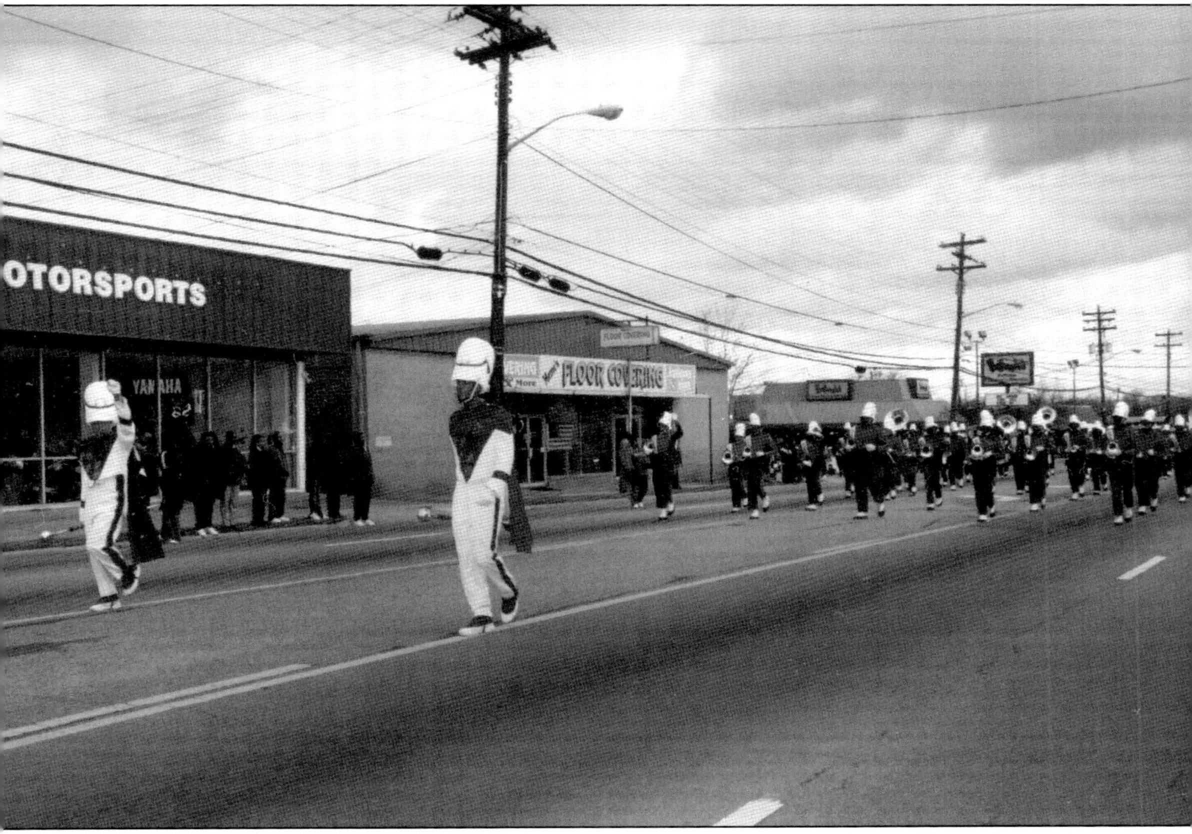

SAVANNAH STATE UNIVERSITY BAND (SSU). The Marching Tigers have traditionally performed in the Elbert County MLK parade since 1994. (Courtesy Jimmy O. White.)

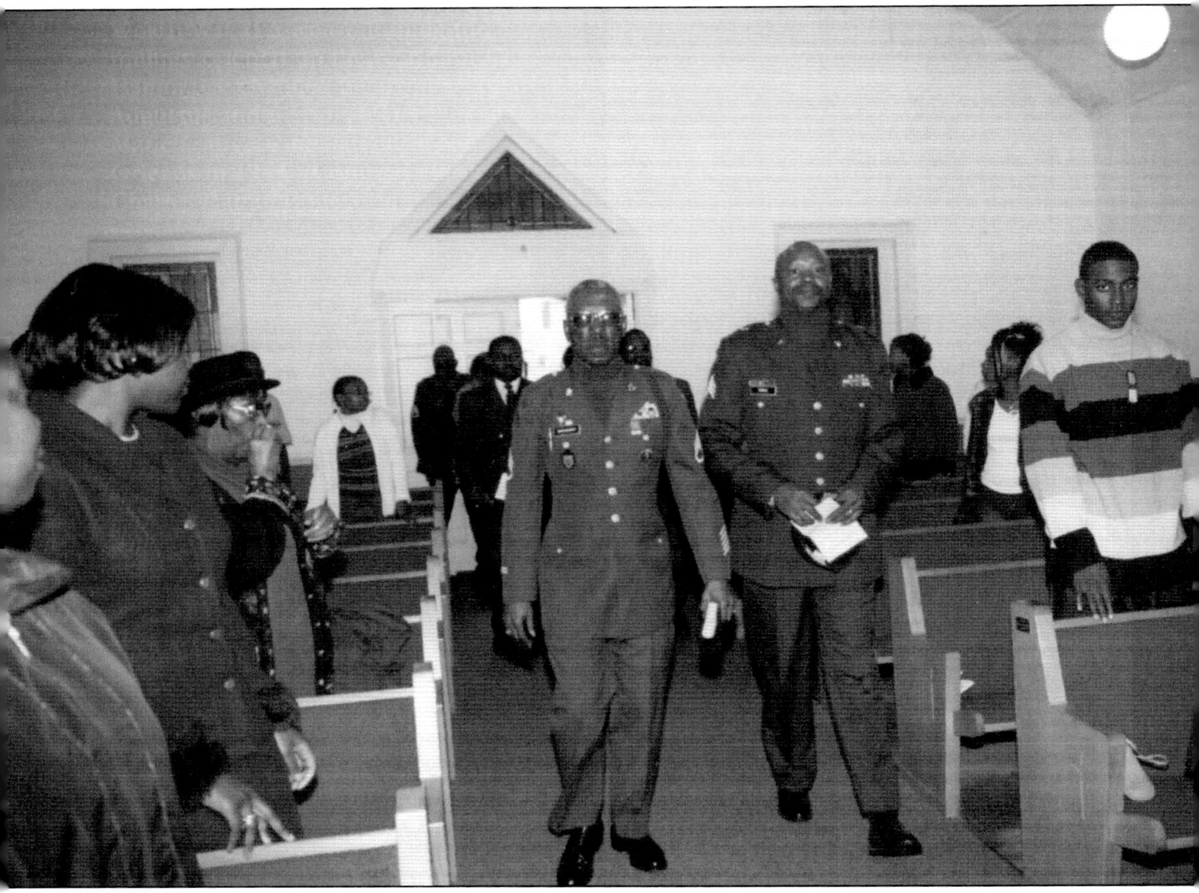

Brothers and Sisters of the Guard. Retired national guardsmen usher in the ministers during the Emancipation Proclamation Celebration. The annual event, in recent history, has been hosted on a rotating basis by Blackwell Memorial Cultural Center, Lofton Grove Baptist Church, Mount Calvary Baptist Church, New Era Baptist Church, and St. Mary's C.M.E. Church. Pictured are Robert Gibbs, at left, and George Benny Elberhart. (Courtesy Jimmy O. White.)

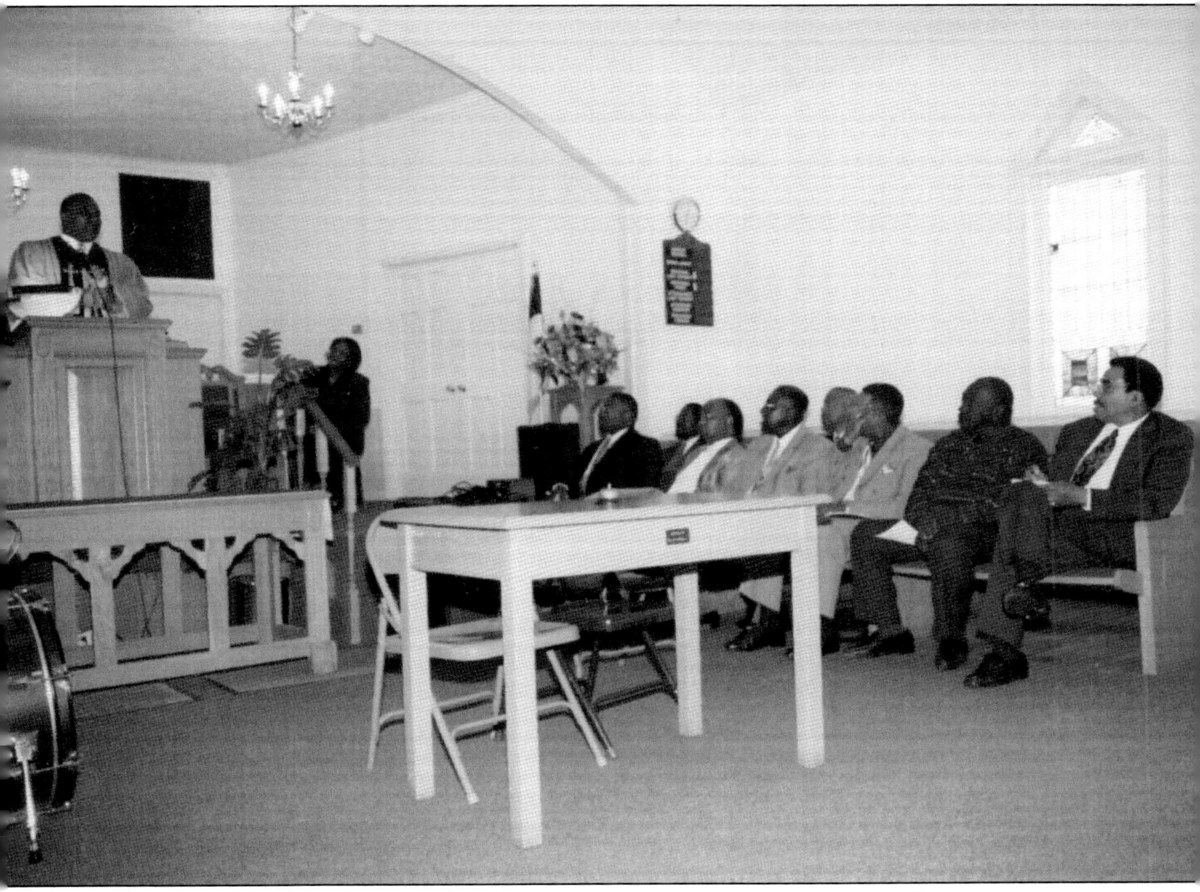

Emancipation Proclamation Commemoration. The tradition of celebrating the Emancipation Proclamation in Elbert County was accredited to Dr. James P. Thompson (1873–1915). (Courtesy Jimmy O. White.)

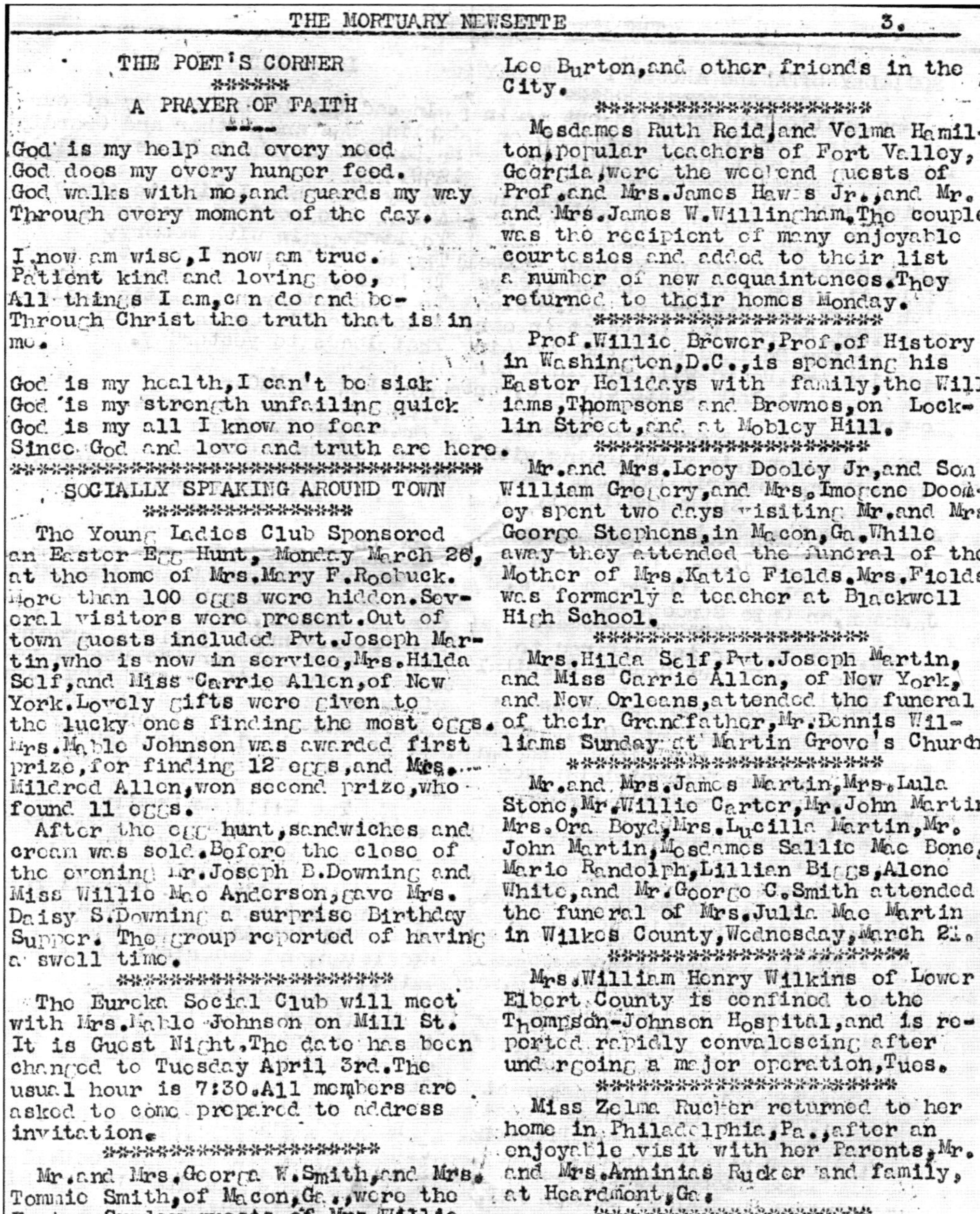

THE MORTUARY NEWSETTE 3.

THE POET'S CORNER

******

A PRAYER OF FAITH

God is my help and every need
God does my every hunger feed.
God walks with me,and guards my way
Through every moment of the day.

I now am wise,I now am true.
Patient kind and loving too,
All things I am,can do and be-
Through Christ the truth that is in me.

God is my health,I can't be sick
God is my strength unfailing quick
God is my all I know no fear
Since God and love and truth are here.

******

SOCIALLY SPEAKING AROUND TOWN

******

The Young Ladies Club Sponsored an Easter Egg Hunt, Monday March 26, at the home of Mrs.Mary F.Roebuck. More than 100 eggs were hidden.Several visitors were present.Out of town guests included Pvt.Joseph Martin,who is now in service,Mrs.Hilda Self,and Miss Carrie Allen,of New York.Lovely gifts were given to the lucky ones finding the most eggs. Mrs.Mable Johnson was awarded first prize,for finding 12 eggs,and Mrs. Mildred Allen,won second prize,who found 11 eggs.

After the egg hunt,sandwiches and cream was sold.Before the close of the evening Mr.Joseph B.Downing and Miss Willie Mae Anderson,gave Mrs. Daisy S.Downing a surprise Birthday Supper. The group reported of having a swell time.

******

The Eureka Social Club will meet with Mrs.Mable Johnson on Mill St. It is Guest Night,The date has been changed to Tuesday April 3rd.The usual hour is 7:30.All members are asked to come prepared to address invitation.

******

Mr.and Mrs.George W.Smith,and Mrs. Tommie Smith,of Macon,Ga.,were the Easter Sunday guests of Mrs.Willie Lee Burton,and other friends in the City.

******

Mesdames Ruth Reid,and Velma Hamilton,popular teachers of Fort Valley, Georgia,were the weekend guests of Prof.and Mrs.James Hawes Jr.,and Mr. and Mrs.James W.Willingham.The couple was the recipient of many enjoyable courtesies and added to their list a number of new acquaintences.They returned to their homes Monday.

******

Prof.Willie Brewer,Prof.of History in Washington,D.C.,is spending his Easter Holidays with family,the Williams,Thompsons and Brownes,on Locklin Street,and at Mobley Hill.

******

Mr.and Mrs.Leroy Dooley Jr,and Son William Gregory,and Mrs.Imogene Dooley spent two days visiting Mr.and Mrs George Stephens,in Macon,Ga.While away they attended the funeral of the Mother of Mrs.Katie Fields.Mrs.Fields was formerly a teacher at Blackwell High School.

******

Mrs.Hilda Self,Pvt.Joseph Martin, and Miss Carrie Allen, of New York, and New Orleans,attended the funeral of their Grandfather,Mr.Dennis Williams Sunday at Martin Grove's Church

******

Mr.and Mrs.James Martin,Mrs.Lula Stone,Mr.Willie Carter,Mr.John Martin Mrs.Ora Boyd,Mrs.Lucille Martin,Mr. John Martin,Mesdames Sallie Mae Bone, Marie Randolph,Lillian Biggs,Alene White,and Mr.George C.Smith attended the funeral of Mrs.Julia Mae Martin in Wilkes County,Wednesday,March 21.

******

Mrs.William Henry Wilkins of Lower Elbert County is confined to the Thompson-Johnson Hospital,and is reported rapidly convalescing after undergoing a major operation,Tues.

******

Miss Zelma Rucker returned to her home in Philadelphia,Pa.,after an enjoyable visit with her Parents,Mr. and Mrs.Anninias Rucker and family, at Heardmont,Ga.

******

GO TO CHURCH SUNDAY.

The Mortuary Gazette. The first and only African-American newspaper in Elbert County was *The Mortuary Gazette*. Rev. John R. and Janesta Lyons McKinney were the creators. *The Mortuary Gazette* was in production for about 10 years. (Courtesy Jim-Ree African-American Museum, Inc. Archives.)

WORLD WAR II SOLDIER. Joining the military opened up the world for Charlie Hamm. He changed his name to Charles Augustus and met the love of his life, Marie Louise Anne Parker, in New Orleans in 1943. (Courtesy Marie and Charles Hamm Collection.)

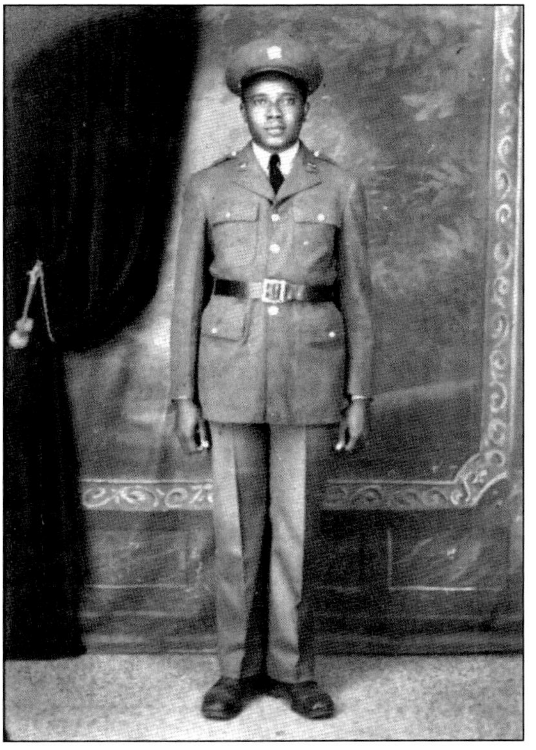

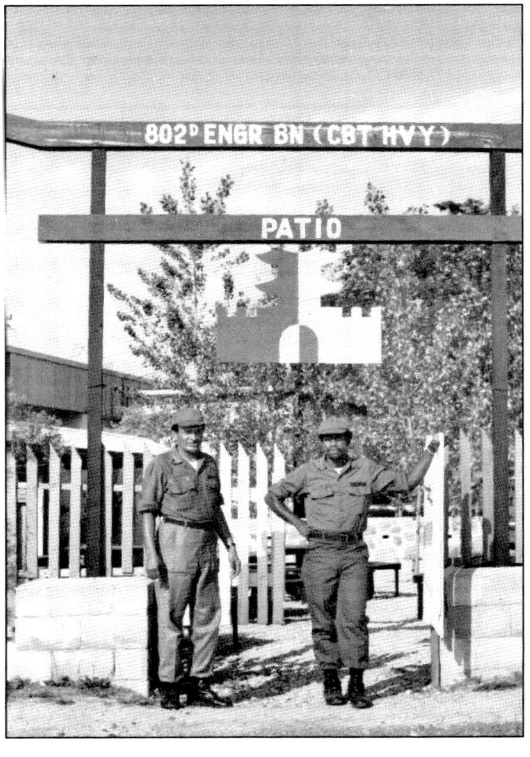

ARMY RESERVES. Mike Fortson and Ronald Hamm traveled to Korea while in the army reserves. (Courtesy Mike Fortson.)

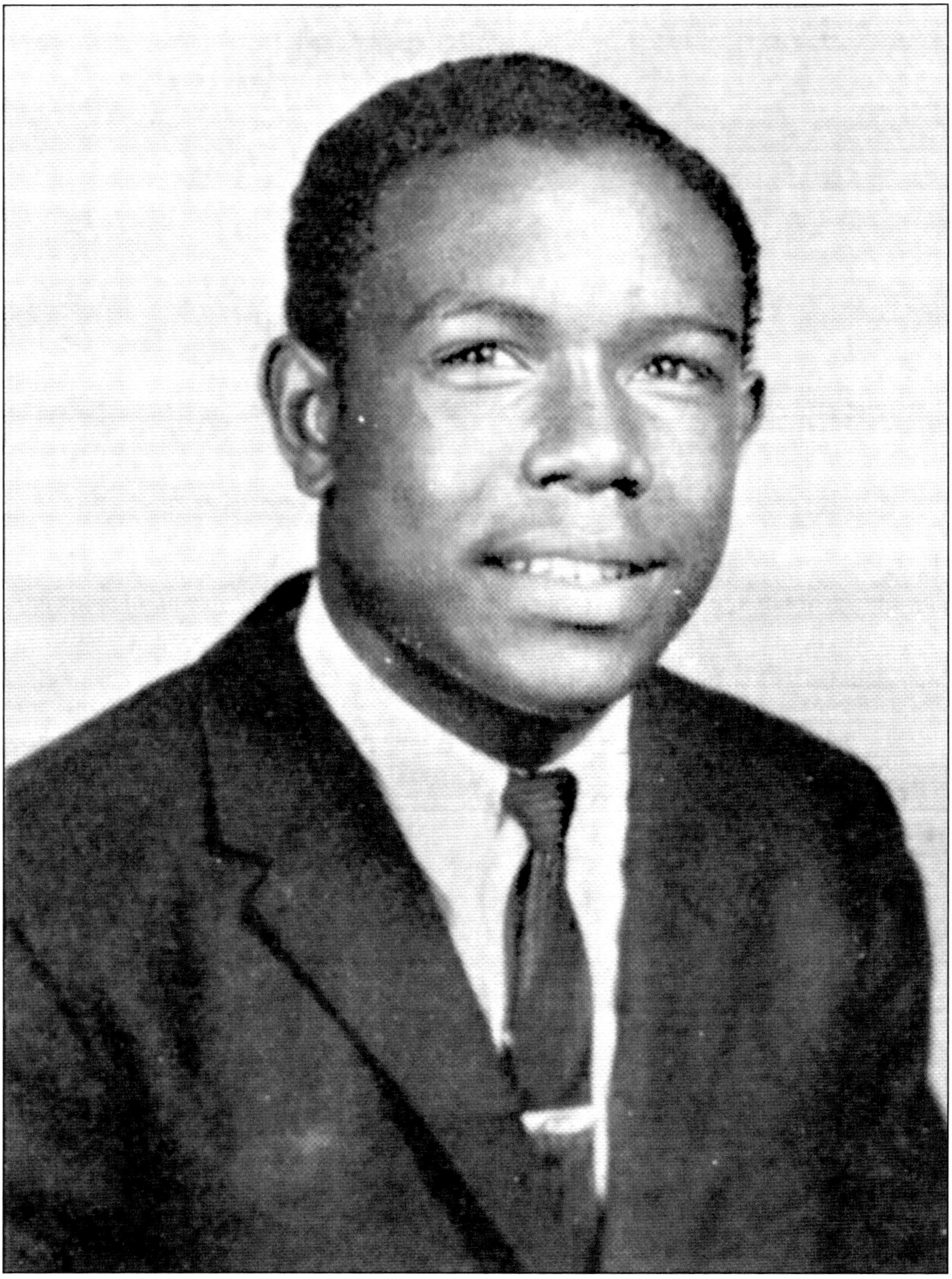

Spotlight. Allen Winton Jones, better known as "Wint," lost his life in 1966 in the Vietnam War at the age of 22 years. His family started the Allen Winton Jones Tutoring Center in honor of his memory in 2004.

Five

Politicians Represent Communities

Intolerance, someone has said, is violence to the intellect
and hatred is violence to the heart.
—Mahatma Gandhi

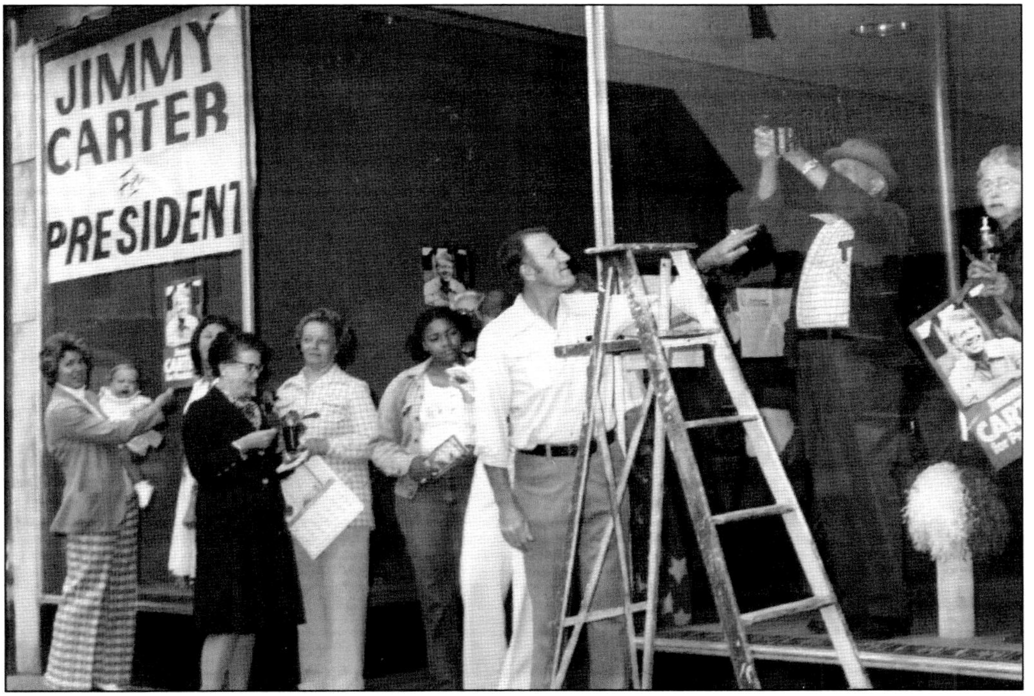

Young Democrat. Sandra Lee Hamm (Gibbs) joined the Democratic Party to assist in getting Gov. Jimmy Carter elected as the next president of the United States of America. Sandra Lee Hamm is pictured with other democrats in 1975. (Courtesy Jim-Ree African American, Inc. Archives.)

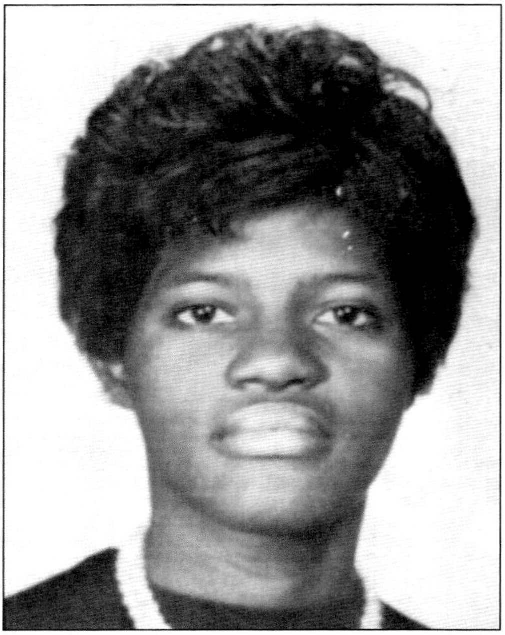

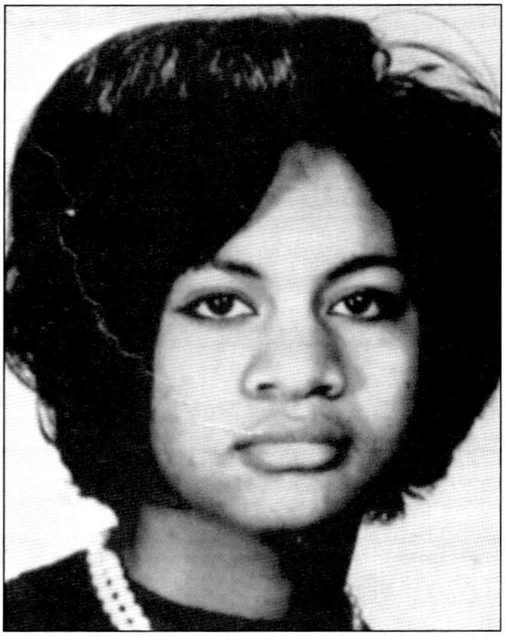

Initiated Sit-Ins. Tired of their second-class citizenship, students of Blackwell Memorial High School organized sit-ins at Elberton Drugstore and Ward Pharmacy in 1965. At the time, African Americans could not sit at the counters to be served from the fountains. They had to stand to place their orders and stand to wait on their orders. Their senior year in high school, Lillie Bolton, Shirley Thornton, Mary Booker, and Berta Power helped organize the sit-ins and helped organize the local branch of the NAACP. Pictured are Lillie Bolton (above left), Shirley Thornton (above right), Mary Booker (lower left), and Berta Power (lower right). (Courtesy Marie and Charles Hamm Collection.)

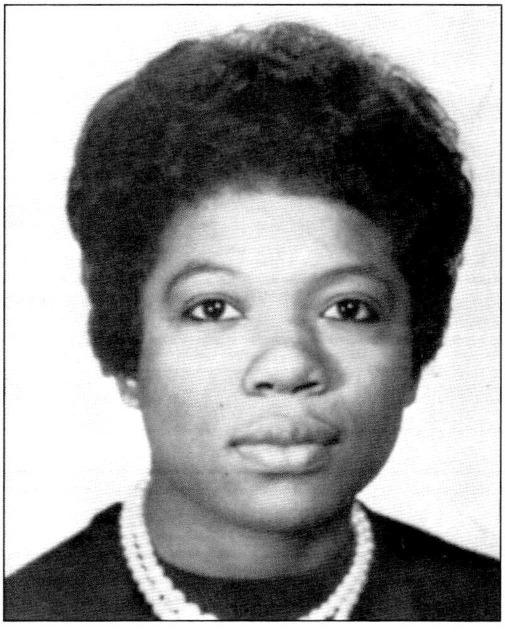

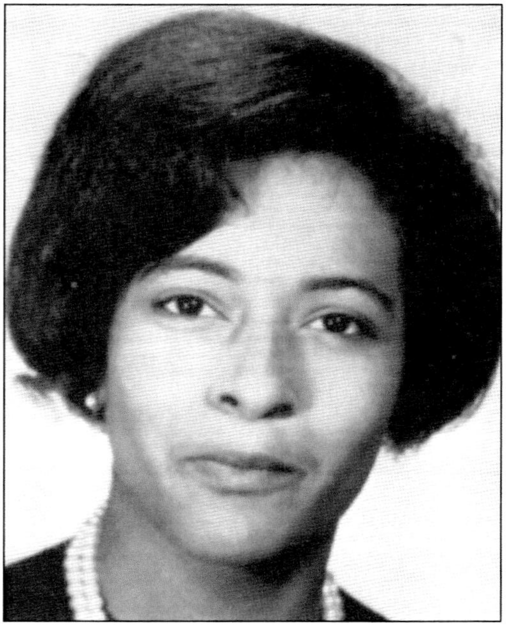

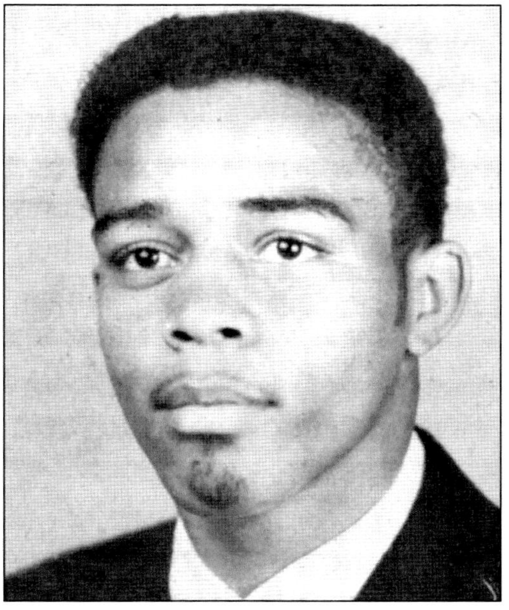

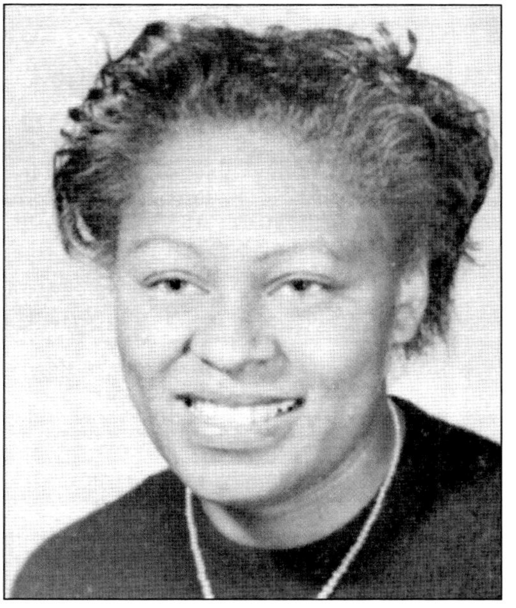

CIVIL RIGHTS MOVEMENT. Prompted by civil unrest throughout the community after Curtis Brawner, an African-American man, accidentally killed his boss, John McLanahan, a white man, young African-American men and women organized the local branch of the NAACP in 1965. A lawyer from Savannah, along with students from Savannah State College, helped the officers of the chapter organize a voter-registration drive. Pictured are John Phelps, president (above left); Bobby Joe Fortson, vice president (below left); Imogene Holland Willis, secretary (above right); and Jimmy Dubose, treasurer (below right). Rev. Eddie Burt and Charlie Tate, both of St. Mary's C.M.E. Church, assisted the group. (Courtesy Jim-Ree African American, Inc. Archives.)

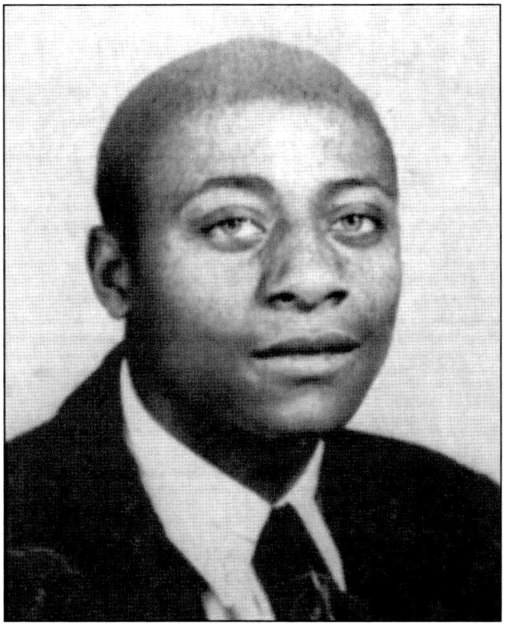

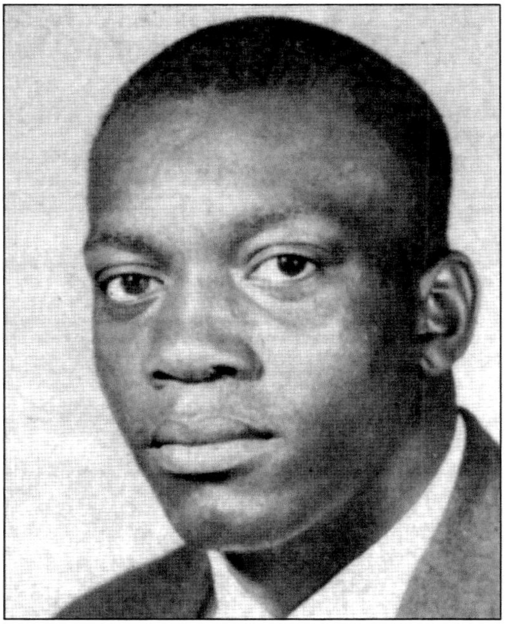

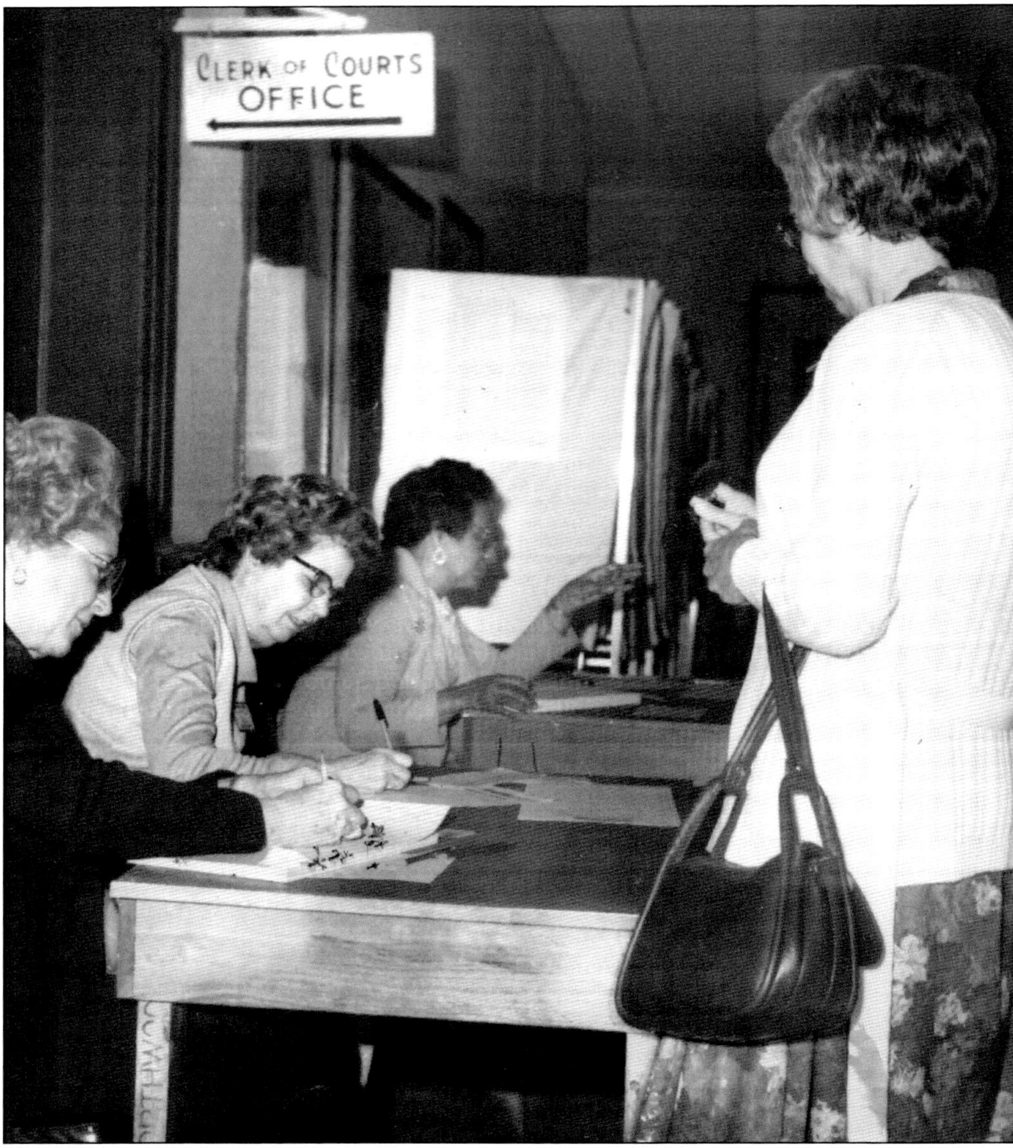

AT THE POLES. Genora Biggs, seated near the booths, worked at the polls on Election Day, November 2, 1976. (Courtesy Jim-Ree African American, Inc. Archives.)

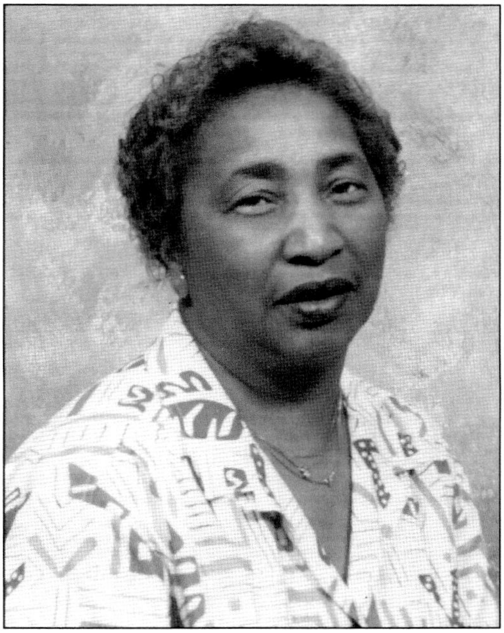
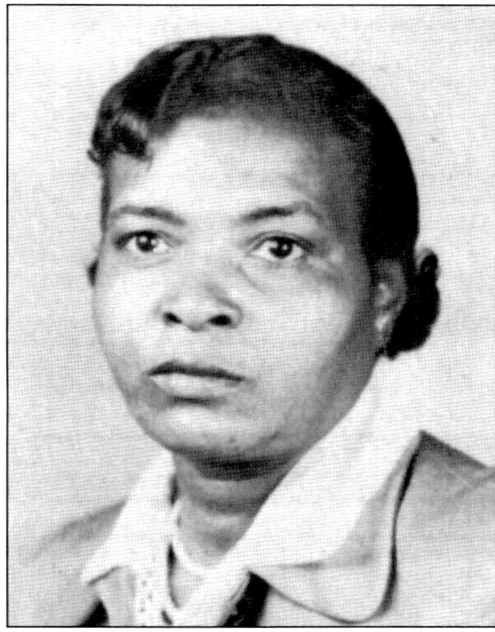

CLASS-ACTION LAWSUIT. Mozelle Mattox (above left), Lillie Pressley (above right), and Imogene Willis Holland (lower left) were plaintiffs in a class-action lawsuit filed in 1982 to get the City of Elberton to change its system of voting from an at-large system to a ward system. At the time, no African American had been elected to public office in Elbert County. Robert Mattox (lower right), the president of the NAACP local branch, and Rev. H.E. McRae, pastor of Saint Mary's C.M.E. Church, were involved in the organization of the lawsuit. (Courtesy Mozell Mattox and Jim-Ree African American, Inc. Archives.)

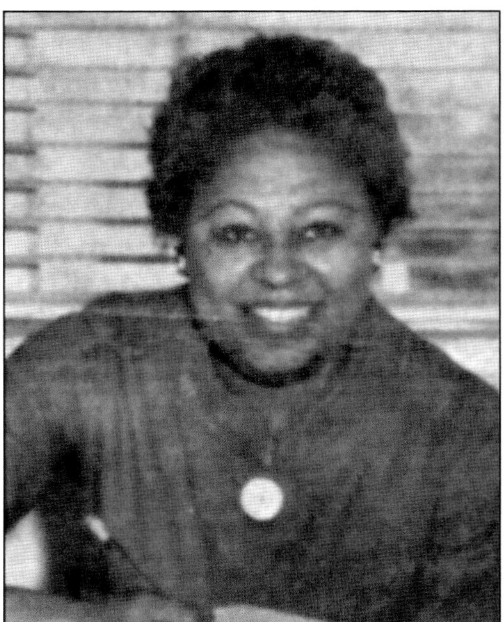
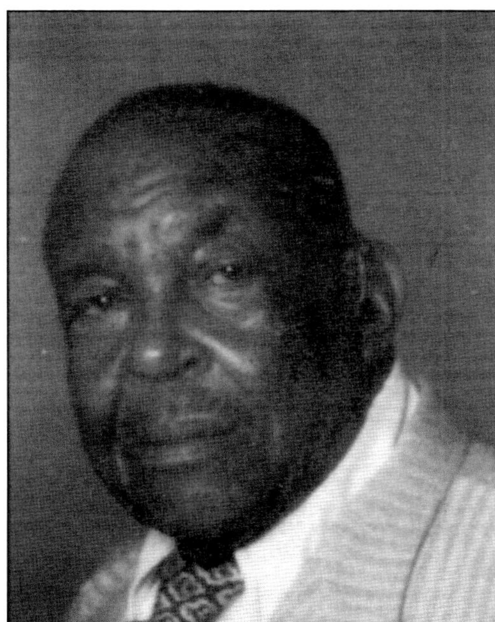

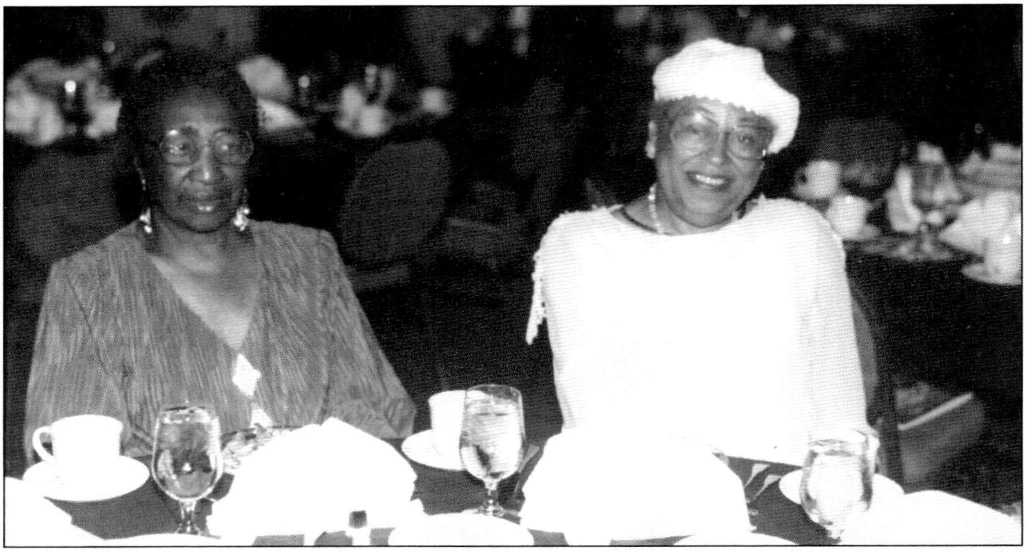

Mozelle Mattox. Mozelle Mattox, left, is pictured with Imogene Willis Holland at an NAACP banquet in Atlanta. Mattox, who attended Elberton Colored School, dropped out of school in her 10th grade year to marry. During that time, students graduated from school after completion of their 11th grade year. Of the lay people involved in the class action lawsuit, Mattox is the only one still living. Mattox says that concern for the rights of all people is what prompted her to be involved in the lawsuit in 1982. (Courtesy Jimmy O. White.)

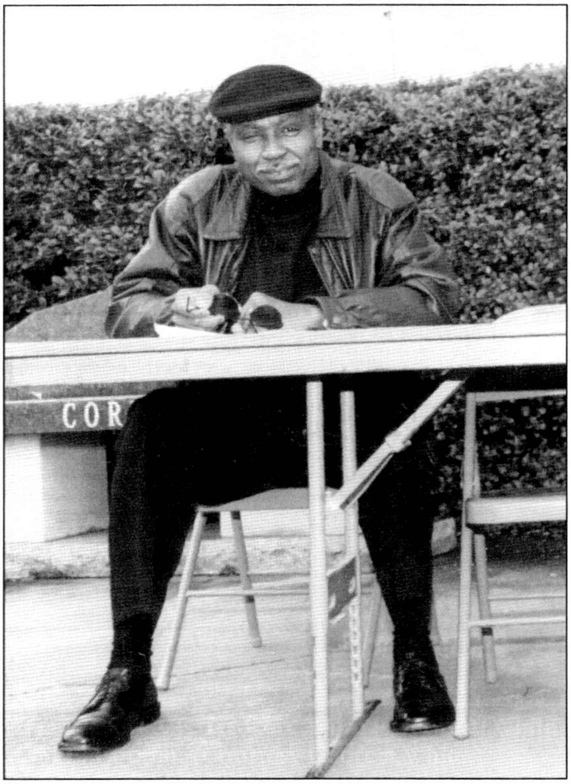

Attorney Kenneth Dious. Mozell Mattox says that she, Pressley, Holland, and McRae met in secret, strategizing on actions that they would take against the City of Elberton, so African Americans would have chance at being elected to public office. They approached Kenneth Dious of Athens, Georgia, with their plight. Dious took the case. After Attorney John Clark opened his practice in Elberton, he along with George McGriff of Atlanta, Georgia, joined Dious to work on the case.

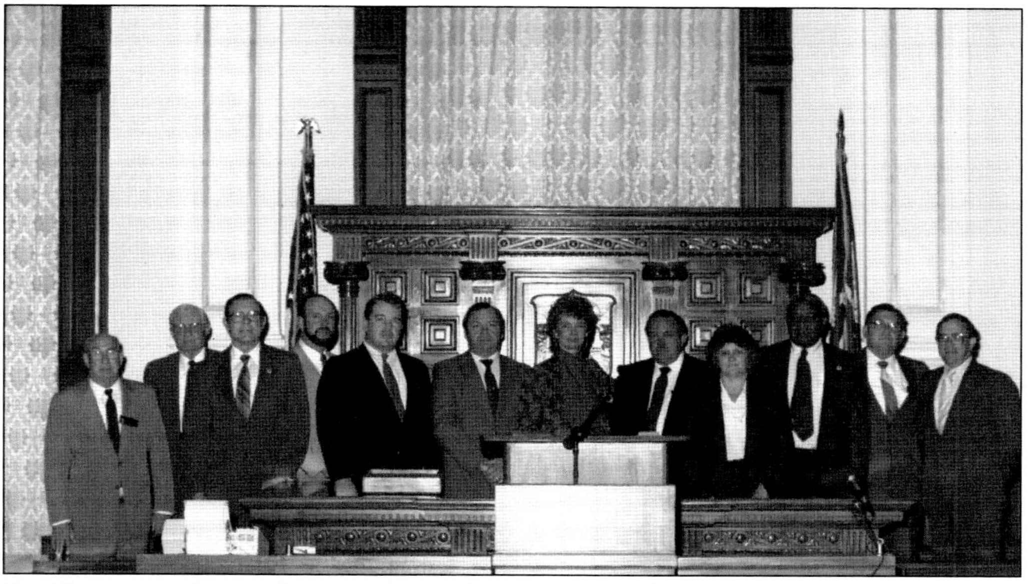

The Honorable Charles Augustus Hamm Sr. Hamm was the first African American elected to public office in Elbert County and was the first African American elected to public office from Ward 1. He served as a councilman from January 1, 1985, to January 3, 1994. Hamm poses for a picture with other public officials from Elbert County at the state capitol of Georgia. (Courtesy Marie and Charles Hamm Collection.)

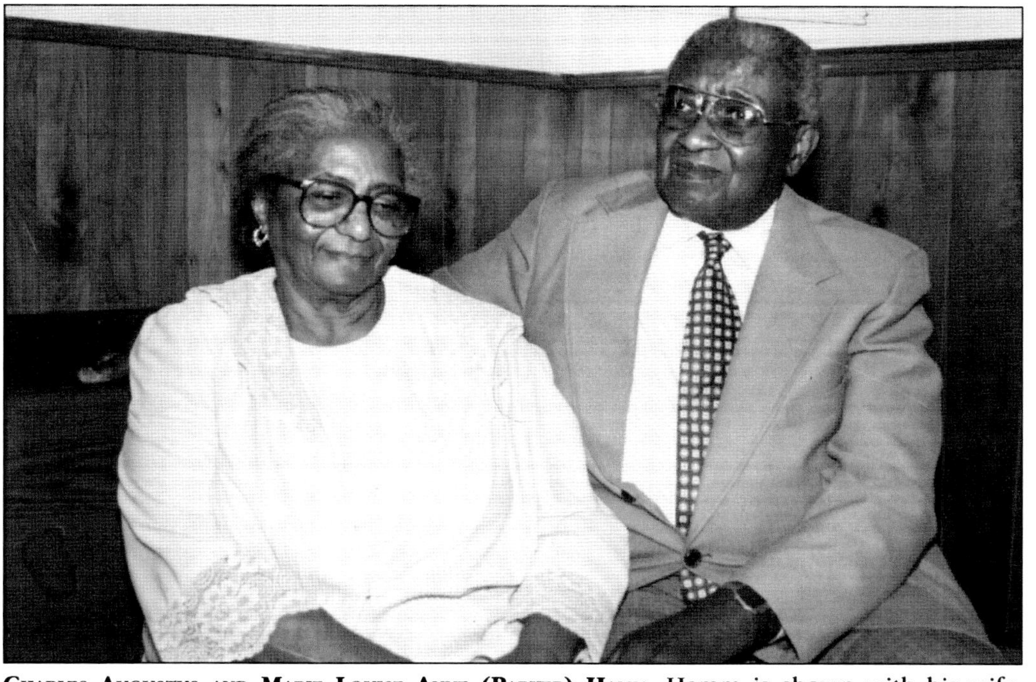

Charles Augustus and Marie Louise Anne (Parker) Hamm. Hamm is shown with his wife, Marie. They met at a USO dance in New Orleans in 1943. (Courtesy Marie and Charles Hamm Collection.)

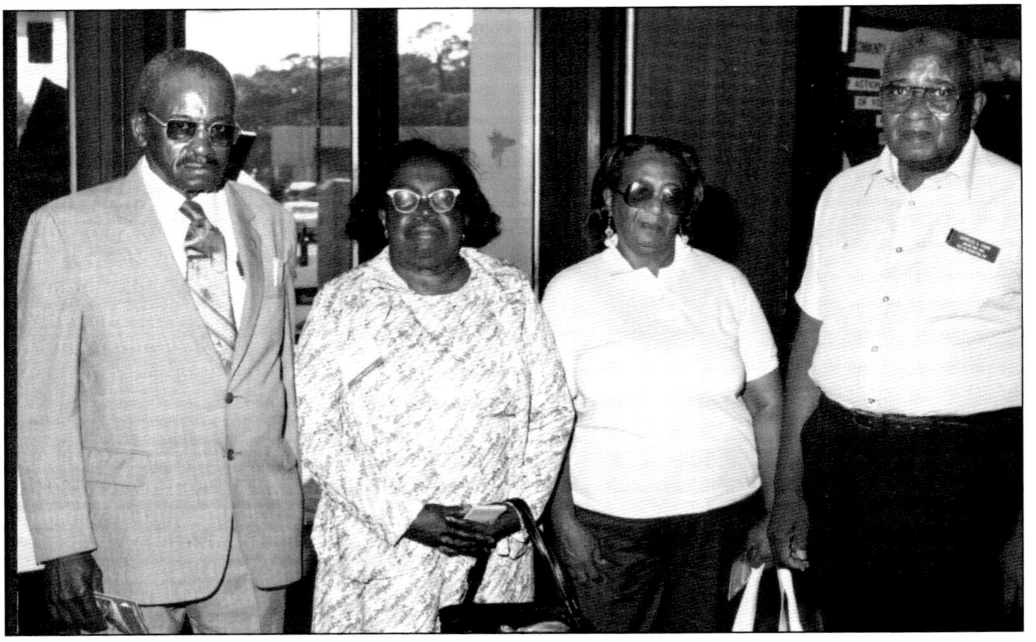

Hon. Walter Rucker. Rucker was the second African American elected to public office in Elbert County and the first African American elected as a city councilman from Ward 2. He served from January 1, 1986, to January 1, 1988. Pictured are Walter and Lillian Byrd Rucker and Marie and Charles A. Hamm Sr. (Courtesy Marie and Charles Hamm Collection.)

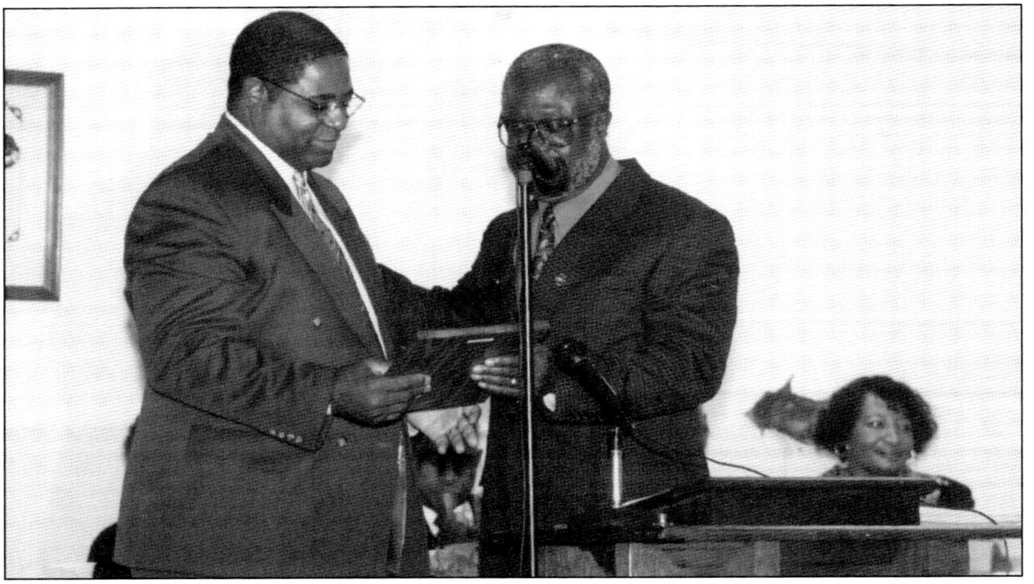

Civil Rights Issues. Attorney John Clark was involved in other important area lawsuits: initiating equity in the hiring practices at Elberton's fire department and changing Hart County's system of voting for county commissioners to a district system. The last case almost cost him his life. In 1989, the Hart County Klan offered a $5,000 reward to anyone who would kill him. Clark is pictured to the right of Clark Gaines. (Courtesy Jimmy O. White.)

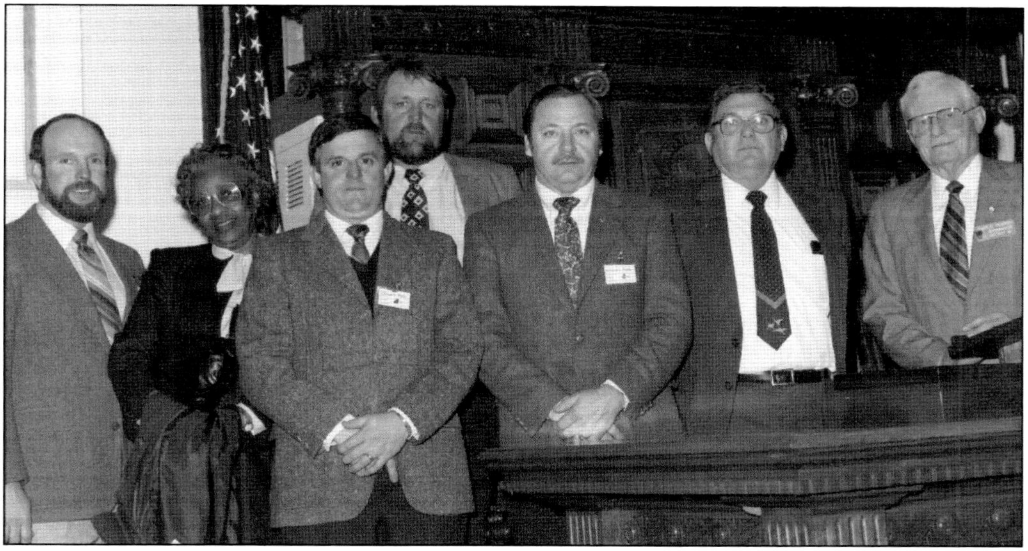

Hon. Georgia White. White is the first African-American woman elected to public office in Elbert County and the first African American elected as a county commissioner in Elbert County. She served as a commissioner from the fifth district from January 1, 1987 to January 1, 1992. She resigned after serving two years of her second term due to heath concerns. White's first term was for three years and her second term would have been for four years had she served it to its completion. (Courtesy Georgia White.)

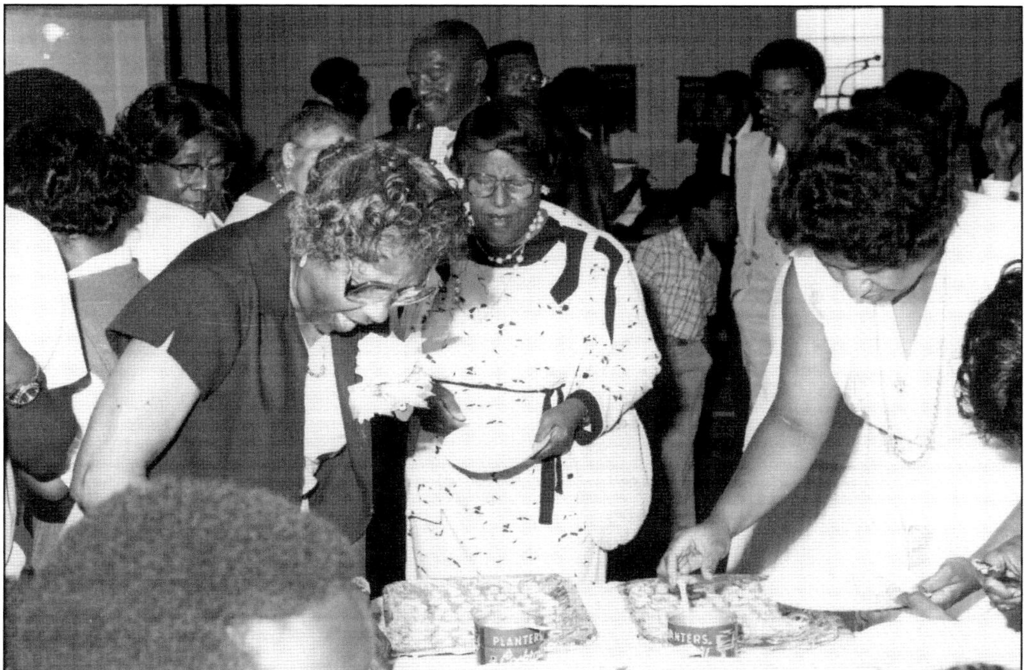

Happy Birthday, Georgia White! Georgia White celebrates her birthday at White Chapel C.M.E. Church. (Courtesy Georgia White.)

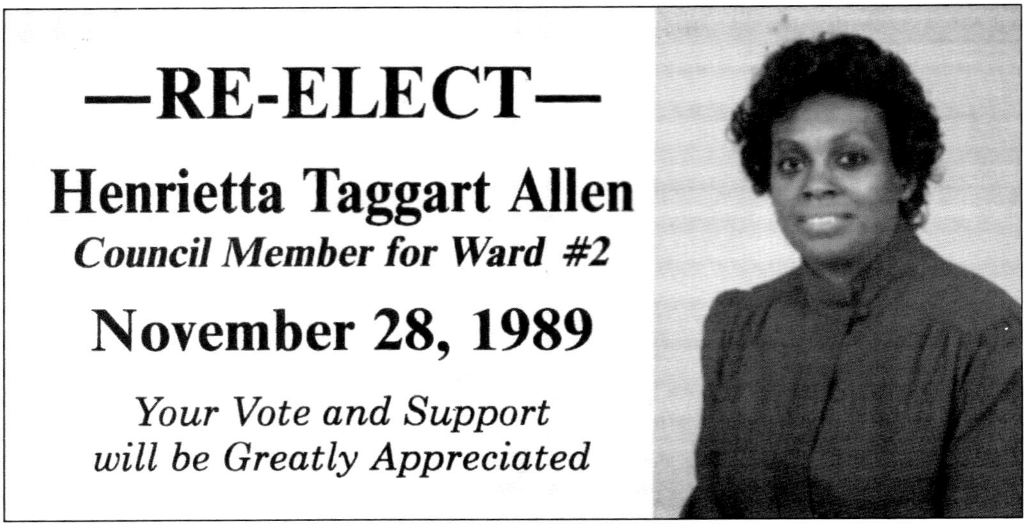

The Honorable Henrietta Taggart Allen (Williams). Allen has the distinction of being the second African-American woman elected to public office in Elbert County and is the first African-American woman elected to public office in the city of Elberton. Allen represented Ward 2 for eight years, from 1988 to 1996. Allen was educated in the Elbert County School System, graduating from Blackwell Memorial High School. (Courtesy Henrietta Taggart Williams.)

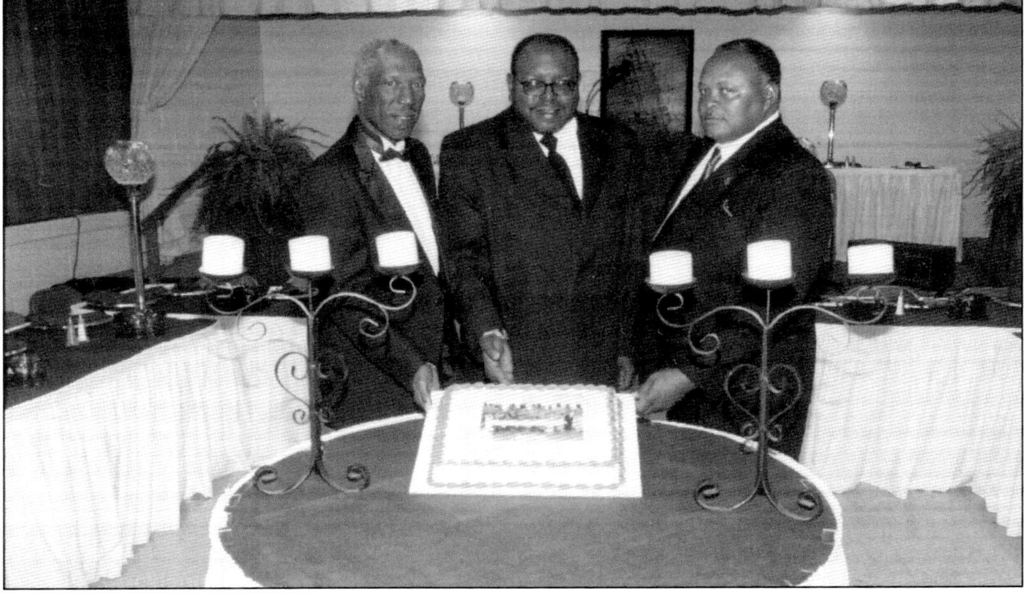

Wilbert Williams. Williams was the first African American elected to the city council in Bowman, Georgia. He is also the first African American to seek office on Bowman's city council. He qualified to run for office in 1985, 1986, and 1987, being elected in 1987 and serving from January 1, 1988, to January 1, 2004. Williams is a Vietnam veteran and retired from the national guard with 22 years of service. Williams is third from the left. (Courtesy Jimmy O. White.)

Sallie Walker Hood. Sallie Hood grew up in Athens, Georgia, and graduated from Athens Industrial High School. She earned a bachelor's degree and master's degree in education from the University of Georgia. She has taught in Elbert County for 34 years and served as the county commissioner of District 5 for 10 years, from 1992 to 2002. Hood completed the last two years of Georgia White's term and chaired the board of the county commissioners from 1999 to 2001. (Courtesy Sallie Walker Hood.)

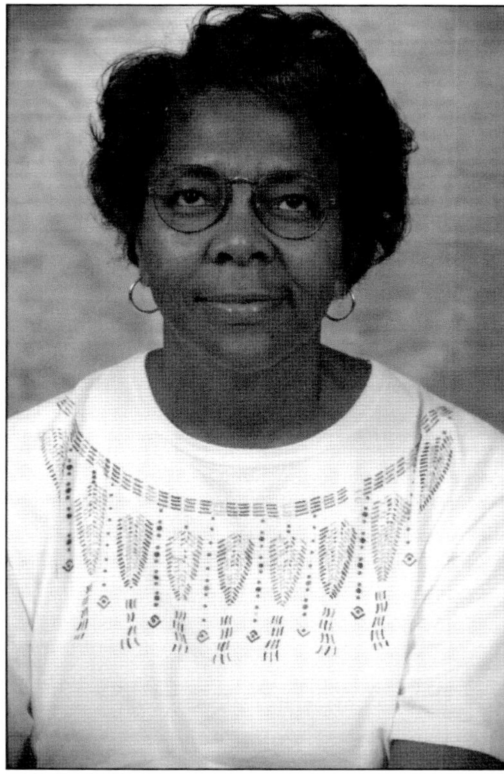

Bobby G. Hunt. After graduating from Blackwell Memorial High School, Hunt enlisted in the army and served for 20 years. Returning to Elbert County, he worked as a 911 dispatcher for Clark County. He was elected as a city councilman to Ward 2 in 1995 and is presently in his third term. He is a member of the NAACP, the Coalition of Concerned Citizens, and a board member of the Jim-Ree African-American Museum, Inc. (Courtesy Jimmy O. White.)

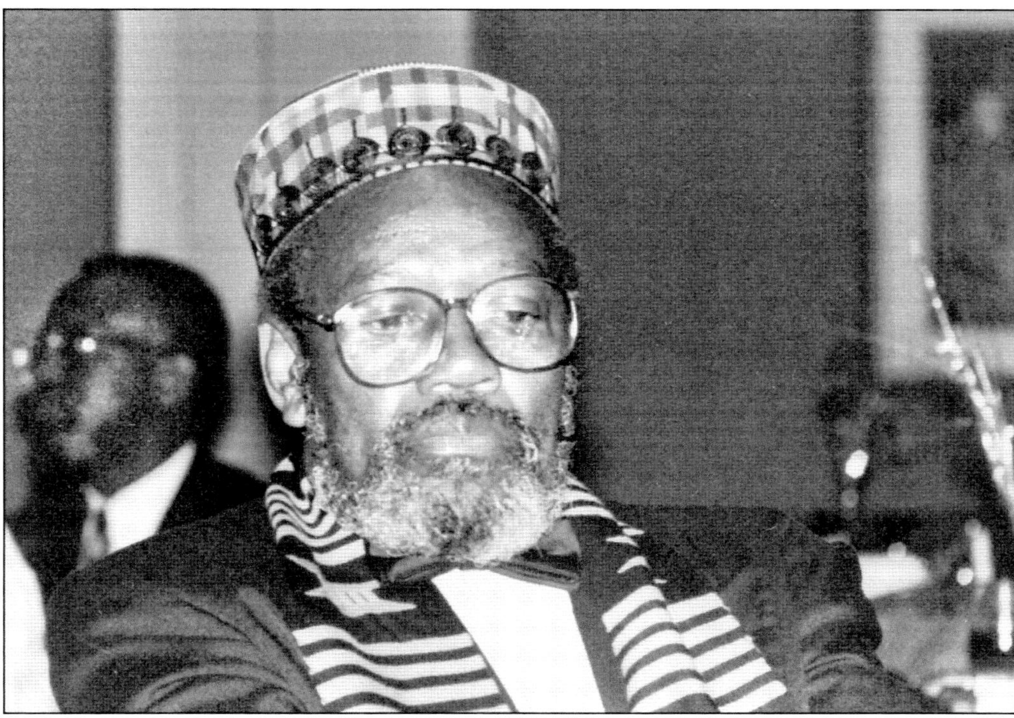

Spotlight. Mary Morrison Clark is the first African-American female elected to public office in Bowman, Georgia. Clark is the 9th of 11 children of J.T. and Azzie Lee Williams Morrison. She attended Bowman Elementary, Blackwell Memorial High School, Savannah State University (SSU), Brenau University, the University of Georgia, and Clemson University. She holds a master's degree in early childhood education and teaches at Bowman Elementary. She was teacher of the year from 1998 to 1999 and authored a *History of Bowman Elementary School* in 2002. Clark is pictured with Tom Joyner at a fund-raiser gala at Savannah State University. Clark is a volunteer in numerous service organizations, including Alpha Kappa Alpha Sorority, Inc., SSU National Alumni Association, and the NAACP. She is the founding chairperson of the Elbert County Martin Luther King Parade Planning Committee. (Courtesy Mary and John Clark.)

Six

People Make Communities

What can you do to promote world peace? Go home and love your family.
—Mother Teresa

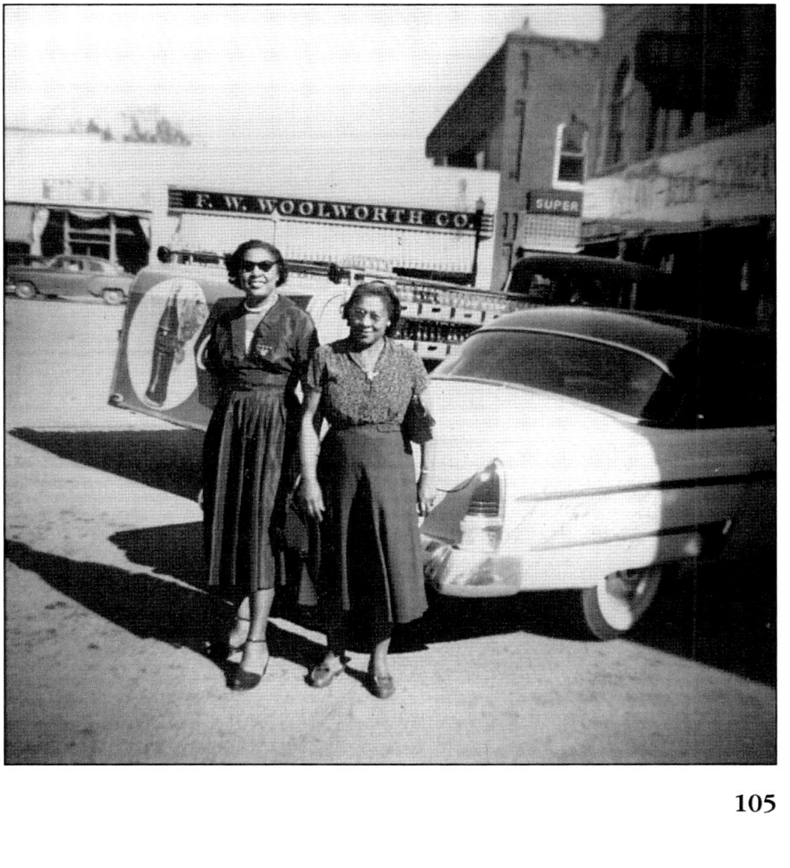

Downtown. Sisters Lois Strickland Fleming and Delree Strickland White take a moment to pose for a picture as they shop. (Courtesy Jimmy O. White.)

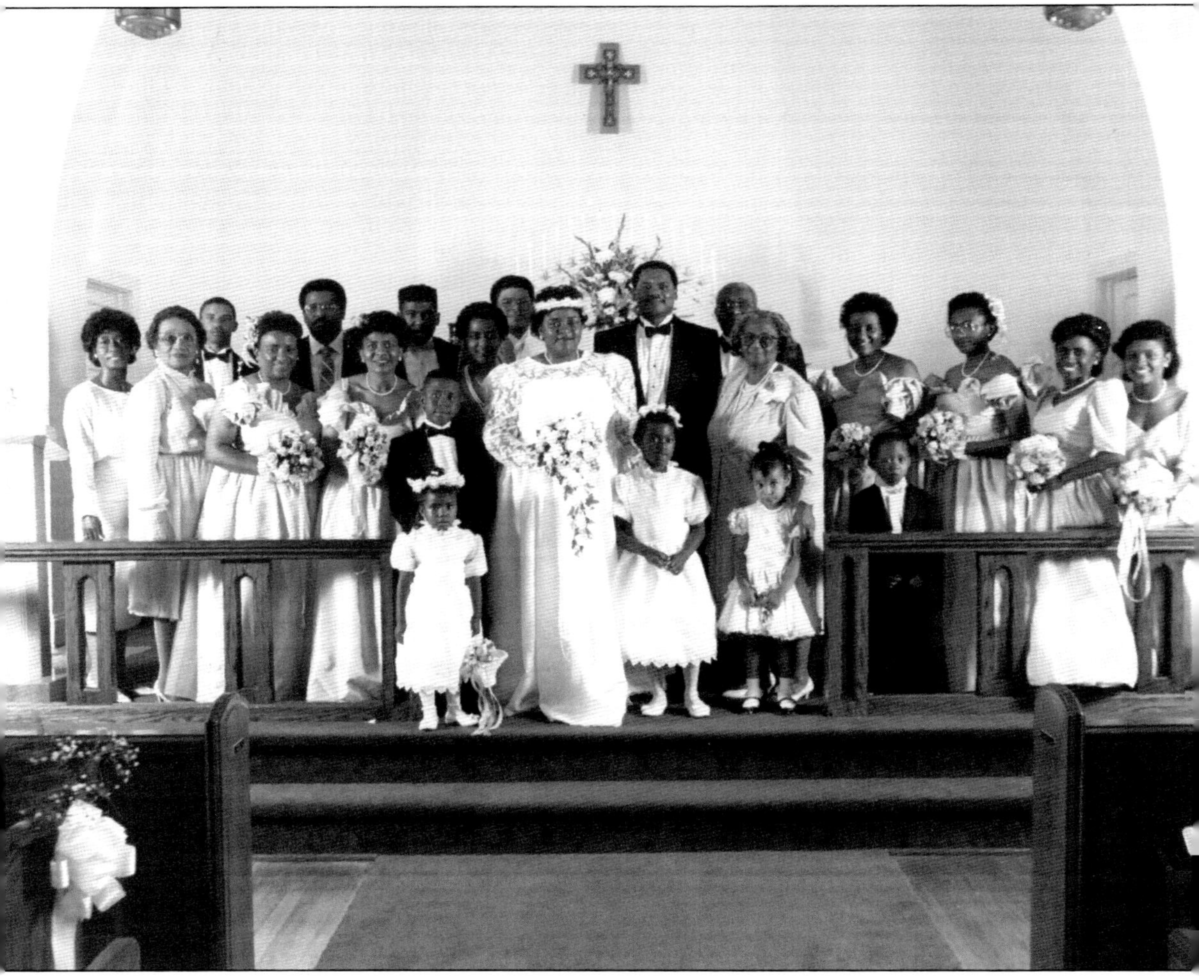

Family Portrait. Weddings provide opportunities for families to get together. Pictured at Saint Mary's Catholic Church are, from left to right, (first row) Aldra Patricia Mathis (Walker); (second row) Terry Joseph Hamm Jr., Dr. Sandra Hamm Gibbs (bride), April Michaela Hamm, and Portia Sabb; (third row) Gwendolyn Anderson Hamm, Genora Hamm Biggs, Janice Hamm Gallimore, Patricia Hamm Allen, Michelle Hamm, Henry Gibbs (groom), Marie Parker Hamm, and Alan McKenzie Hamm; (fourth row) James Elliott Gallimore Jr., Terry Joseph Hamm Sr., "Jelani" William Michael Hamm, Charles Augustus Hamm Jr., Dr. Charles Augustus Hamm Sr., Mr. Barbara Lois Hamm, Aurolyn Melba Hamm, Sonja Marie Hamm (Sardin), and "Chubby" Terrace Latrice Allen. (Courtesy Sandra Hamm Gibbs.)

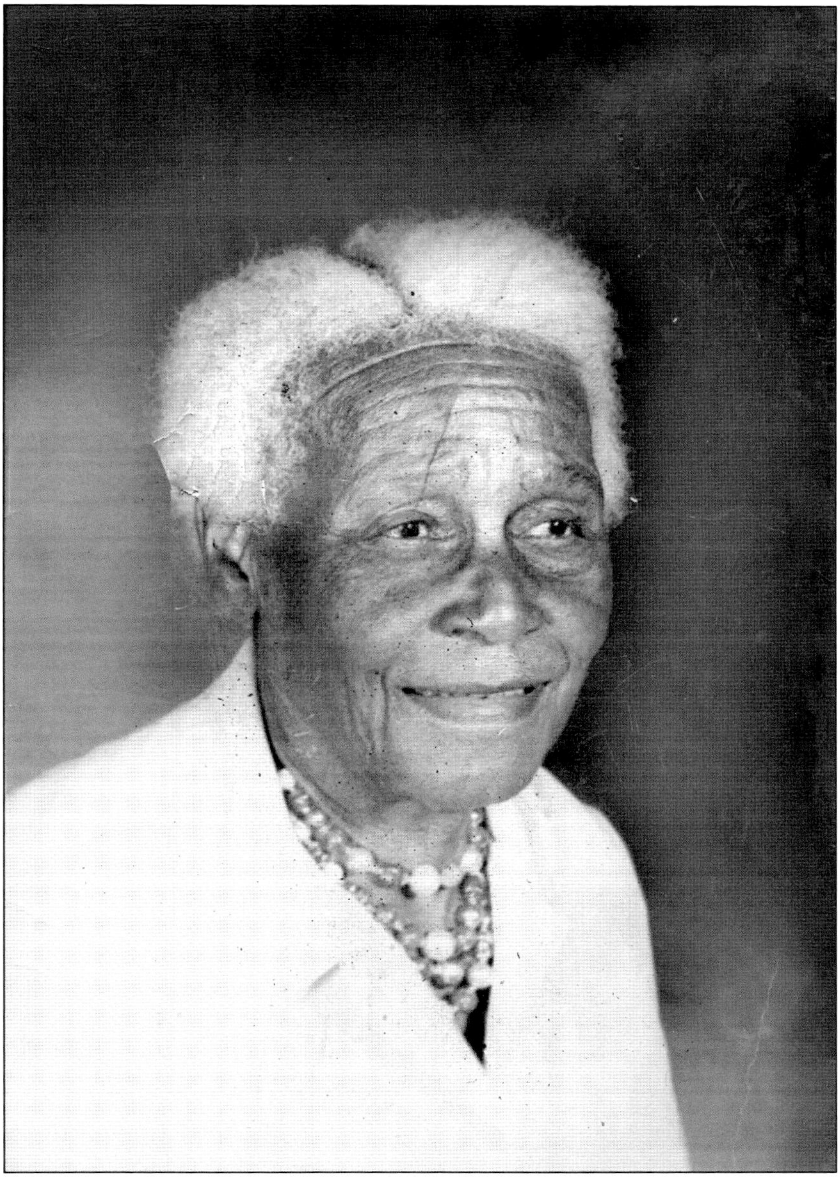

Oral History. Mary Wall Hamm spoke of a lynching. The subsequent rioting compelled her family to move to another part of Elbert County. "The white folks sho' didn't like coloreds," she said. "The Klan went from one colored house to the next, looking for that man. When they didn't find him in our house, they set the beds on fire. Pa begged them not to. 'There ain't nowhere for him to hide in here!' Them folks didn't care. They put a torch to the beds anyway. They was nothing but straw covered with a blanket. We couldn't put the fire out and escaped through a window. What the Klan did to that colored man, when they found him, weren't right." Then she said, "I heard that story so much, I started telling it like I was the one who tried to put the fire out. One day I asked my ma, 'What happened to that baby in your arms?' Ma laughed. 'Nothing. She sitting right here looking at me.'" (Courtesy Marie and Charles Hamm Collection.)

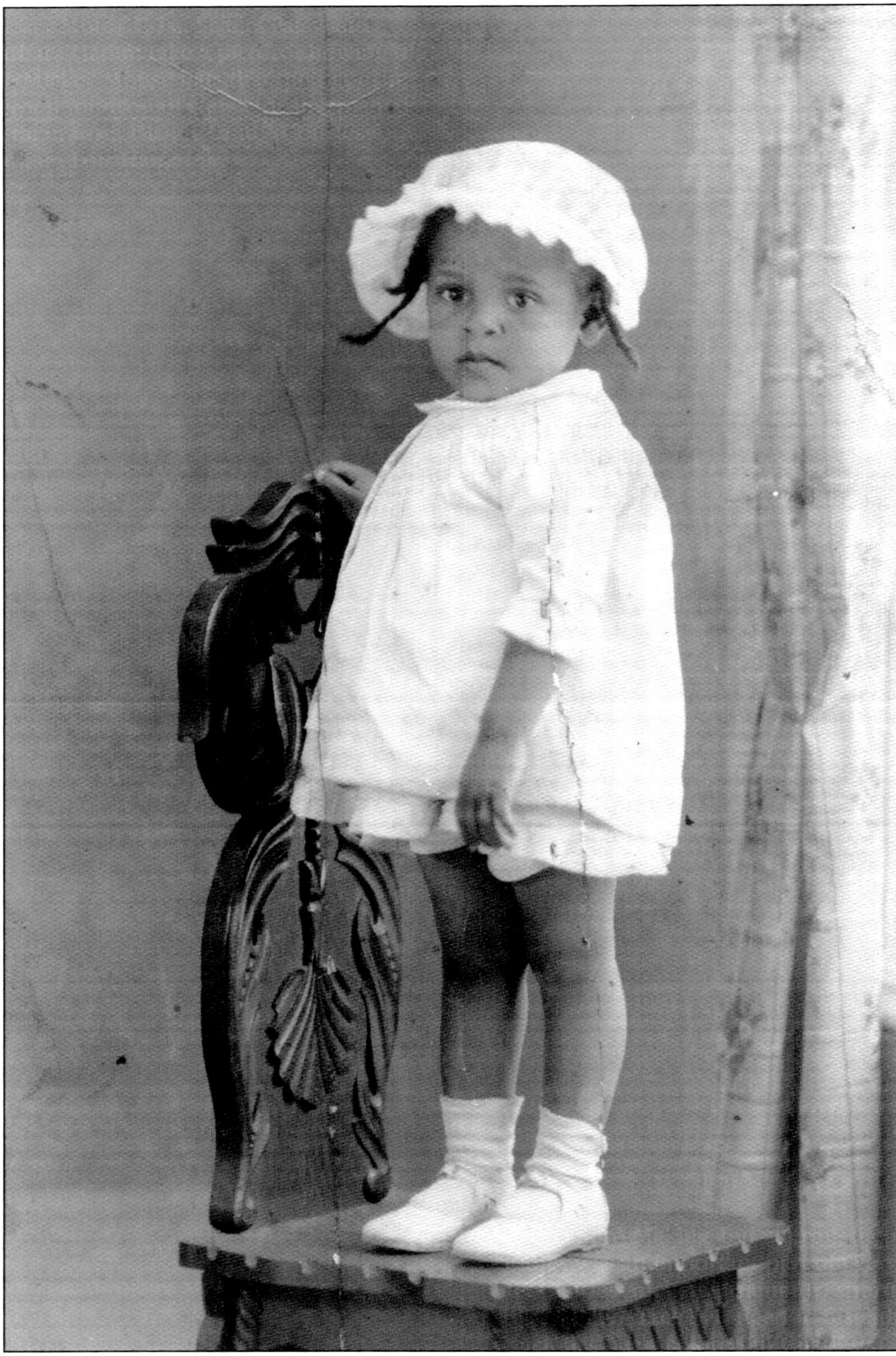

A Captured Moment. Two-year-old Azalee Biggs takes a break from playing to pose for a picture. (Courtesy Genora Hamm Biggs.)

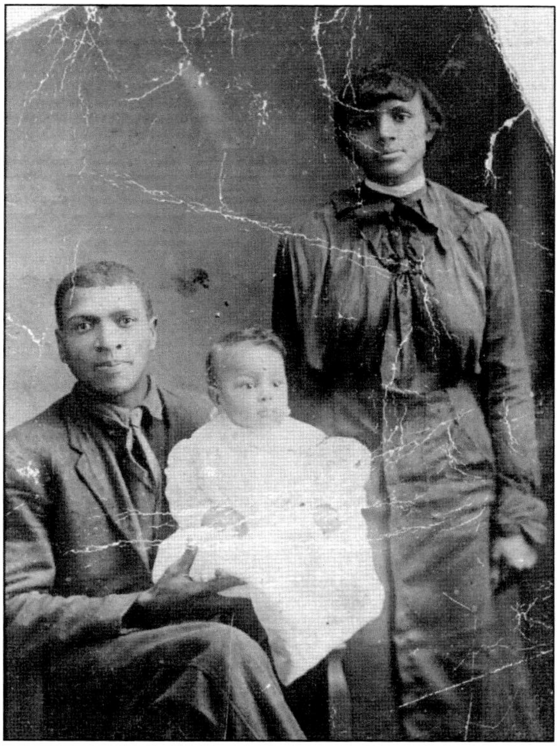

A Farming Family. Dock and Rosa Fortson owned 400 acres of land in the Sweet City community. They purchased the land at $10 an acre. Dock Fortson Sr. also owned and operated a saw mill. They are pictured with their first-born child, Dock Fortson Jr. (Courtesy Mike Fortson.)

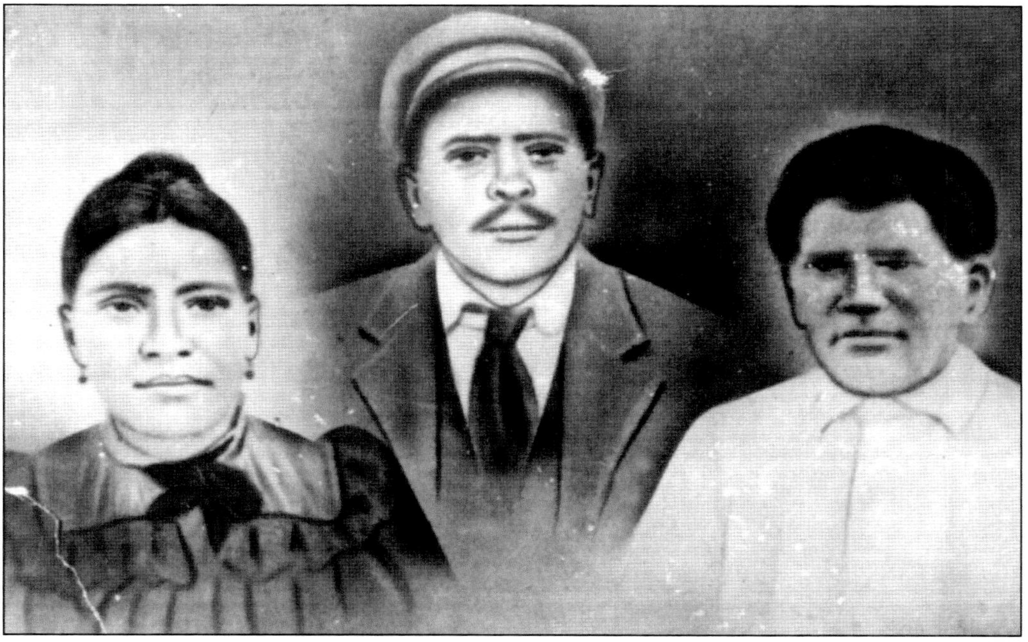

Former Slave. Dock Fortson Sr.'s grandmother was born a slave in Oglethorpe, Georgia. As a slave, her job was to run a store. After slavery, she settled in the Wyche district of Elbert County. Pictured from left to right are Sally Fortson, Clyde Maddox, and "Vic" Maddox.

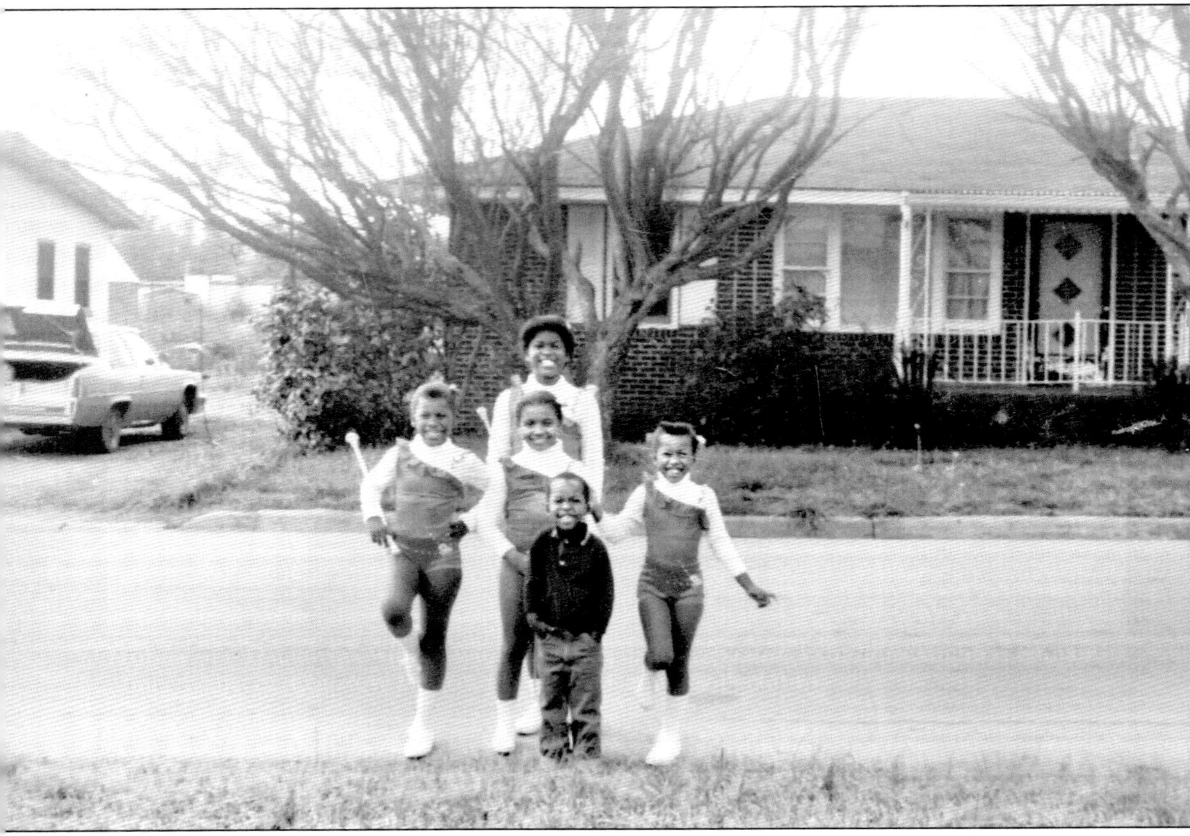

Christmas Parade Participants. Ready to march in the parade, the children take a moment to pose for the camera. Pictured are, from left to right, (front row) Joseph McIntosh Martin; (middle row) Jelyne Valencia Martin, Terrace Latrice Allen, and Ruthea Genae Martin; (back row) Joniata Arlice Martin. (Courtesy Marie and Charles Hamm Collection.)

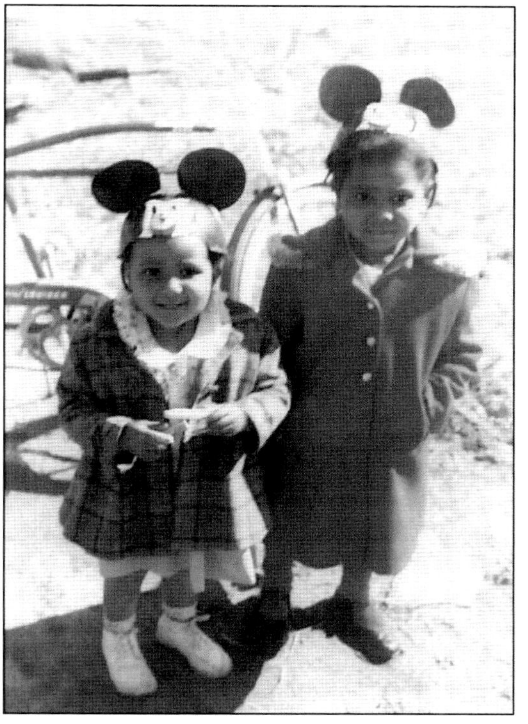

Mickey Mouse Club. Sisters Patsy and Barbara Hamm take a picture showing off the Mickey Mouse hats that their cousin, Bernell Johnson of New Orleans, mailed to them from Disney Land. (Courtesy Barbara Lois Hamm.)

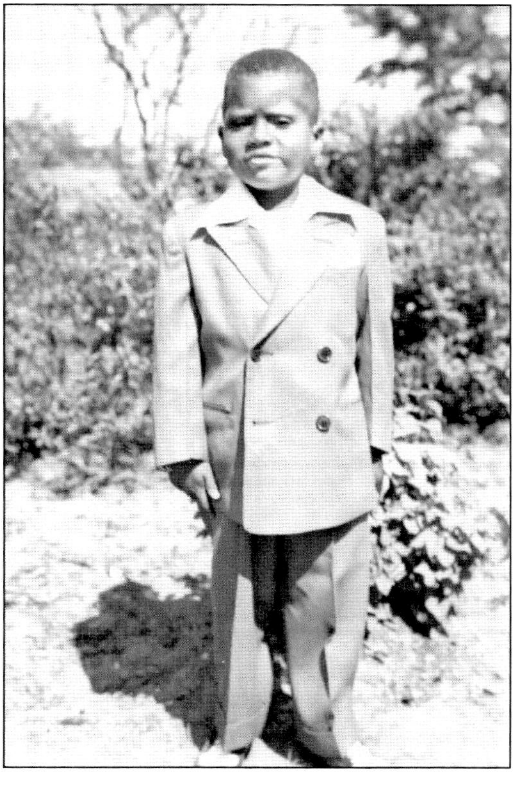

Resized Suit. Making and altering their clothes was an important part of everyday life. Charles Augustus Hamm Jr. sports a suit that had once belonged to his father, which has been tailored to Charles's height. (Courtesy Marie and Charles Hamm Collection.)

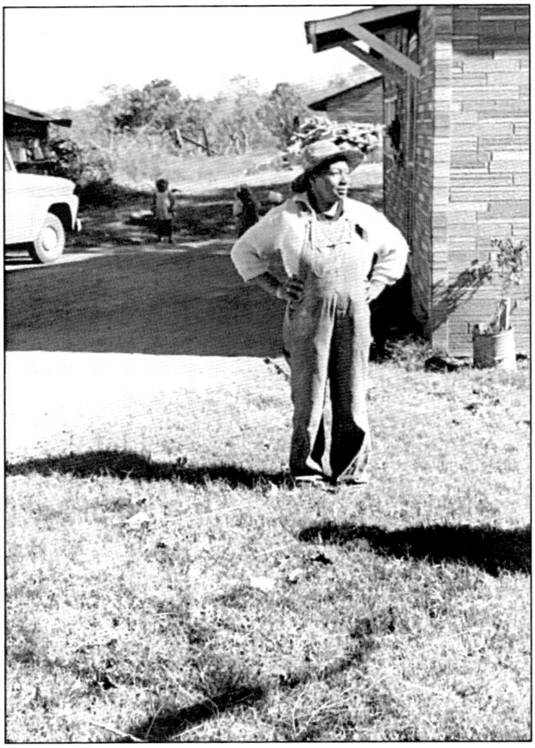

Bessie Mattox. Mattox's dream came true when all 12 of her children had graduated from college. Mattox and her late husband farmed on their land in Bowman. (Courtesy Jimmy O. White.)

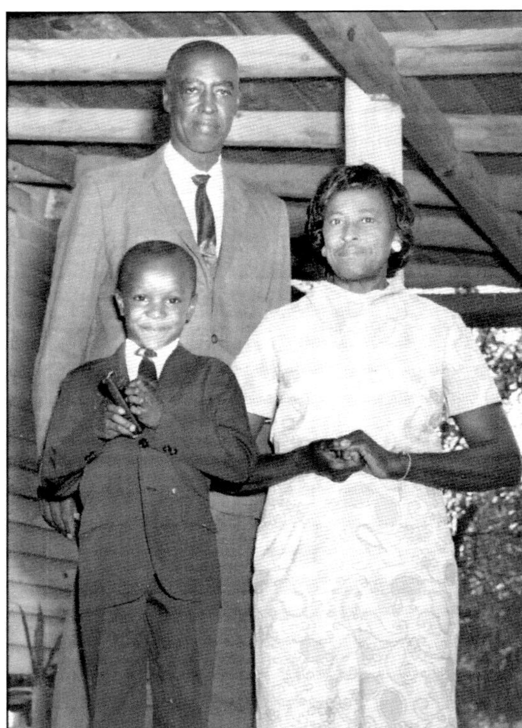

Foster Parents. Lula and Johnny Rucker decided to become foster parents to help children in need of a temporary home. (Courtesy Jim-Ree African American, Inc. Archives.)

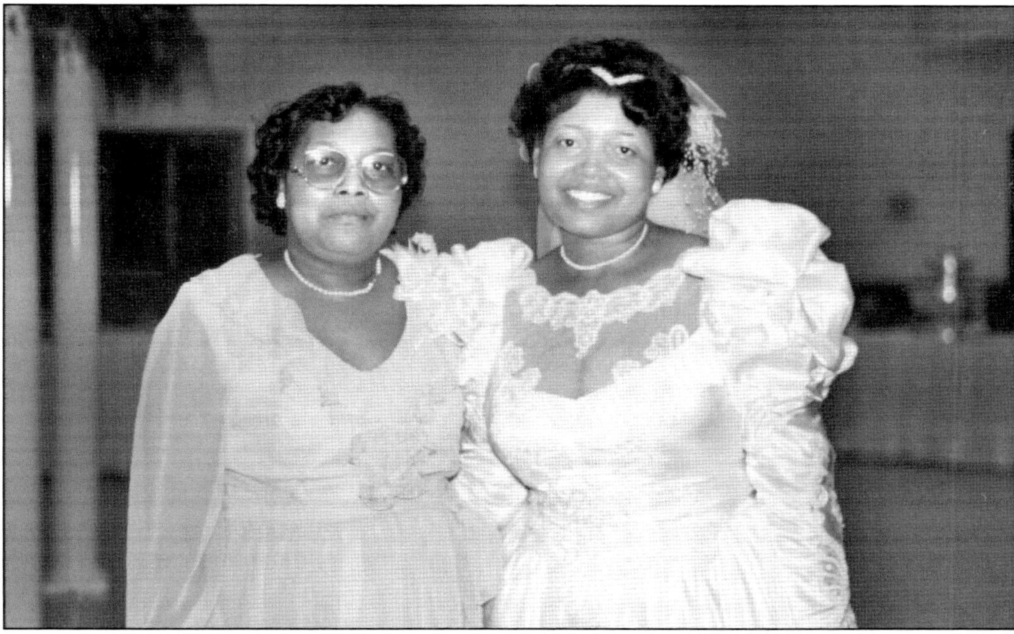

Mother and Daughter. Minnie Winston Abner takes a picture with her daughter, Samantha Abner Wallace. (Courtesy Marie and Charles Hamm Collection.)

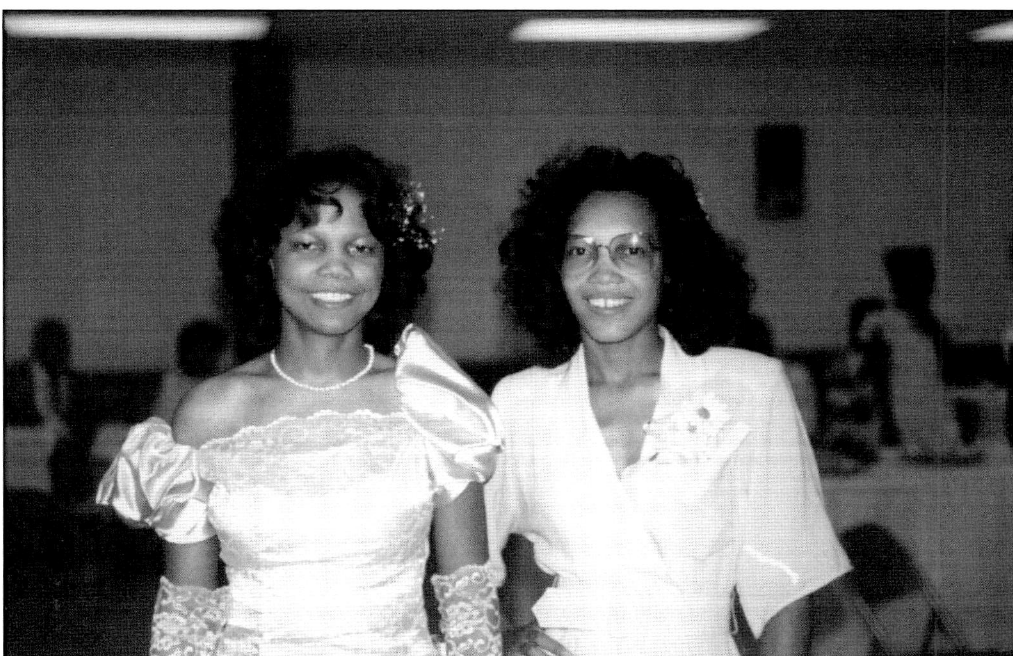

Say Cheese. Sisters Sojanna P. Abner and Suwena Abner Richardson smile for the cameraman. (Courtesy Marie and Charles Hamm Collection.)

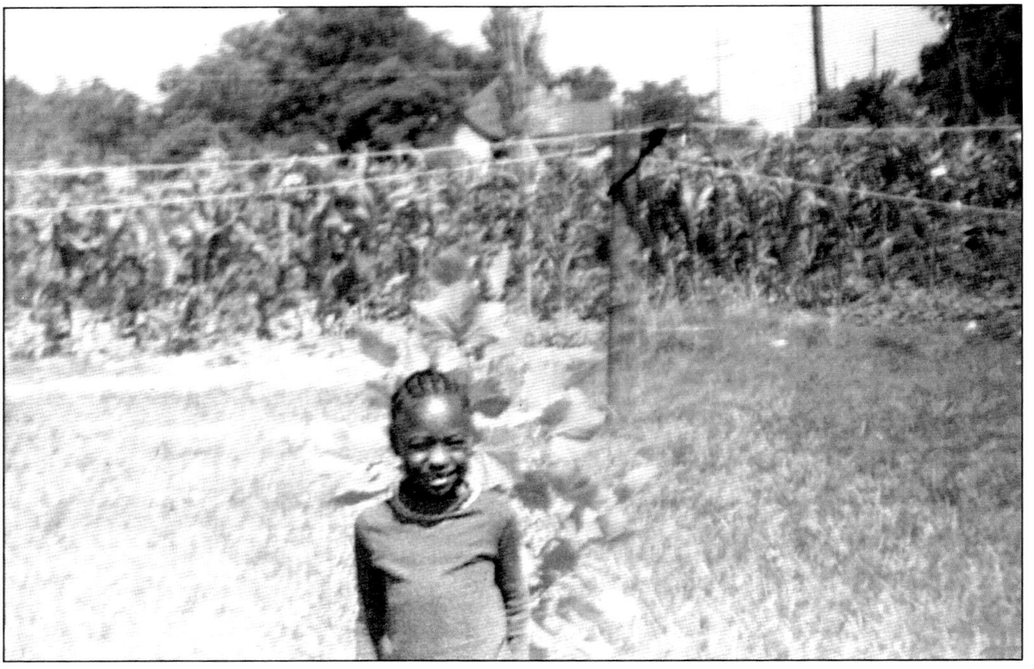

VEGETABLE GARDENS. Even though farming was not a lucrative business for many African Americans, they continued to keep vegetable gardens for their own personal use. A young girl poses by a cornfield. (Courtesy Marie and Charles Hamm Collection.)

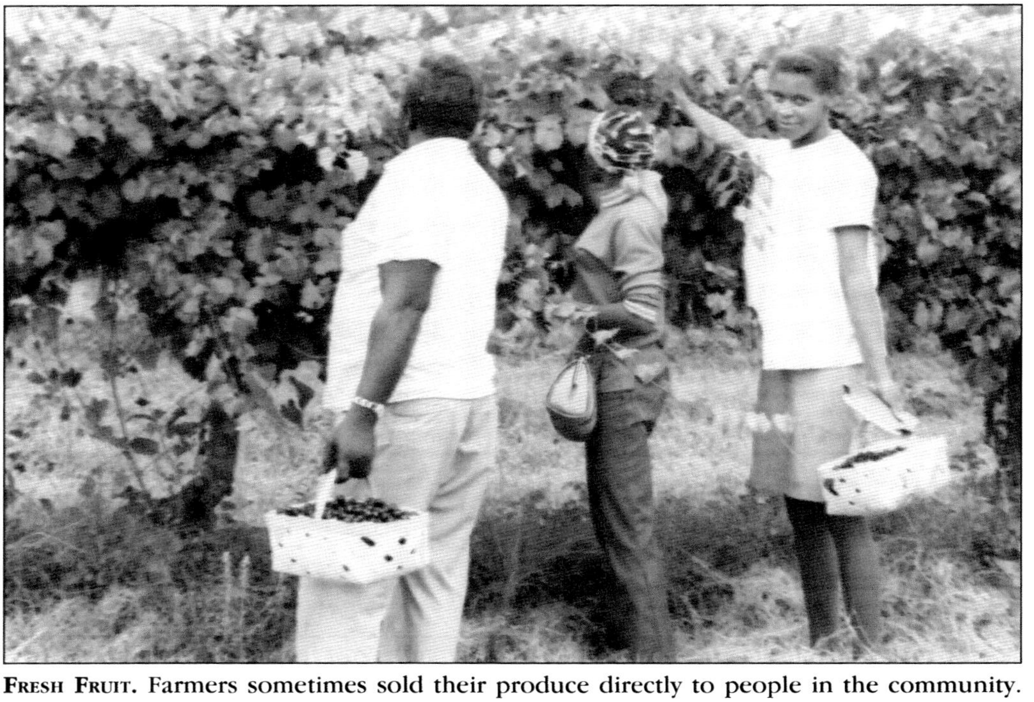

FRESH FRUIT. Farmers sometimes sold their produce directly to people in the community. (Courtesy Jim-Ree African-American Museum.)

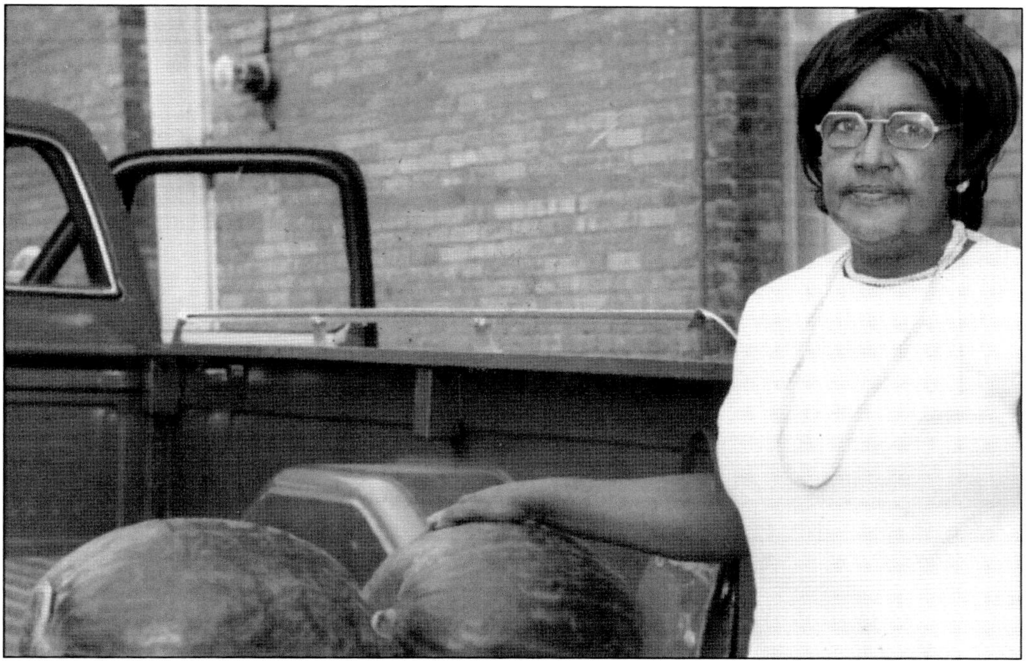

Lena Biggs. Biggs loved gardening. Often too impatient to wait to have her garden plowed, she would use her hoe to turn the earth. (Courtesy Jim-Ree African-American Museum, Inc. Archives.)

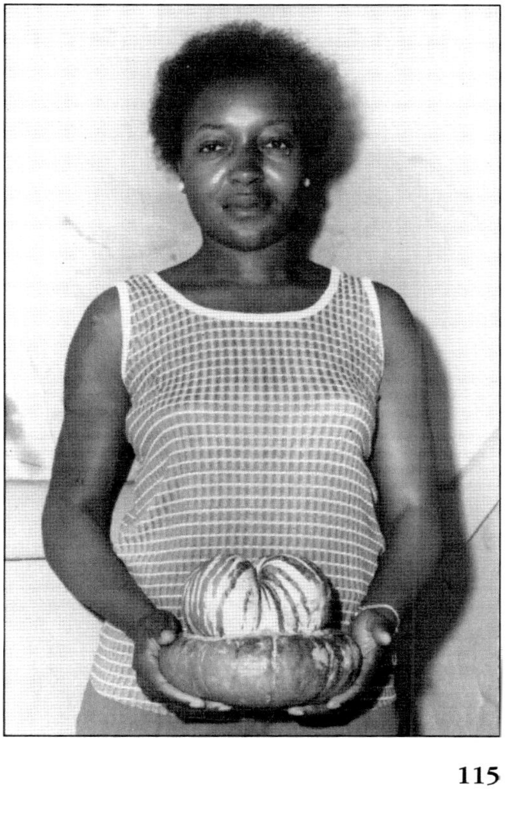

Emma Heard. Heard shows off a squash that her sister grew in the garden. (Courtesy Jim-Ree African-American Museum, Inc. Archives.)

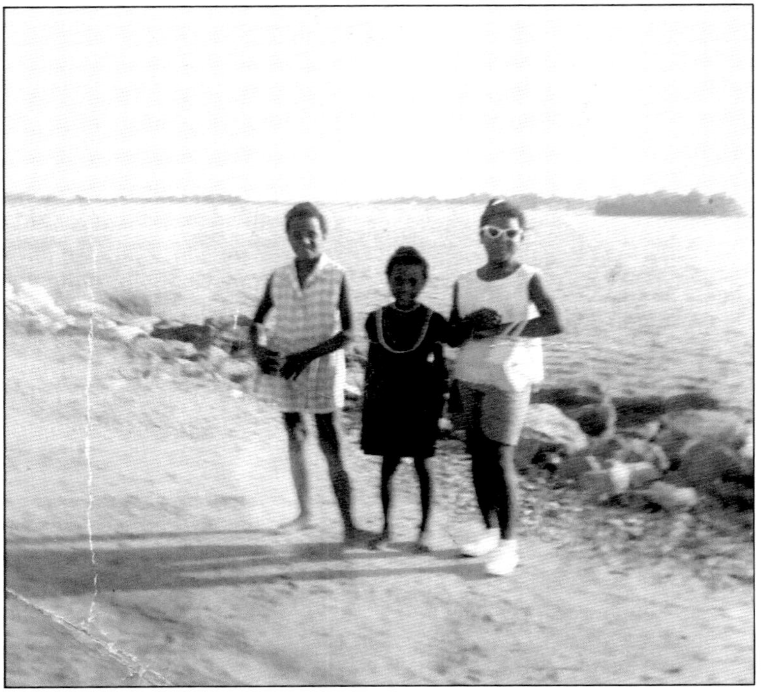

Lake Hartwell. The construction of Hartwell Dam provided temporary jobs for some Elbertonians, while the resulting lake offered enjoyment for families. Pictured from left to right are Barbara, Aurolyn, and Patsy Hamm. (Courtesy Barbara Lois Hamm.)

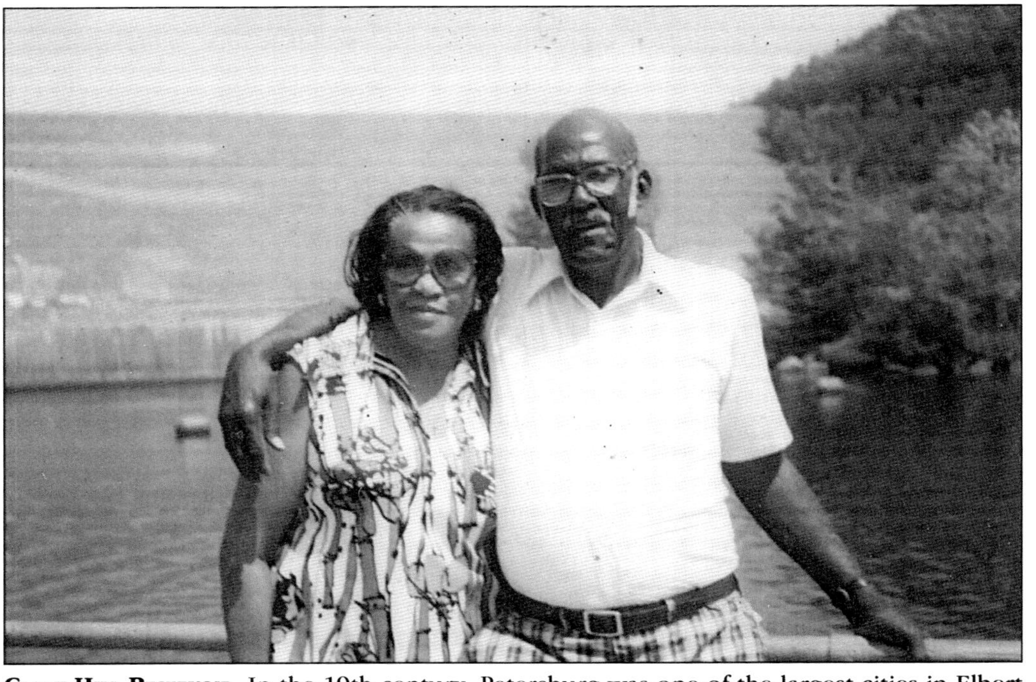

Clark Hill Reservoir. In the 19th century, Petersburg was one of the largest cities in Elbert County and in Georgia. Its location on the Savannah River made it a major transportation site. The railway, however, changed all of that. The city now lies under the lake. "Billie" William and Nell Barnes Rucker are pictured. (Courtesy Nell Barnes Rucker.)

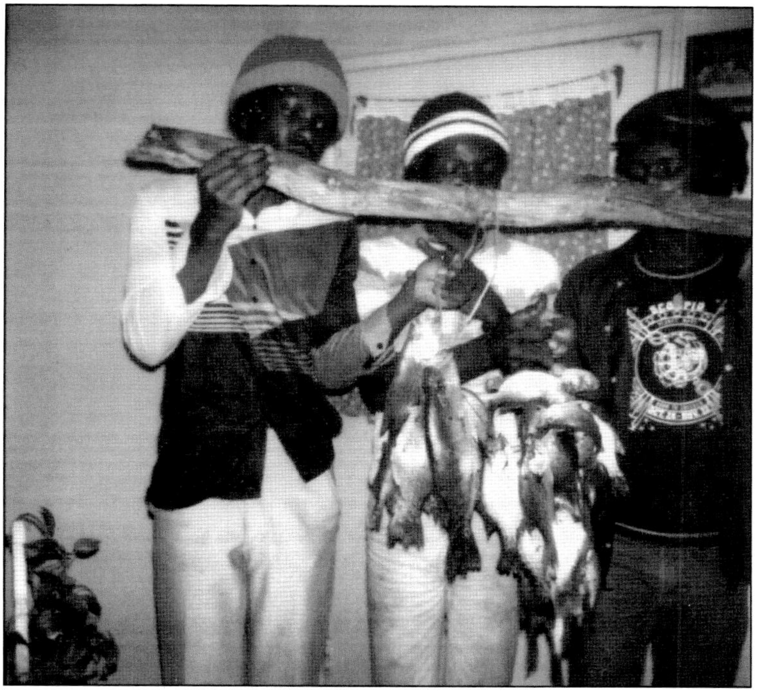

Catch of the Day. Living near the Broad and Savannah Rivers had at least one advantage. (Courtesy Emma Bradford Heard.)

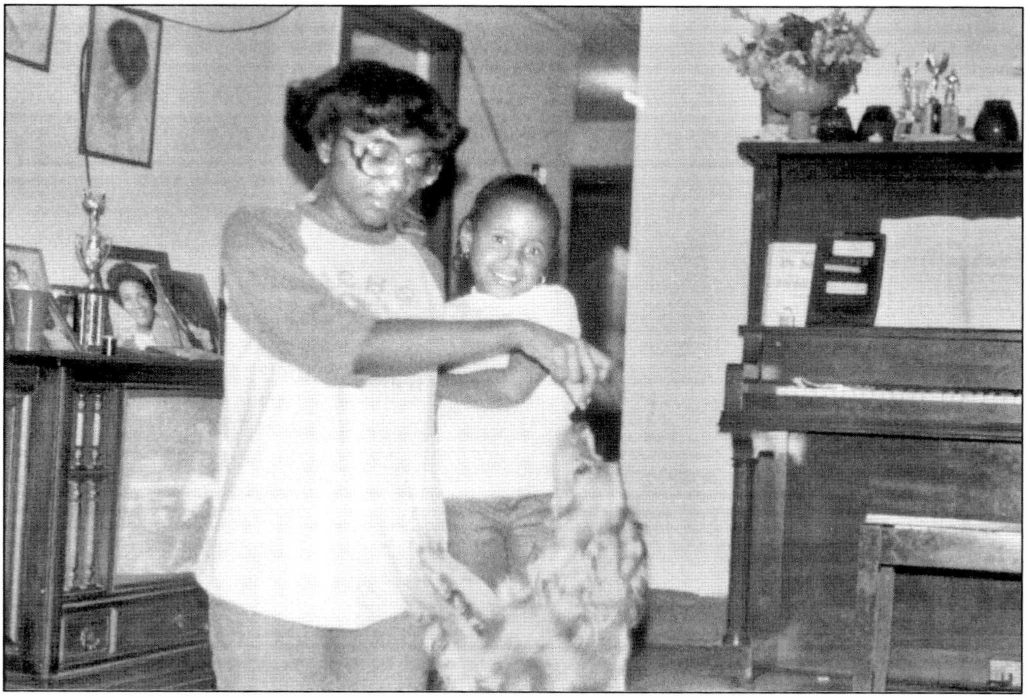

Taking a Break. Terrace Latrice Allen takes a break from practicing the piano to play with her aunt Aurolyn Melba Hamm and Knoxie the pooch. (Courtesy Marie and Charles Hamm Collection.)

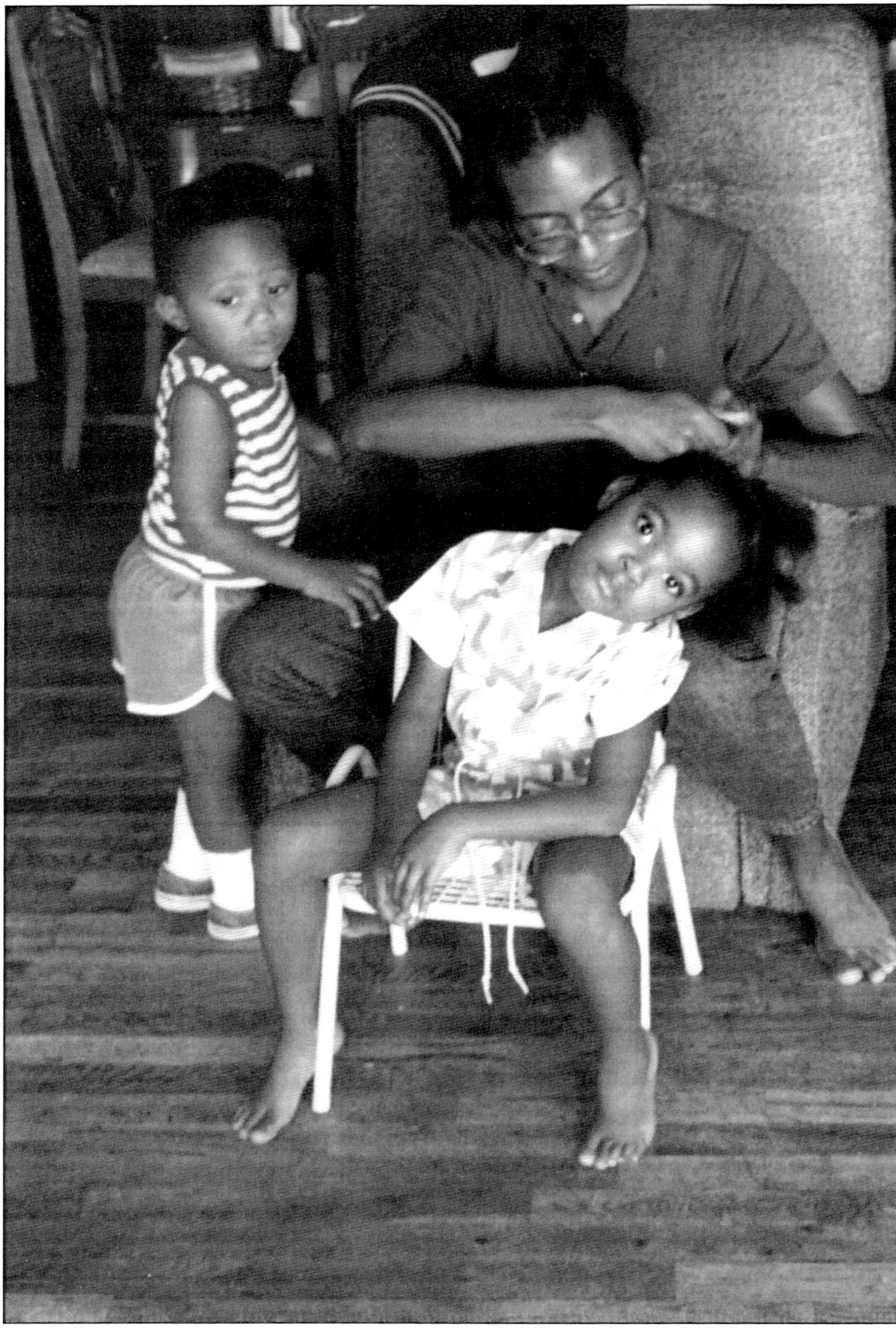

A Candid Moment. Little girls learn to sit quietly when getting their hair combed. Alan waits impatiently for his mom, Aurolyn Melba Hamm, to finish his sister April's hair. (Courtesy Marie and Charles Hamm Collection.)

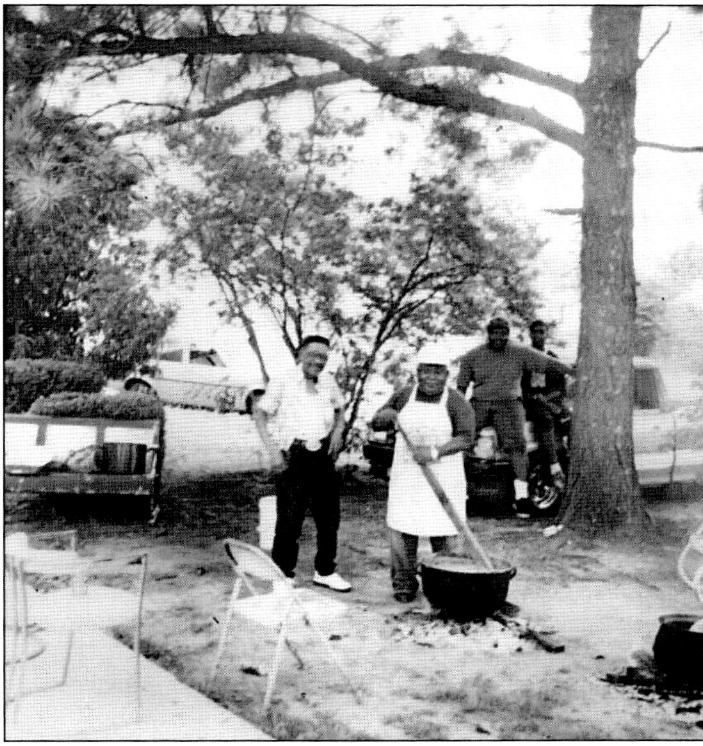

SECRET INGREDIENT. Joe Allen Harper says that the secret to making good Brunswick stew is using a good cast-iron pot on an open flame. Cooking it slow allows the smoke from the fire to permeate the ingredients, giving the stew extra flavor. Pictured are Joe Allen Harper and Lance H. Heard. (Courtesy Emma Bradford Heard.)

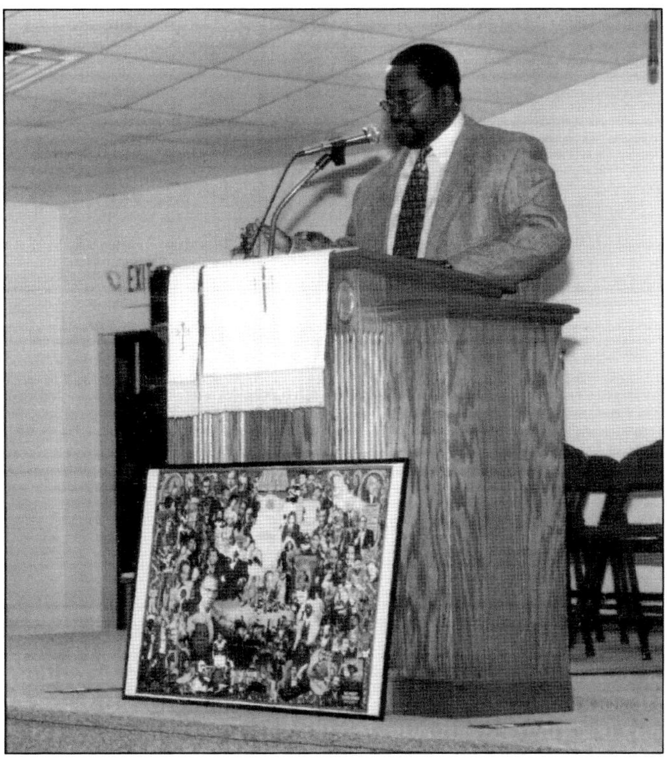

REV. QUINCY FORTSON. Fortson was educated in the Elbert County School System. He is pictured speaking at Mount Calvary Baptist Church to commemorate the Emancipation Proclamation.

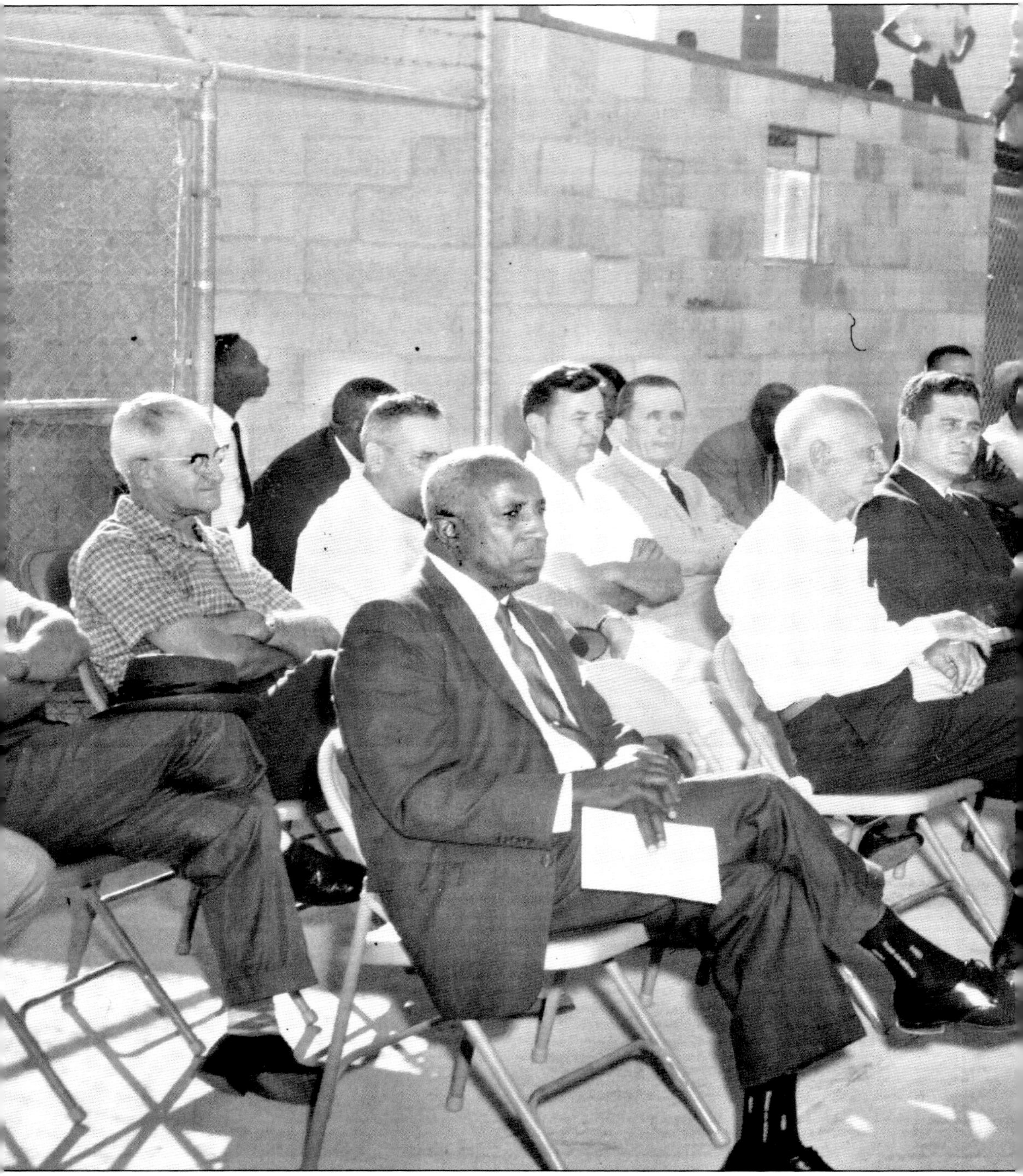

Burke Street Recreational Center. The Burke Street Recreational Center had its grand opening in the summer of 1962. The planning committee and people from the community attended the opening ceremony in the swimming pool area. Due to financial constraints in the 1990s, the pool was filled in and the recreational center was leveled. Considerations

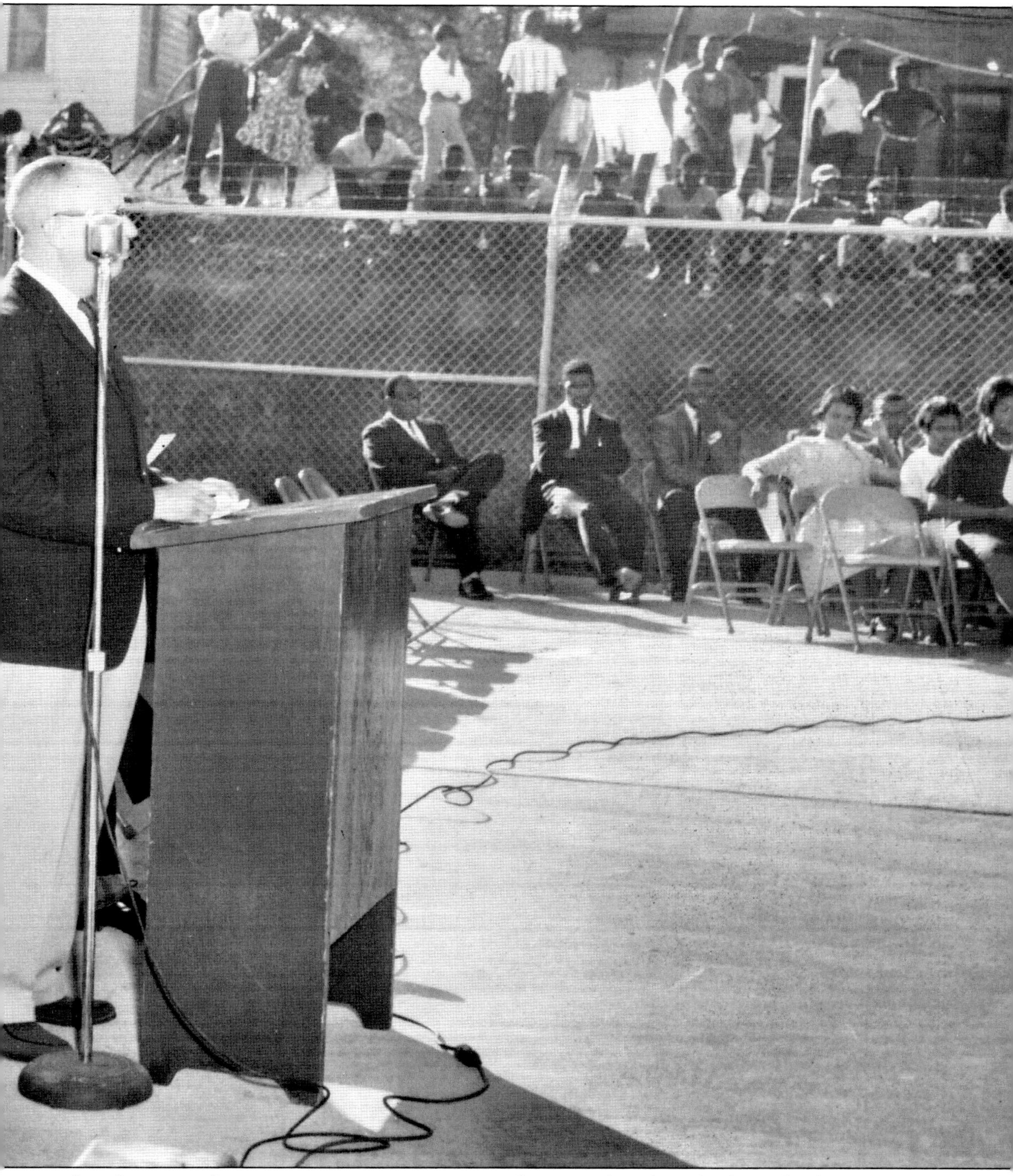

for changing this area into a community park were abandoned after Charles Augustus Hamm Sr. lost his seat on the city council. (Courtesy Jim-Ree African-American Museum, Inc. Archives.)

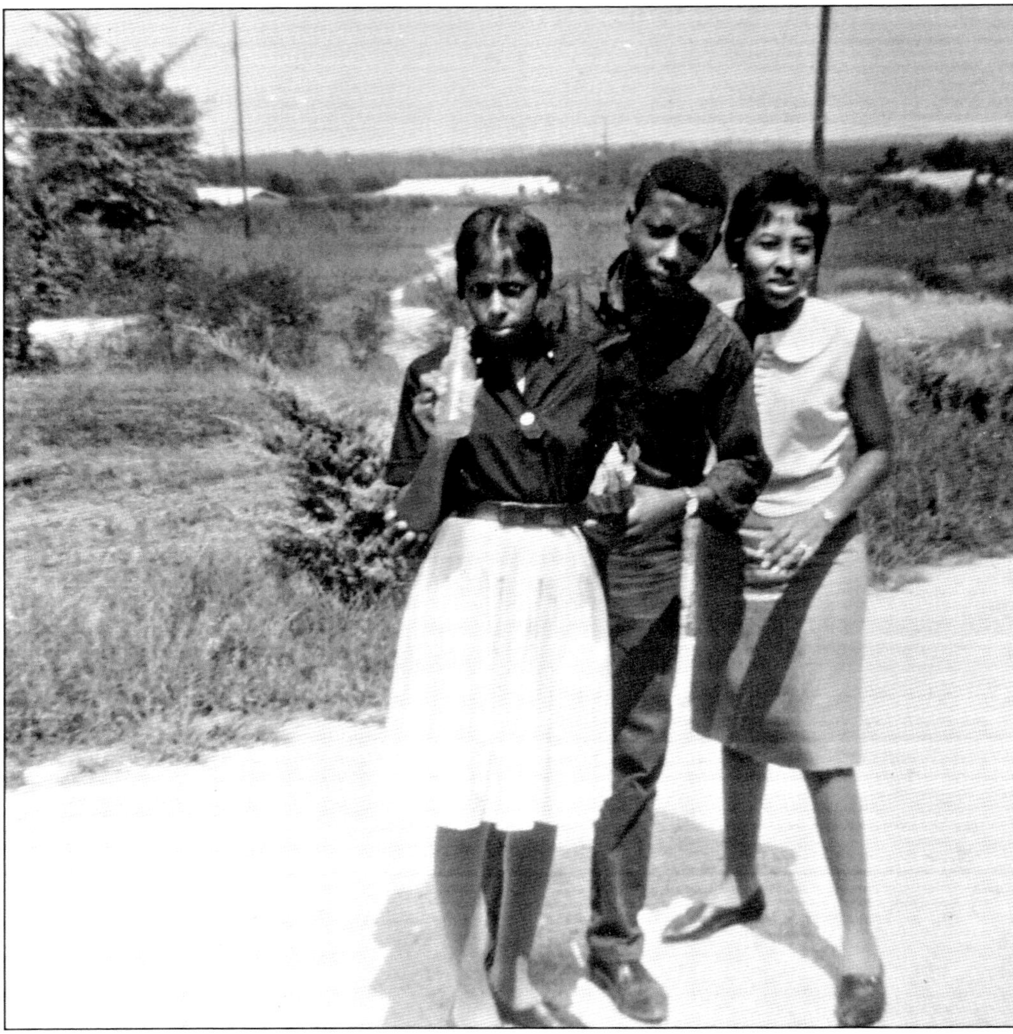

TERESEA DAVIS (BARNETT). Davis, right, was a member of the Future Teachers Association while she attended Blackwell Memorial High School. She graduated from Blackwell in 1961, and eventually became a teacher, a principal and director of the Special Education Program in the Elbert County School System.

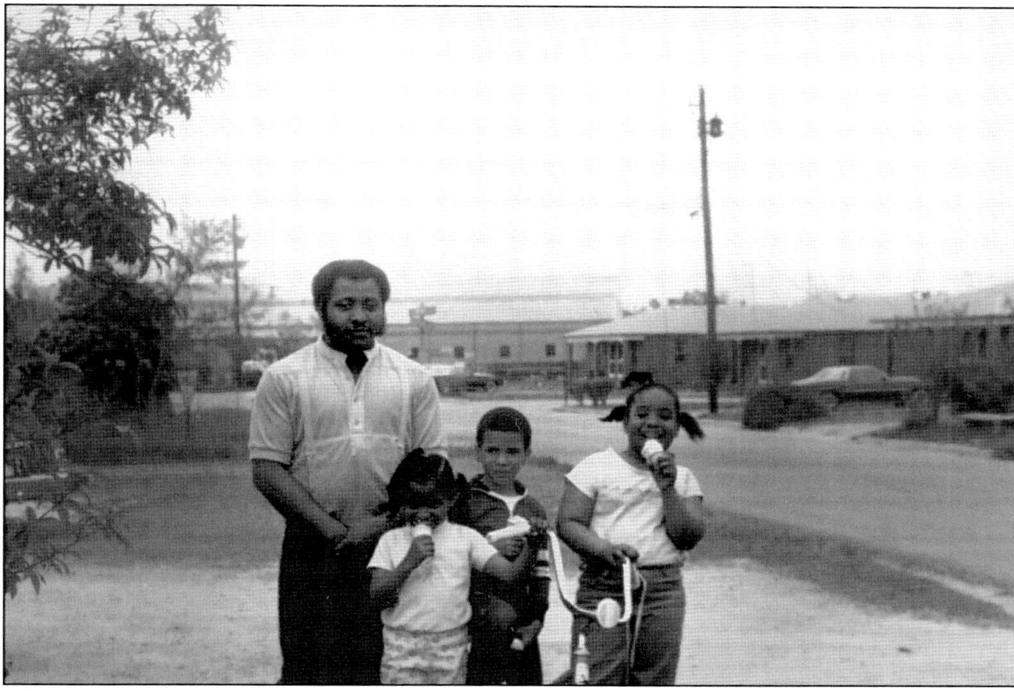

Summer Time. Taking a break from playing and eating their ice cream, these cousins pose for a picture with William Carter "WC" Allen. (Courtesy Marie and Charles Hamm Collection.)

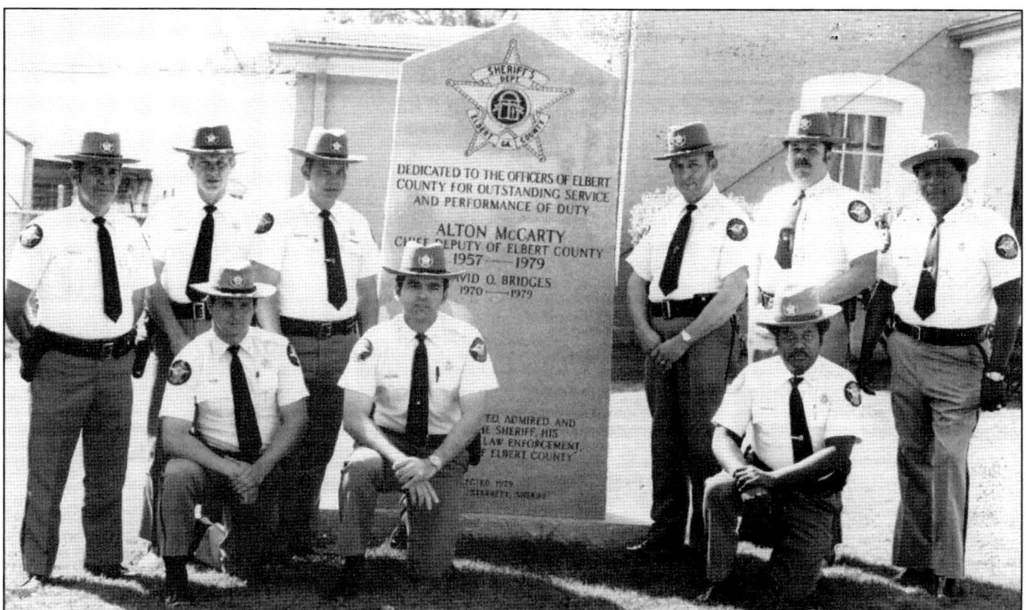

Sheriff's Deputy. Willie Hubbard and James Perlotte were two of the first African-American sheriff's deputies. (Courtesy Jim-Ree African-American Museum, Inc. Archives.)

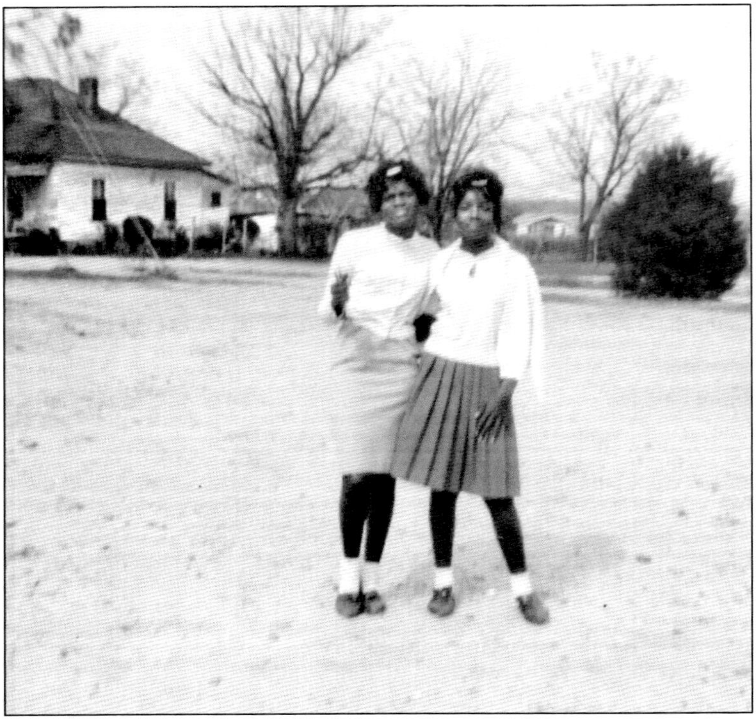

After School. Lillie Bolton and Carolyn Heard pose for a picture on the grounds of Blackwell Memorial High School. (Courtesy Jim-Ree African-American Museum, Inc. Archives.)

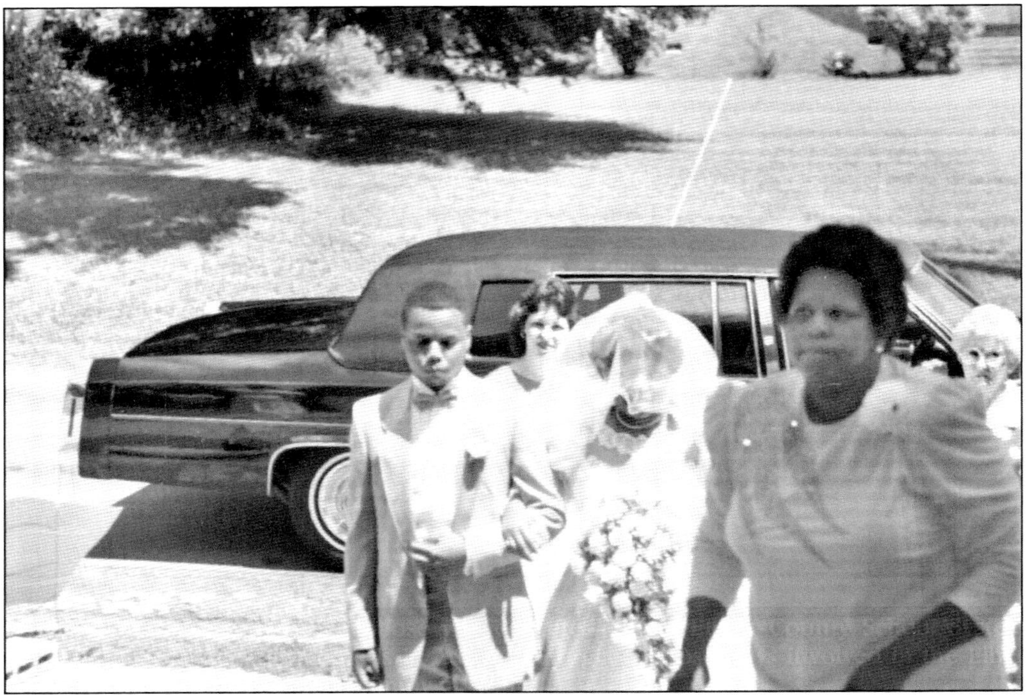

Wedding Planner. Vertis McIntosh Martin enjoys planning and organizing weddings. (Courtesy Marie and Charles Hamm Collection.)

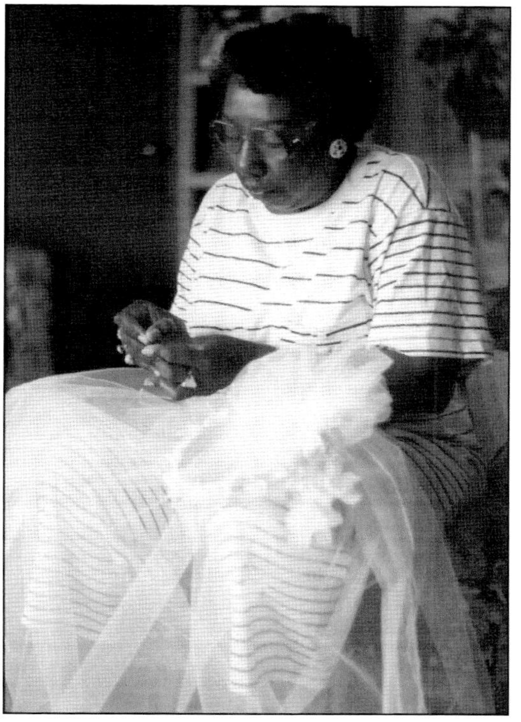

LAST-MINUTE TOUCHES. Lois Johnson Rankins makes last minute changes to a bride's veil. (Courtesy Marie and Charles Hamm Collection.)

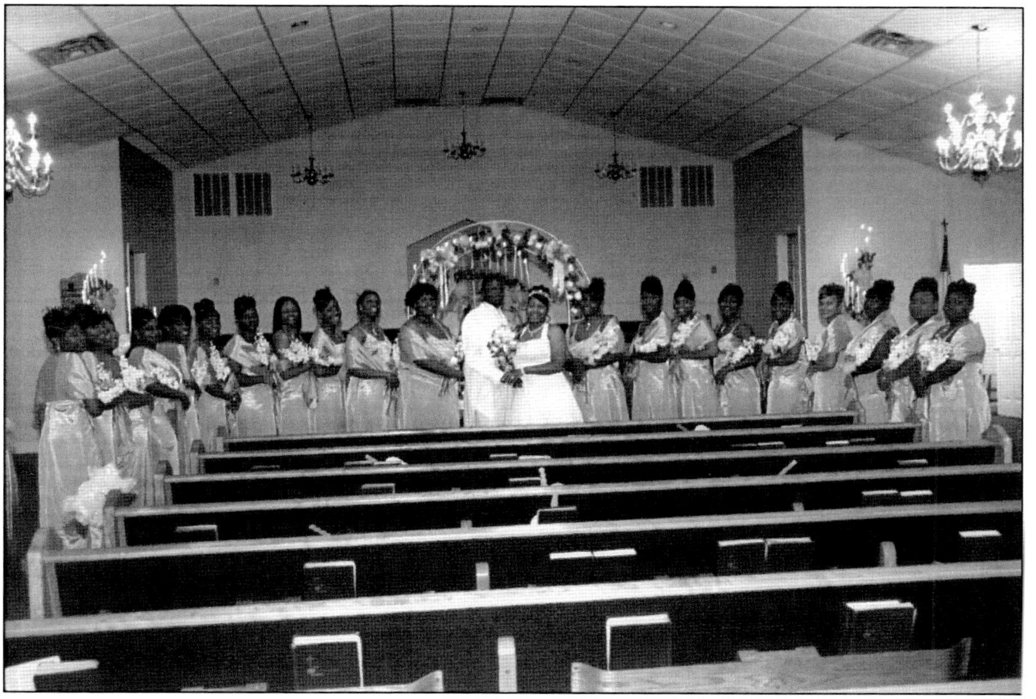

BRIDAL PARTY. Tim and Lashondra Williams Baker take a picture with their bridesmaids. (Courtesy Jimmy O. White.)

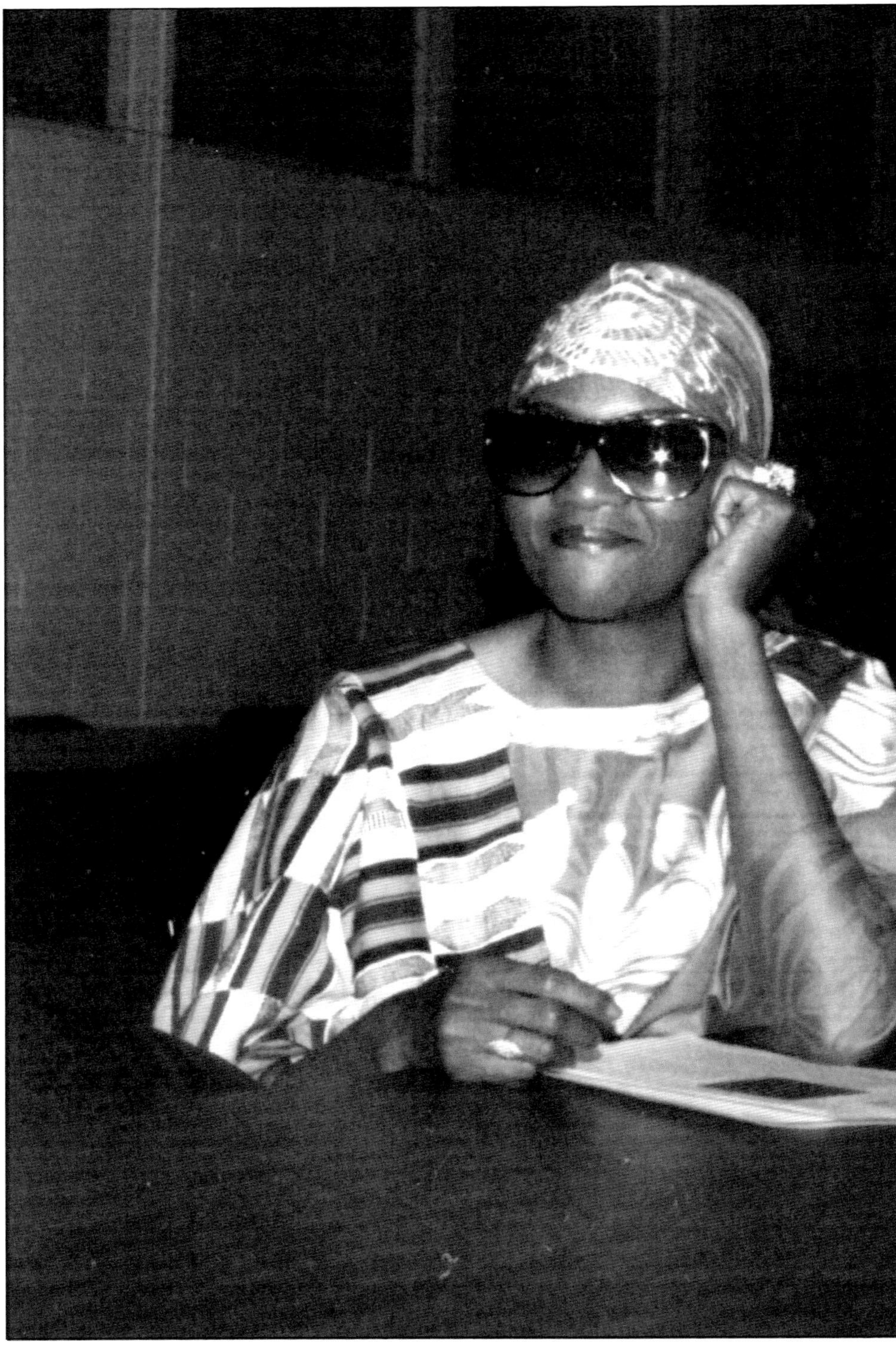

BRENDA HARPER (HOLT) SARKODIE. Sarkodie poses for a picture at the Blackwell Memorial Cultural Center. (Courtesy Jimmy O. White.)

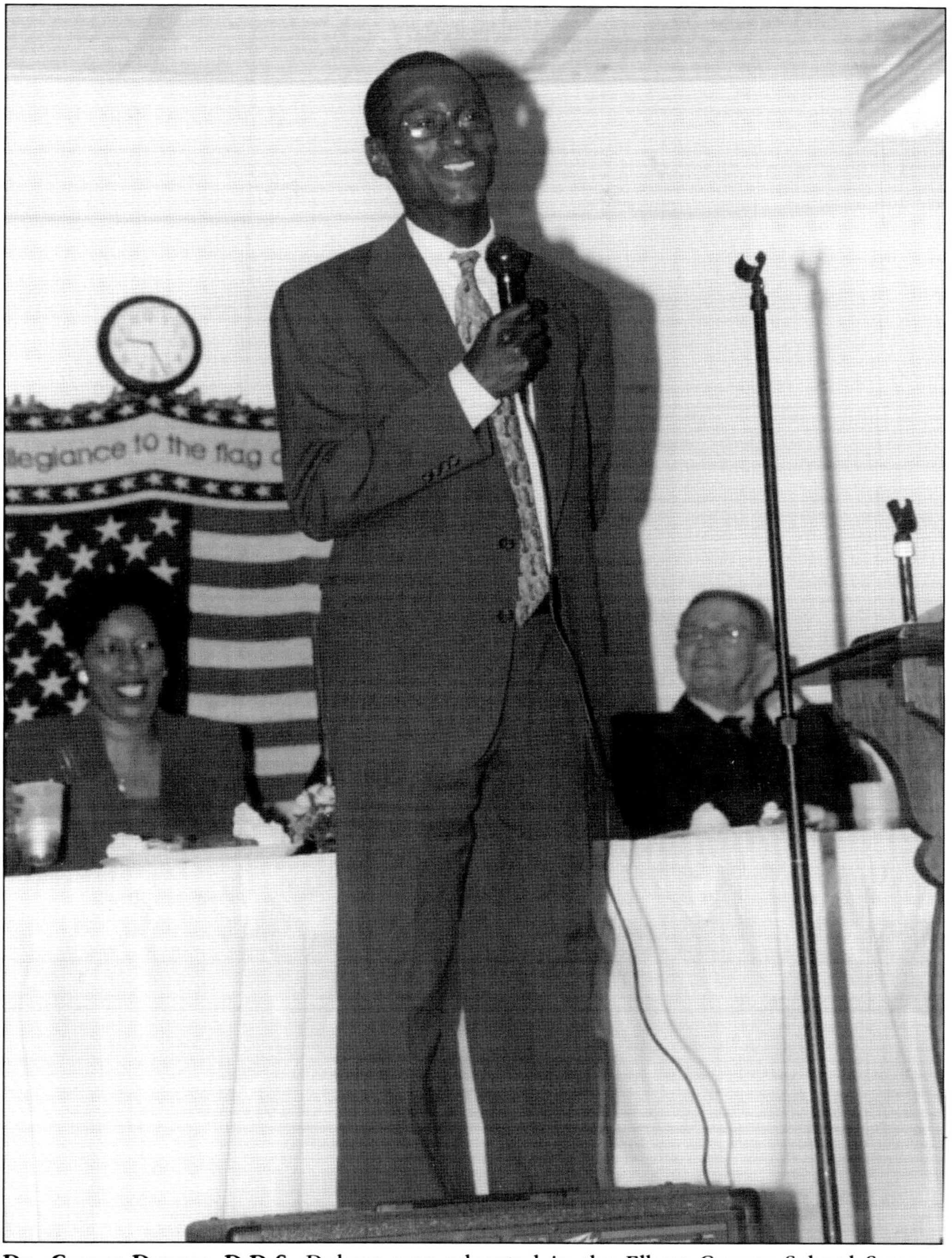

Dr. Claude Dubose, D.D.S. Dubose was educated in the Elbert County School System. Though his practice and home is in Athens, Georgia, Dubose stays involved in the Elbert County community. (Courtesy Jimmy O. White.)

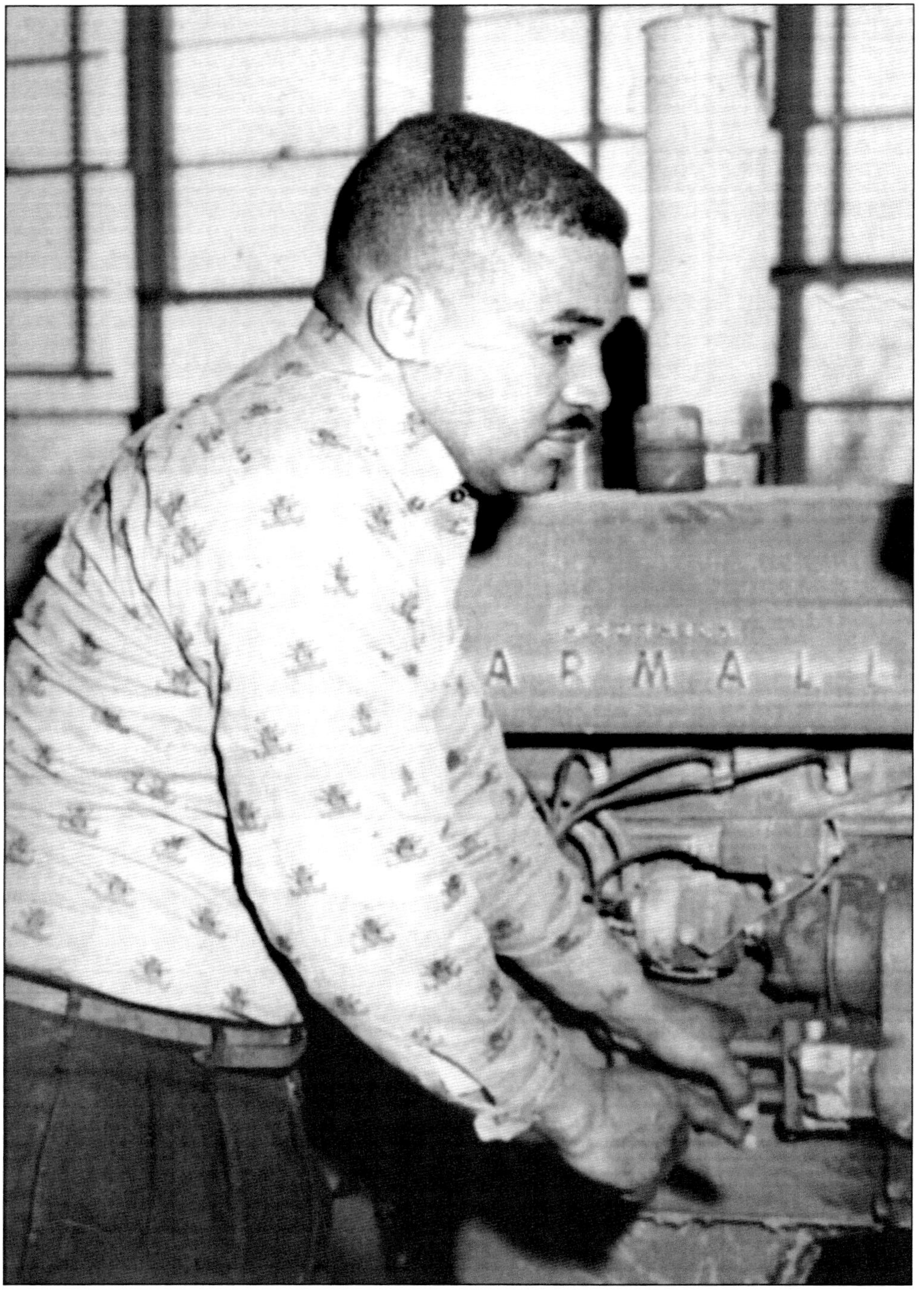

SPOTLIGHT. Welchel Long, a retired educator, was also a farmer. In 1999, he and other African-American farmers won a class-action lawsuit they had filed against the government, claiming that the United States Department of Agriculture discriminated against them based on their race. (Courtesy Jimmy O. White.)